THE HOMESICK TEXAN COOKBOOK

THE HOMESICK

TEXAN

COOKBOOK

LISA FAIN

HYPERION

NEW YORK

Library of Congress Cataloging-in-Publication Data

Fain, Lisa.
  The homesick Texan cookbook / Lisa Fain.—1st ed.
      p. cm.
  Summary: "Stories and photographs that will both reconnect and introduce people to
the joy of Texas, and 150 versatile recipes that highlight the state's rich food traditions,
appropriate for both Texans and non-Texans alike"—Provided by publisher.
  ISBN 978-1-4013-2426-1 (hardback)
  1. Cooking, American—Southwestern style. 2. Cooking--Texas. I. Title.
TX715.2.S69.F35 2011
  641.59764--dc23   2011018471

Hyperion books are available for special promotions and premiums. For details contact
the HarperCollins Special Markets Department in the New York office at 212-207-7528, fax
212-207-7222, or email spsales@harpercollins.com

BOOK DESIGN BY SHUBHANI SARKAR

First Edition

10 9 8 7 6 5 4 3 2 1

For my family—
thank you for always
keeping me well fed

CONT

ENTS

ACKN★WLEDGMENTS

So many generous people have helped me create this book—it's a pleasure to give them proper thanks and praise.

First, a Texas-size thank-you to my agent Brettne Bloom, for not only seeing a book inside of me but cheering me as I created it, every step of the way.

Of course, this book wouldn't have happened without the terrific team at Hyperion, sso thank you to all who spent time producing the book, especially Laura Klynstra and Shubhani Sarkar for fine design, and to my editors Elisabeth Dyssegaard and Leslie Wells for not only pushing me to do my best but also giving the thumbs-up to that batch of Mexican Chocolate Chewies.

It was a blast creating a collection of new recipes, but I couldn't have done it without the wise suggestions and hearty appetites of my wonderful recipe testers: Mike Bierschenk, Rachel Branyan, Erin Bryan, Kristine Laudadio Devine, Travis Dubose, Sharon Dunn, Linda Ford, Kirsten Furl, Bill Gunter, Shawnda Horn, Gary Jones, Jennifer Jones, Celeste Lipp, Erika Lomas, Kathi Malin, Iim Mazurek, Mijke Rhemtulla, Cheryl Rode, Aaron P. Shoop, Ann Tate, Carolyn Woolley, and Sarah Whetsell.

The food-blog community is warm and welcoming, and I'm very grateful to Penny De Los Santos, Elise Bauer, Matt Armendariz, Jaden Hair, Deb Perelman, Shauna James Ahern, Kalyn Denny, and Tara Austen Weaver for their encouraging words and reminders to breathe. Likewise, thank you to Robb Walsh, Elizabeth Karmel, and Amy Mills Tunnicliffe for wise counsel in navigating the publishing process. And Kat Kinsman, thank you for having a pork drawer and a freezer filled with offal.

Before I started hanging out in my kitchen, I worked with a smart group of folks at *Advertising Age*. A hearty thank-you for being such willing taste testers over the years, and for being patient with me when I was thinking about food instead of magazine production.

I couldn't have done any of this without my family, who graciously provided me with recipes and amusing anecdotes. Much gratitude goes to Grandma for her patience while being photographed; Mom for making the best scones; and Dad for teaching me the finer points of chicken-fried steak. I'd also like to give special mentions to my late grandpa, Dr. A. J. Jernigan, and grandma, Mrs. Jeannine Ashner; while they didn't get to see this book, I think they would have enjoyed it.

And lastly, thank you to my blog readers. Your comments and encouragement have made sharing stories and recipes a true joy.

★ ix

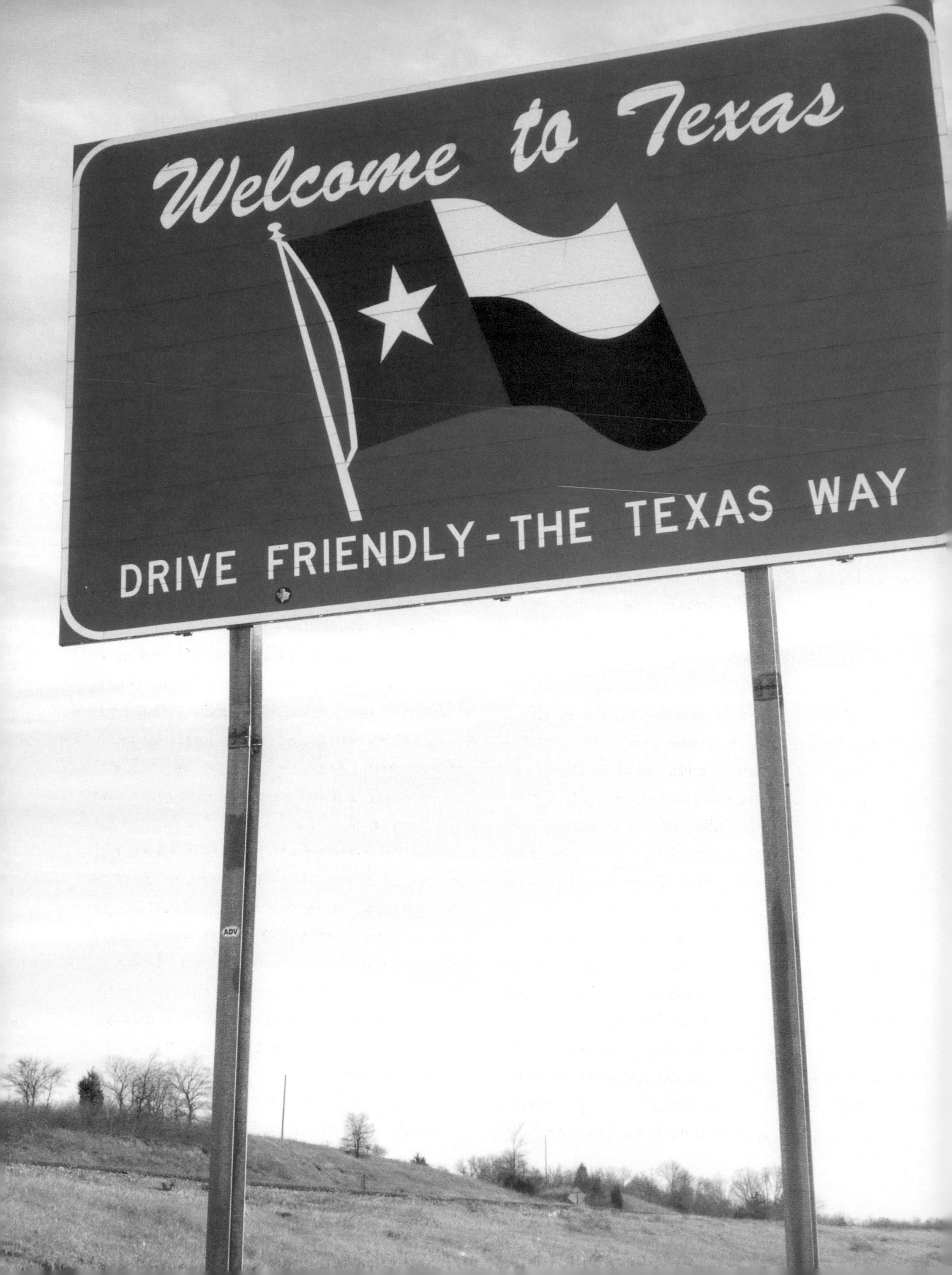
Welcome to Texas
DRIVE FRIENDLY - THE TEXAS WAY
ADV

INTRODUCTION

If you had told me before I moved to New York that one cold and blustery day I'd find myself walking along a New Jersey highway in search of food,

I would have said you were nuts. OK, so I wasn't on the hunt for just any food; I was looking for Ro-Tel, a spiced-up can of tomatoes and chiles that is a standard ingredient in any Texan's larder, not to mention a crucial component of chile con queso, a dish I hoped to serve to my friends that night. But perhaps I'm getting ahead of myself.

I am a Texan, a seventh-generation Texan, in fact. My formative years were spent on the outskirts of Houston, with crude-oil tanks, barbecue stands, and rice fields all practically in my backyard. My summers were spent outside Dallas, driving a tractor, picking black-eyed peas, and shucking corn at my grandparents' long-standing farm. These were the places that I knew, the places that I loved. But for some reason, from an early age I had a hankering to live in New York City—it was an itch that I just had to scratch. Movies, magazines, and books made New York City appear sophisticated, fast paced, and electric—which in my young, unformed opinion were things that Texas was decidedly not. So when I was offered a job in Manhattan at the age of twenty-five, it was no surprise to my family that I didn't think

twice before packing up a truck and telling Texas good-bye.

At first I was pleased that I had traded big sky for skyscrapers, backyard barbecues for Broadway shows. In Manhattan I couldn't be happier, or so I thought. But soon, a certain something started to gnaw at me; there was definitely a lack in my citified life. Sure, I missed my family, my friends, and my land, but I also missed those foods that I loved, the foods that had always been central to my life. In Texas, food played a key role in all situations no matter how big or how small. Not a wedding, funeral, summertime holiday, Friday-night football game, after-school study session, Sunday evening at church, or any other excuse for people to gather occurred without a huge spread of varied and delicious things to eat. Brisket and ribs, smoked until tender; jalapeño beef sausage, each bite with a snap; cheese enchiladas, oozing with chili gravy; chicken-fried steak, so large it's barely contained on the plate; fiery chili always prepared without beans; freshly caught catfish battered in cornmeal and fried; pillow-soft kolaches, stuffed with sweet prunes and apricots; and a bowl of said chile con queso, where melted cheese, chiles, and tomatoes became a perfect match. Growing up, I didn't consider Texan food special, however, as it was simply what we ate. I guess you could say I took it for granted. So I was shocked when I moved to New York City and discovered that these beloved foods weren't readily available. Only then did I understand how unique and wonderful my home state's cuisine was.

When you meet new people, you want to share yourself. And that's how it was in New York with my new friends. They were curious about Texas, so I'd prepare for them—to the best of my ability—these cherished dishes that both explained Texan culture and helped me feel closer to home. Which brings us back to that highway. Everyone knows that you can't make chile con queso without Ro-Tel. But this can of fiery tomatoes had eluded me since I'd arrived; I had scoured markets in all five boroughs with no success. That morning, however, I had read in the *New York Times* about a behemoth of an international grocery store in New Jersey that was thirty-four thousand square feet filled floor to ceiling with foods from around the world. If anyplace had my tomatoes, this would be it. So I hopped on a train and made the trek across the river. The paper had said that the store was close to the train station, but I soon realized that this was a lie. It took me almost an hour to reach the store, situated in a suburban area more accessible to cars than to people on feet.

In hindsight, I probably should have called before my trip. This store's impressive inventory boasted foods from all corners of the globe—England; Malaysia; Brazil; South Africa; heck, even Canada—but my beloved tomatoes were not to be found. Tired, I left without buying anything and made the long journey home. That evening I still made my queso for my friends, but with regular tomatoes and chopped jalapeños instead. While it wasn't perfect, they didn't know any different and thoroughly enjoyed it; the evening turned out fine after all.

Not having easy access to Texan food made me feel homesick. But taking to my tiny New York City kitchen and cooking the foods that I had grown up with went far to help cure what ailed me. And as I made each dish I slowly began to reconnect with the home that I had left, which, I now realized, was a place that I dearly loved.

To the uninitiated, Texan cuisine is stereotypically comprised of only three things: Tex-Mex, barbecue, and chicken-fried steak. And while it's true that we love and cherish these foods, our large state is geographically and culturally diverse, so there is a much greater variety to our cuisine than just these three iconic categories.

Take West Texas. There's little rainfall in that part of the state, so ranching is the dominant means of food production. Beef simmered with dried chiles is common, as are stacked cheese enchiladas topped with a fried egg.

Along the Gulf Coast, you'll find redfish cooked on the half shell, shrimp steeped in a thick gumbo, and tacos stuffed with chile-soaked fish. In the Rio Grande Valley, sweet and juicy Ruby Red grapefruit picked from the tree can be eaten fresh, or can liven up foods such as sweet rolls. Meanwhile, vaqueros cook up carne guisada and pan de campo over mesquite-fueled pits.

The eastern part of the state is more closely aligned with the Deep South, so there you'll find fried catfish, collard greens, and big pots of black-eyed peas. The lush Hill Country is rich in pecans and peaches, while its strong German heritage guarantees smoked meat and hot links.

Then there are the cities, each with its own distinct flavor. The sour cream enchiladas you eat in

Dallas can't be found in El Paso. The creamy green table sauce enjoyed in Houston is unheard of in Amarillo.

This variety is what I missed, what I longed for. And this is why I cook—so that I can feel closer to home.

In New York, I spent a large amount of my free time wandering neighborhoods in search of tastes of Texas. I'd take the train out to Brooklyn in search of dried chiles, and I'd venture up to Harlem for fresh black-eyed peas still in the pod. A trip to Chinatown could sometimes get me frog legs, while in Queens I found corn husks for my tamales.

At first, I felt that I was alone in my quest. But in 2005, I started a food blog called Homesick Texan to document with stories, photos, and recipes my trials of re-creating Texan food in my tiny Manhattan kitchen. Soon I found a community of readers worldwide that felt the same as I did.

Homesick Texan, the Web site, has united a large community of readers by our shared love of Texas food. This book aims to enhance this passion and interaction with a collection of stories and over 125 versatile recipes that highlight the state's rich food traditions, appropriate for both Texans and non-Texans alike.

Texan food isn't overly complicated—its palette is based on indigenous ingredients such as chiles, cilantro, citrus, tomatoes, tomatillos, seafood, beef, pecans, peaches, and beans. The recipes that I share are authentic, either created through much experimentation or culled and adapted from family, friends, and old community cookbooks. But this isn't to say that my recipes are encased in amber, as I've been known to replace the ubiquitous cream of mushroom soup

in my King Ranch Chicken with a creamy béchamel sauce; the liquid smoke common in baked barbecue briskets with chipotle chiles and smoked paprika; and the Velveeta found in chile con queso with milk and cheddar.

Of course, some dishes don't require much tinkering, as a simple enchilada sauce requires little more than chiles, aromatics, and broth; ice cream is comprised of nothing more than cream, eggs, and sugar; and chicken-fried steak is still best made with a simple batter of flour, eggs, and milk.

My emphasis in cooking is to use whole ingredients that are seasonal and local, when available. Of course, this hasn't always been possible in New York City, as items such as citrus don't grow here, and many of the dried chiles I buy come from Mexico. But I eschew fast solutions such as canned cream soups, prepared sauces, and boxed mixes, as I find that food tastes better when made from scratch.

My recipes are dishes that I have known and discovered in Texas. They are the foods that I grew up with, and the foods that remind me of home. The power of these dishes is that other Texans love them as well, and making them helps all of us feel closer to the state that we love, whether we are there or not. Yet despite the nostalgic tug, these recipes are accessible to anyone —even if they don't have a relationship with Texas—as our food is alive with flavor as well as comfort.

I dearly love Texas. While I'm currently hanging my hat in New York City, I try to reconnect with home as often as I can. My goal is to help others make this connection as well and to celebrate with me the bounty and joy that is Texan cuisine.

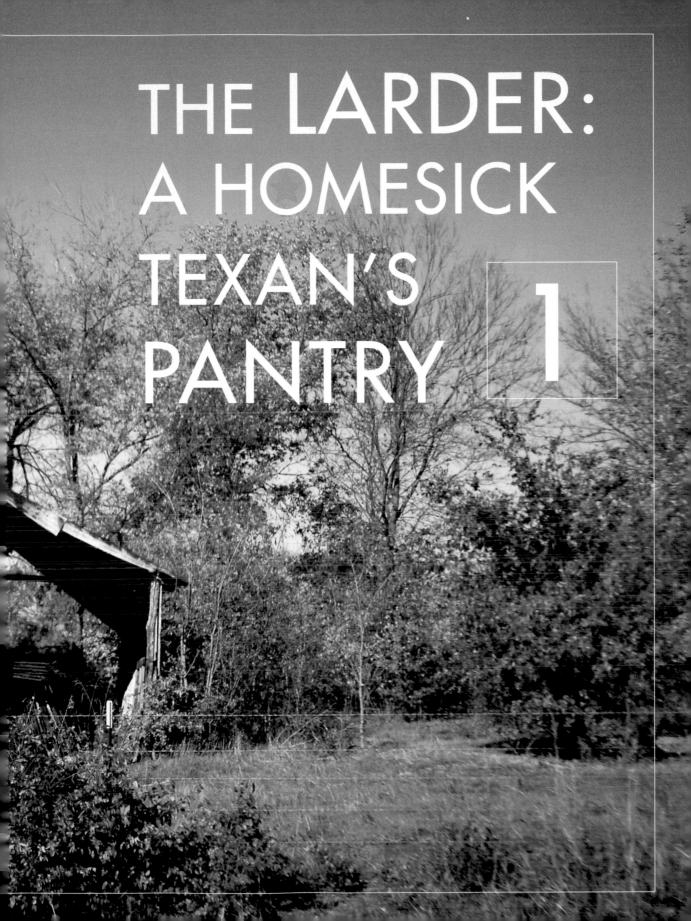

THE LARDER: A HOMESICK TEXAN'S PANTRY

1

After I moved to New York City, one of the first things that struck me was the unavailability of certain items usually found in a Texan's pantry. Dried chiles, Mexican chocolate, and masa harina were just some of the ingredients that I loved to use, but they weren't available at my corner market.

It didn't take long, however, for me to discover that New York City has a large Mexican population. In these neighborhoods, I discovered a host of stores that did sell the ingredients I needed for cooking. At the same time, I learned to be creative with what was available.

Here are a few of the ingredients found in my recipes that might not be familiar to you, with suggestions on both where they can be found if they're not at your usual grocery store, and substitutions you can make with more commonly found ingredients.

FRESH CHILES

Fresh chiles are in season throughout the summer and early fall, though you can usually find them year-round at most grocery stores. When buying them, you want the color to be bright and the texture to be firm; mushiness means the chile is old. I find that the best fresh chiles give off a scent and may even make your eyes water a bit. Don't worry, that's a good sign!

To store fresh chiles, keep them wrapped separately in the crisper drawer of a refrigerator. When cooking with fresh chiles, if you want to temper the heat, remove the seeds, as that's where most of the fire lives. I recommended that you wear gloves, as the chile's oils can burn you. If you don't wear gloves, you can run milk over your hands to get rid of the heat. And never, *ever* touch your eyes or your nose after working with chiles.

Here are the fresh chiles found in my recipes, and a few notes about their flavor and heat levels.

Anaheim chile: The Anaheim chile is long, light green, and has a pointed end. It tends not to be very fiery but has a bright and slightly sweet flavor. Its skin is tough, so it usually needs to be removed before using.

Habanero chile: This is one of the hottest chiles available, so be very careful when working with it. It's a squat, lantern-shaped chile that comes in bright, festive colors such as red, yellow, and orange, though you might see light green ones as well. Even though the habanero chile is super hot, its fire is tempered by a fruity, sweet flavor.

Hatch chile: This light green, long, pointed chile comes from the same family as the Anaheim, but it tends to be more hot and to have a brighter flavor. Hatch chiles are not a variety; the name refers to where it is grown, in the Hatch Valley of New Mexico. They are found only in the late summer and early fall; if the store says that it's a Hatch chile that's been grown in, say, Florida, then it's not truly a Hatch chile, it's an Anaheim.

Jalapeño chile: If Texas had a state chile, it would be the jalapeño. This medium-size, pointed chile is ubiquitous in Texan cuisine—found in everything from salsas to jams. Jalapeños have a fruity, warm flavor that can be very hot, though there are mild breeds as well. Unfortunately with jalapeños, you usually don't know how hot it will be until you bite into it. I have found, however, that if you hold a fresh one close to your nose, you can detect its heat. Jalapeños should be firm, and they will either be a deep bright green color or a bright red. There's no

Poblano and Anaheim chiles

DRIED CHILES

I love dried chiles and use them all the time. As the name implies, a dried chile is simply a chile pepper that's been dried and sometimes, as in the case of chipotle chiles, smoked. Their concentrated, robust nature gives dishes a wonderful depth of flavor. When buying dried chiles, freshness is key. You want your dried chiles to be pliant and soft, like raisins. If they are hard and brittle, it means that they are old and might not have as much impact as their fresher counterparts. Likewise, I find that older chiles can be more bitter.

When storing dried chiles, keep each type in a separate airtight container, as they have distinct flavors. You wouldn't store cornmeal in the same container as sugar, and so it should be with chiles.

To use dried chiles, you need to rehydrate them first. To do this, simply remove the stems and seeds of the chiles and then, in a dry cast-iron skillet on medium-high heat, cook them for few seconds on each side until they begin to puff up a bit. Add water to the skillet, turn off the heat, and let the chiles soak for thirty minutes or until they are moist. I then drain the soaking water (because it can be bitter), rinse the chiles, and proceed with the recipe.

Here are the dried chiles I use in my book, with an explanation about what they are and the flavors they impart.

Ancho chile: The essence of Tex-Mex is found in this chile, which is a dried version of a poblano pepper. It's colored dark red to brown and has a conical shape with a wide top that tapers to a point. Its flavor is earthy and almost sweet, with hints of raisins and chocolate. Commercial chili powders use the ancho chile as a base, so its flavor will probably be familiar to you if you've eaten Tex-Mex cheese enchiladas or a bowl of Texas chili. Its heat is mild, though sometimes you may come across a batch that is hot.

difference between the two; all jalapeños start out green and then will eventually turn red, the longer they ripen. Some believe that red jalapeños are more hot, but I haven't always found this to be true. Sometimes jalapeños will have white lines running through the skin; they are still fine to buy, as long as the chile isn't mushy.

Poblano chile: This long, heart-shaped chile is dark green with a wrinkled skin. It has a mild, slightly earthy flavor, and it's not too fiery.

Serrano chile: This small, thin chile has a bright, crisp bite and packs a lot of heat. They are usually bright green, though as they age on the vine, they will turn red. They look like a jalapeño that's been on a diet, but please note that they have a lot more heat, so be careful when working with them.

FROM LEFT, CLOCKWISE:
Pasilla chile, guajillo chile, ancho chile,
pequin chiles, chile de arbol, and chipotle chile

which is simply dried chipotle chiles that have been ground.

Guajillo chile: This slender, long, bright red chile has a berrylike flavor that tends to stay in the background—guajillos will not dominate a dish. It's not too hot, which also makes it an accessible chile. Its skin is tough and thick, so the guajillo needs to be soaked longer than most chiles before it's smooth and moist. If you can't find guajillo chiles, then use the more widely available red New Mexican chiles.

Pasilla chile: The pasilla chile is a dried version of the chilaco chile. Pasillas are long and slender, with a deep red-to-brown color. They have a bitter-sweet, earthy flavor that isn't too hot but can have a bit of an afterburn.

Pequin chiles: Be very careful when using these tiny, oval-shaped chiles, as they are very hot. In Texas, they grow wild throughout the more arid southern and western portions of the state, and you can buy them both fresh and dried. Outside the state, however, they're usually only found dried, and will be a dark red color. Because of their size, you don't need to re-hydrate these chiles; you just throw them into the pot.

GROUND CHILES

Chiles that are already ground provide a simple way of giving dishes flavor and heat quickly.

Cayenne: The cayenne pepper in its natural state is slender and red, though most commonly you'll buy it already preground into a powder, which is how I use it in my recipes. It has a bright, lively heat that has the benefit, when used in moderation, of making other flavors sing.

Chile powder: Chile powder consists of ground chiles that have been roasted and then ground in a spice or coffee grinder. The flavor is intense and

Chile de arbol: This small, pointed bright red chile is very hot. Its bright, perky flavor can liven up a dish.

Chipotle chile: This is a dried jalapeño chile that has been burned over coals; therefore it has a smoky flavor. It's a hot chile, and its presence in a dish is loud—the chipotle likes to assert itself! Often, dried chipotle chiles are a dusty brown, though sometimes you'll see them in a dark red color. While you can buy these chiles dried, they are more commonly found canned in an adobo sauce, which is a sauce made up of tomatoes, onion, sugar, and vinegar. If using canned chipotle chiles, be sure to throw in some of the adobo sauce from the can, as it has a lot of flavor. Some of my recipes call for chipotle powder, concentrated. There are several recipes that call for chipotle or ancho powder. You can often find these in the spice aisle of a grocery store or at a Mexican grocery. You can also, however, make your own. To do this, in a dry skillet heated on high, toast two ounces of chiles on each side for about ten seconds, or just until they start to puff. Remove from the skillet and place chiles in a spice grinder; pulse until finely ground.

Chili powder: Chili powder, not to be confused with *chile* powder, is a blend of ancho chile powder, allspice, granulated garlic, and clove. It's found in the spice aisle; choose a powder that is dark red. This spice blend is used in Tex-Mex recipes such as carne guisada and fideo.

Smoked paprika (pimentón): This Spanish chile powder is made from chiles that are dried over oakwood smoke. It doesn't have much heat, but it does have a potent, smoky flavor.

SPICES AND HERBS

Texans like to use certain spices and herbs to give their dishes a distinct flavor. Here are the spices and herbs found in a large portion of my dishes. My recipe ingredients list will most often call for spices to be ground. You can buy these spices preground, or you can buy them as seeds and grind them yourself in a spice grinder or a coffee grinder. As for the herbs, I will note if they should be fresh or dried.

SPICES

Allspice: A sweet, warm spice that has hints of both cinnamon and clove.

Cinnamon: This warm, slightly bittersweet spice is used in both stick form and ground.

Clove: A warm and sweet spice that, when used with a heavy hand, can quickly take over a dish and give it an almost bitter flavor, so always use sparingly.

Cumin: This earthy, bitter spice is what distinguishes Tex-Mex from Mexican food. It has a strong presence that can easily dominate a dish if you're not too careful, so always taste your dishes when using it so it doesn't overpower the rest of the flavors.

Ginger: While ginger is a root that can be used either fresh or ground, my recipes call for it to be added in the latter form. Ground ginger has a bright and strong flavor that has a bit of heat.

HERBS

Cilantro: A most contentious herb—people either love or hate cilantro. I adore it and throw it into almost all of my savory dishes, as I love its unique sweet-and-sour flavor. Unfortunately, some people have a genetic inclination to think that cilantro tastes like soap. There's not a good substitution for cilantro, so if you don't like it, simply don't use it.

Cilantro

Oregano: This pungent herb has a slightly grassy flavor. I tend to use dried oregano, as it has a deeper flavor than fresh. Also, due to availability, I use the common dried Mediterranean oregano found at most supermarkets. Don't confuse it with an herb called Mexican oregano, which isn't related to this common dried oregano. Mexican oregano is instead related to sage and has more of a floral flavor.

DAIRY

As Texas is cow country, we love our dairy. Whether it's buttermilk in our dressings and desserts, or cheese in our Tex-Mex and side dishes, many Texan dishes call for some sort of milk product. Here are the ones most commonly found in my recipes.

Asadero cheese: This mild cow's milk cheese comes from Mexico. It is a bit tangy, but the flavor is not pungent. It's an excellent melting cheese. If you can't find it, however, Muenster or Monterey Jack can work as a substitute.

Buttermilk: In the old days, buttermilk was a by-product of butter production, hence the name. These days, however, it's regular milk that's been fortified with cultures, which provides its distinct flavor. I use it in baked goods such as cakes and breads because it makes for a softer, moister product. If you can't find buttermilk, you can make your own by adding one tablespoon of vinegar to one cup of milk and letting it stand for a few minutes to acidify. Some people also substitute kefir, which is a thick dairy liquid with added live cultures.

Cheddar cheese: This sharp, hard, cow's milk cheese comes in many varieties. It can range in color from white to bright orange; the latter is created by adding annatto for color. When cheddar is young, it will be smooth and almost rubbery. But as it ages, it becomes more crumbly. It also melts very well. The orange, half-moon-shaped form is known as longhorn cheese, and that's what was commonly used in old-fashioned Tex-Mex. Longhorn cheddar tends to be milder than other cheddars.

Cotija cheese: This crumbly, soft cow's milk cheese comes from Mexico. It is usually sold in a block; to use it, you simply pinch off a bit and sprinkle it into or on top of the dish. It has a salty flavor and makes for a fine finishing garnish. If you can't find Cotija cheese, Parmesan or a mild feta will be a good substitution.

Monterey Jack cheese: This mild cow's milk cheese is white with a soft milky flavor. It's not aged for long, so it's very smooth and melts well. If you're looking for a livelier flavor, you can use pepper Jack, which is studded with bits of jalapeños.

Muenster cheese: This mild yet slightly tangy American cheese is white with an orange exterior. It melts very well and is an excellent substitution for asadero cheese if the latter cannot be found.

FATS

Don't worry, I'm pretty conservative with the amount of fat that I call for in my recipes, but I don't completely eliminate it, as fat adds moisture and flavor. Here are the ones I like to use.

Bacon grease: I think the name says it all—bacon grease is simply the rendered fat found at the bottom of your skillet after you've cooked a mess of bacon. It has a salty, smoky flavor that adds a quick jolt of flavor to any dish. Our ancestors may have kept it in a coffee can over the stove, but this might not be the healthiest storage option, as it can go rancid. To save your bacon grease, simply pour the cooled bacon grease into a glass jar and then store it in the

you want to purchase lard that is refrigerated, which you can find at butchers, Mexican markets, or at a farmers' market.

Lard's flavor is neutral. What it adds to a dish, however, is silky texture and a rounded mouth-feel. There are two types of lard—regular lard, which is rendered from back fat; and leaf lard, which is rendered from the fat surrounding the belly. Regular lard works well in savory dishes, whereas leaf lard is more tender and works well in baked goods.

If you are feeling bold, you can render your own lard. To do this, ask your butcher for unrendered back fat or unrendered leaf lard. Each pound of fat will render to about a pint of lard. Take the fat and cut it into one-inch cubes. Place the cubes in a large pot and cover with a half cup of water per pound. Set the heat on medium low and stir every ten minutes.

After about an hour, the fat will begin to melt. At this point, you should start stirring more frequently so it doesn't burn. Note that there will be some popping, so be careful. This popping comes from the cracklings, which are small, light brown pieces of fried pork (not fat) being formed.

Once the cracklings rise to the top of the pan and then sink, the lard has been rendered. After it's cooled, line a colander with cheesecloth and strain the lard through the cheesecloth into glass jars; the cracklings that are left behind make for a tasty snack, or can be stirred into cornbread or used on top of a salad.

The lard, while liquid, may be a light yellow color. But once it's been refrigerated for a few hours and solidified, it should turn white. Don't be distressed, however, if the solid lard isn't snowy white. Sometimes lard can be light brown— this doesn't mean it's not good; it's just the nature of the fat.

refrigerator. Bacon grease will keep for six months when refrigerated.

Lard: Don't shake your head—lard isn't nearly as awful as its reputation has made it out to be. Lard, which is rendered pig fat, has less saturated fat (the bad fat) and more than twice as much monosaturated fat (the good fat) as does butter. And it has none of those pesky trans fats—that is, if it hasn't been hydrogenated to prolong its shelf life.

Now, that's the key to buying lard—if it's not refrigerated, then it's been hydrogenated to keep it shelf-stable and is, therefore, awful for you. Instead

OTHER PANTRY INGREDIENTS

Cactus: Edible cactus, which in Spanish is known as *nopal*, comes from the prickly pear cactus, a beautiful plant that dots the landscape of West Texas. The plant has wide paddles that resemble a beaver's tail, and with a little care (yes, you remove the thorns) the paddles make for a delicious vegetable. It's also extremely nutritious, as some studies have noted that eating cactus helps treat diabetes and lower cholesterol levels. You can find cactus paddles, both fresh and canned, at any Mexican grocery or in the Mexican-food section of your grocery store.

Coffee: Most people have coffee on hand, though I use it so frequently in my cooking that I also keep a high-quality instant coffee in my pantry as well. I tend to use decaffeinated coffee when cooking, just in case people are sensitive to caffeine.

Masa harina: Many Tex-Mex foods are made from masa, which is corn that has been treated with lime (the mineral, not the fruit) so it can bloom and be ground into a paste. This is known as nixtamalization. But producing fresh masa takes a lot of work, and finding companies that make it outside of the Southwest can be difficult. Enter masa harina, which is a dry corn flour that is used as a base for many Tex-Mex dishes such as corn tortillas, tamales, and gorditas. Because it's been treated with lime, however, it is not the same as cornmeal, and sadly you can't make tortillas from the latter. People will say that the flavor of a tortilla made with masa harina is not as good as a tortilla made with fresh masa. But when it's all you have, I think it's just fine. Masa harina can be found at Mexican groceries and at many larger grocery stores.

Molasses: This thick syrup, a by-product of sugar production, has a uniquely strong bittersweet flavor. Its distinctive flavor adds depth to barbecue sauces.

Tomatoes: I love to use fresh tomatoes when they are in season, but since that time is limited, I've provided canned tomato measurement equivalents as well. When I was growing up in Texas, Ro-Tel tomatoes, which are a canned tomato that's been mixed with green chiles, were a common ingredient. In New York, however, as finding these tomatoes eluded me for years, I turned to alternatives. I'm now a big fan of fire-roasted canned tomatoes, which can be found most anywhere.

Tomatillos: This squat, green fruit is actually a member of the gooseberry family, not the tomato family. Its tangy, tart flavor is essential to many Tex-Mex dishes. In their natural state, they come wrapped in a husk, which needs to be removed before using. When buying fresh, try to find the smallest ones, as they have the best flavor. If you can't find them fresh, you can use canned—but be careful, as they're pre-salted; so adjust your recipe accordingly.

Tomatillos

KITCHEN EQUIPMENT

I have a small kitchen with little storage space, so I keep my equipment inventory low. Here are the things that I use most often.

Candy thermometer: This valuable tool can measure liquid temperatures up to 500 degrees. They're not very expensive and make frying foods and cooking candies much simpler.

Cast-iron cookware: I make the majority of my dishes in a ten-inch cast-iron skillet that belonged to my great-grandmother; it's a family treasure. I find that cast iron is excellent at retaining heat and, if you treat it well, will also be practically nonstick. The key to cast iron is to keep it seasoned by lightly rubbing the inside with either bacon grease, lard, or vegetable oil, and then baking it on a foil-lined sheet upside down for one hour in an oven set at 200 degrees. If rust appears on your cast iron, gently scrub it with steel wool until the rust disappears, and then proceed with seasoning. To clean cast iron, try to avoid soap, as this removes the seasoning. Instead, scrub it with coarse salt and warm water. Then place the cast iron on the stove, turn the heat on high until all the water has evaporated, and rub a quarter teaspoon of vegetable oil over the surface.

Tortilla press: While a tortilla press isn't necessary for making corn tortillas, it does facilitate pressing them into a round shape. They come in both wooden and iron forms; I prefer the latter, as it's sturdier. You can find tortilla presses at many kitchenware shops and Mexican markets. If you don't have a press, however, you can use a heavy object, such as a cast-iron skillet or a large book.

PICKLES AND PRESERVES

2

felt a gentle nudge. I slowly opened my eyes and looked out the window. It was barely light outside.

"If we're going to do this right, we've got to get started now," said my grandma.

I had arrived the night before at my grandma's farm north of Dallas in a tiny community called Chambersville. While there wasn't much left of Chambersville save for a cemetery, a Methodist church, and several farms, I was a direct descendant of the area's namesake, Elisha Chambers, and was thrilled to be on Texas land that had been in my family for 160 years. I had come all the way from New York because I wanted to learn how to preserve from a master—my grandma. Upon arrival, she informed me that her Golden Delicious tree was dropping ripe apples like rain and she decided that would be a good place to begin my canning education.

After putting on some clothes and my cowboy boots, we loaded up the back of the pickup truck with tubs and buckets and drove through the pasture over to the small grove of fruit trees. The ground under the tree was studded with a host of apples, all in various states of decay. A swarm of bees was having a feast. "There was so much rain this year, this tree just keeps producing. I haven't been able to keep up with it," said my grandmother. "But look at those bees! The honey this year is going to taste fine—like apples, I reckon!"

As the sun came up, we started to pluck the apples off the tree. Even though my family has always had fruit trees, for some reason I had never been apple picking. While it's a popular autumn pastime near my home in New York City, it felt more authentic and useful to be doing it on my grandparents' farm: these were my apples, fruit from my family's land. We filled two aluminum tubs and a bucket, then drove back to the house. After unloading the apples from the truck, we hauled them into the kitchen and set them by the sink.

Wielding a skinny knife with a twelve-inch blade,

my grandmother grabbed an apple and in a few deft strokes had quartered and removed the skin. "Some people use a small knife, but I've always preferred a larger knife—I have more control," she said.

She handed the knife to me and said, "Here, you try it." I fumbled with the apple and narrowly missed slicing off my thumb. She'd been peeling apples with that blade for over seventy-five years, so of course she made it look easy. "Maybe I should just use a peeler," I said.

She left me alone with the apples, and I got to work: there were over fifty for me to peel and cut before we started canning. An hour later, she came back into the kitchen and helped me with the few apples left in the tubs. In the time it took me to peel one piece of fruit, she had peeled and quartered five with that old knife. I was impressed.

There were several large pots filled with the apple slices—enough to yield over a gallon of jarred goods. I'd never seen so much sliced fruit in my life. My grandmother noted that this was not anything spectacular: with fruit trees, it was a constant battle trying to preserve the fruit before it rotted.

As we prepared to start canning, I was in awe of how calm she remained in the face of so much work and so many apples. While I had a few herb plants back in my apartment in New York City, harvesting them was nothing compared to this.

"How do you keep up with all this? How do you do this every day?" I asked.

"Goodness, you just do!" she replied.

I was thankful that I had her seventy-five-plus years of experience to guide me as I attempted to learn some of my family's old methods of putting food on the table. Since that trip, I've become quite keen about preserving. I'll make pickles with summer squash, jalapeños, and peaches; when strawberries are at their peak, I'll slow cook them into a jam. For some, crafting homemade pickles, jams, and relishes can appear to be daunting, but all it takes is a little time and you will be rewarded with condiments that will make anything store-bought pale in flavor.

BLANCHE'S MUSTARD PICKLES

2 QUARTS

½ cup granulated sugar

½ cup kosher salt

½ cup dry mustard

½ cup ground black pepper

½ gallon white vinegar

2 quarts pickling cucumbers
(about 1½ pounds), sliced into
¼-inch-thick rings

SPECIAL EQUIPMENT
2 quart-size jars with lids and bands

Though a schoolteacher, my great-grandma Blanche had some of the most illegible handwriting I've ever seen, save for my grandpa's and mine. My grandpa was a doctor, so that was his excuse, but as for Blanche and myself, I have no idea what happened. I like to think that our thoughts fly too fast for our hands to keep up with our minds.

In my collection of her handwritten recipes, many are difficult to read. Fortunately, this recipe for her famous mustard pickles I can read just fine.

1. Sterilize the jars and lids in either a large pot of boiling water or dishwasher. Remove jars and lids with tongs and place on a clean surface.

2. In a large pot, mix the sugar, salt, dry mustard, and black pepper with the vinegar and heat on medium until thoroughly mixed and dissolved.

3. In the sterile jars, layer the slices of cucumbers. Pour the vinegar mixture in the jars and stir. Seal and refrigerate. In 1 week they'll be ready and will last for 1 month.

I like to store my pickles and preserves in the refrigerator to be used immediately. Sometimes, however, you may want to store them for a longer shelf life. To do this, you can place the covered jars in a canning pot or stockpot, cover the jars with water, bring to a boil, and then cook on high for 10 minutes. Remove the jars with tongs and then allow to cool. If you are processing this way, make sure that the lids have never been used before, as they will seal only once. These jars will not require refrigeration until after opening.

Mustard Pickles

Mix thoroughly:

1 cup sugar, 1 cup salt, 1 cup
dry mustard, 1 cup ground
black pepper.

Dissolve in 1 gal. vinegar
Fill jars stirring constantly. Seal

JALAPEÑO, CAULIFLOWER, AND CARROT PICKLES (ESCABECHE)

4 PINTS

If you're of a certain age, you may remember a time when along with chips and salsa, you were served free corn tortillas, pats of butter, and hot pickle relish at your local Tex-Mex restaurant.

It's a shame you don't see pickled jalapeños in Tex-Mex restaurants more often, especially since its piquancy really wakes up your appetite. But I'm on a mission to bring this one-time favorite back into vogue.

1. Sterilize the jars and lids in either a large pot of boiling water or dishwasher. Remove jars and lids with tongs and place on a clean surface.

2. Heat the oil in a skillet on medium low. Add the jalapeños, carrots, cauliflower, and onions. Cook for 5 minutes, stirring occasionally.

3. Divide among the jars the garlic, peppercorns, cumin seeds, cilantro, and bay leaves, then pack each jar with the cooked pepper mix. Add ½ cup of vinegar to each jar, then fill the rest of the jar with water, leaving ¼ inch at the top. Top each jar with ½ teaspoon of salt.

4. Seal the jar and then give it a good shake. Refrigerate overnight, and they should be ready within 24 hours. They will keep in the refrigerator for a month.

1 tablespoon vegetable oil

1 pound jalapeño chiles, stems and seeds removed, cut into rings

3 carrots, peeled and cut into rings

1 small head of cauliflower, cut into florets

1 medium yellow onion, cut into rings or slivers

4 cloves garlic, minced

4 teaspoons peppercorns

4 teaspoons cumin seeds

4 sprigs cilantro

4 bay leaves

2 cups white vinegar

2 teaspoons kosher salt

SPECIAL EQUIPMENT

4 pint-size jars with lids and bands

BREAD AND BUTTER JALAPEÑO PICKLES

2 PINTS

1 pound jalapeño chiles, stems and
seeds removed, cut into rings

2 cups apple cider vinegar

1 cup granulated sugar

2 teaspoons mustard seed

1 teaspoon whole cloves

1 teaspoon whole allspice

2 cinnamon sticks

SPECIAL EQUIPMENT
2 pint-size jars with lids and bands

I admit that I am not usually a fan of sweet pickles, commonly known as bread and butter pickles, for reasons that remain elusive to me. Perhaps it's because I don't have much of a sweet tooth, or perhaps it's because I think that pickles are a savory condiment that should be tart and salty, never sweet.

All that changes, however, with these bread and butter jalapeños. The fire of the peppers combined with the warm tones of the cloves, allspice, and cinnamon makes for a bread and butter pickle that seems more sophisticated than usual. And sure, there's sugar involved, but it's just enough to round out the flavor without being cloying.

The uses for these are endless, though I'm inclined to add them to my potato salad, swirl them into some softened cream cheese for a quick dip, top them on slices of smoky brisket, or simply eat them straight out of the jar.

1. Sterilize the jars and lids in either a large pot of boiling water or dishwasher. Remove jars and lids with tongs and place on a clean surface.

2. Pack the sliced jalapeños into the sterilized pint-size jars.

3. Bring the vinegar, sugar, mustard seed, cloves, allspice, and cinnamon sticks to a boil, and then pour over the jalapeños. Seal the jars and fasten with rings. Allow to cool and then refrigerate. Will be ready in 4 hours and will last for 1 month in the refrigerator.

SPICY PICKLED OKRA

4 PINTS

A Texan friend had called me, thrilled that she had found Talk o' Texas brand of pickled okra at a New York grocery store. I must have not expressed the appropriate amount of enthusiasm for her discovery because she said, "What's wrong, don't you like okra pickles?" I admitted that okra and I have a somewhat strained relationship. She chided me and told me that my attitude needed to change, as I was missing out on a very good thing.

It took a while, but a few months later, I finally tried my first okra pickle. And you know what? My friend was correct. They're crisp and cool, and while there are still slight texture issues—yes, that's a slight hint of softness in the center of each pod—I find that the tang of the vinegar and fire of the chiles used in the brine make up for what I normally find unappealing.

I like to toss them cold and crisp into salads, use them as a garnish in a glass of vegetable juice, or simply eat plain.

2 pounds okra, stems trimmed
1 cup fresh dill, chopped
4 serrano chiles, stems and seeds removed, cut in half lengthwise
8 cloves garlic
3 cups apple cider vinegar
2 teaspoons red pepper flakes
2 teaspoons cumin seed
4 teaspoons kosher salt

SPECIAL EQUIPMENT
4 pint-size jars with lids and bands

1. Sterilize the jars and lids in either a large pot of boiling water or dishwasher. Remove jars and lids with tongs and place on a clean surface.

2. Evenly divide among the jars the okra, dill, serrano chiles, and garlic cloves.

3. Bring the vinegar, red pepper flakes, cumin seeds, and salt to a boil and pour into the jars. Fill up the rest of the jars with water. Cover with lids and fasten with rings. Allow to cool and then refrigerate. They will be ready after 4 hours and will last for 1 month in the refrigerator.

SUMMER SQUASH PICKLES

1 QUART

1 pound yellow squash and
   1 pound zucchini, sliced into
   ¼-inch rounds

4 cloves garlic, cut in half

2 teaspoons dill seeds

2 teaspoons cumin seeds

2 teaspoons celery seeds

2 teaspoons black peppercorns

2 cups white vinegar

2 tablespoons kosher salt

SPECIAL EQUIPMENT

2 pint-size jars or 1 quart-size
   jar with lids and bands

Many of us reach that point in midsummer when we have so much summer squash, we have no idea how we'll ever be able to eat it all. Why not do what my family's been doing for years—make squash pickles?

If you've never had pickles made from squash, I think you'll be surprised at how they taste. Said one friend who ordinarily doesn't enjoy squash: "They taste almost like pickled cucumbers. What a surprise!"

They make a fine starter on a pickle plate, add bright crunch to hamburgers, and give flair to a green salad. But even if you can't bear the thought of eating any more summer squash, the best thing about preserving them is you can save them until the winter, when you just might be ready to eat them again.

1. Sterilize the jars and lids in either a large pot of boiling water or dishwasher. Remove jars and lids with tongs and place on a clean surface.

2. Divide the sliced squash, zucchini, and garlic cloves and pack into the jars. Add to the jars the dill seeds, cumin seeds, celery seeds, and peppercorns, placing 1 teaspoon in each pint jar.

3. Bring to a boil the vinegar, salt, and ½ cup of water. Pour the boiling vinegar mixture into the jars, leaving a bit of headspace. Cover with lids and fasten with rings. Allow to cool and then refrigerate. They will be ready after 4 hours and will last for 1 month in the refrigerator.

CANNED APPLES

2 PINTS

2 pounds sweet apples such as
    Golden Delicious
1 tablespoon lemon juice
2 cinnamon sticks
1 jalapeño chile, seeds and stems
    removed, cut in half lengthwise
1 cup granulated sugar

SPECIAL EQUIPMENT
2 pint-size jars with lids and bands

My grandma makes these canned apples every year when her Golden Delicious apple tree goes into high production. Watching her make these was my first experience in canning, and even though I make lots of pickles, jams, and relishes, these are still a favorite.

Of course, I wouldn't be me unless I added some chile peppers to this recipe (my grandma calls me Chile Girl), which I do by sliding a sliced jalapeño into the syrup. I enjoy the heat it gives, though this is entirely optional, if you prefer to keep it simple. These canned apples will serve you well as a pie filling, on top of ice cream, or layered on slices of warm biscuits.

1. Sterilize the jars and lids in either a large pot of boiling water or dishwasher. Remove jars and lids with tongs and place on a clean surface.

2. Peel, core, and slice the apples. As you're slicing the apples, toss them with lemon juice to prevent browning. Pack apples into the jars along with a cinnamon stick and half a jalapeño chile.

3. Bring the sugar and 3 cups of water to a boil. Pour over apples. Cover with lids and fasten with rings. Allow to cool and then refrigerate. Will last for 1 month in the refrigerator.

HABANERO PICKLED PEACHES

2 QUARTS

Texas is proud of its peaches. They're soft, juicy, floral, and sweet, and the best I've ever tasted. During the season, when you travel through lush Hill Country Texas towns such as Fredericksburg, or Central Texas towns such as Fairfield, you won't be able to go a mile without seeing a roadside stand or pickup truck filled with baskets of this cherished summertime treat. We also have a peach tree at my grandma's North Texas farm, and every July it delivers a bounty of peaches that she'll put up for later in the year.

Pickling fruit is a common method of fruit preservation in Texas. Yes, there's vinegar involved, as with other types of pickles. But you also add enough sugar and warm spices to give the fruit a balance of both acidity and sweetness. If you've never tried pickled fruit, you'll be pleasantly surprised.

Pickled peaches are perhaps my favorite fruit to preserve, as I love how the peaches' sweet juice combines with the piquant brine. Of course, I've added a bit of heat to my peaches, which is decidedly *not* traditional, but I find that the habanero's flowery notes go very well with the peaches' floral tones.

These go well with a bowl of ice cream, on top of your morning oatmeal, with a freshly baked biscuit, or yes, simply eaten straight out of the jar.

3 pounds fresh peaches

1 cup apple cider vinegar

1 cup granulated sugar

1 habanero chile, stem and seeds removed, cut in half

2 cinnamon sticks

½ teaspoon whole cloves

SPECIAL EQUIPMENT
2 quart-size jars with lids and bands

1. Sterilize the jars and lids in either a pot of boiling water or dishwasher. Remove jars and lids with tongs and place on a clean surface.

(CONTINUED)

2. To peel the peaches, fill a large pot with water and bring to boil. Cut a small x on the top and bottom axes of each peach. Carefully drop them into the pot of boiling water and let them cook for 30 seconds. Using tongs or a long spoon, remove peaches, rinse with cold water, and then peel off the skin by gently rubbing the peach. Halve and pit the peeled peaches and put them in the jars.

3. In another pot, bring to a boil the cider vinegar and the sugar. In each jar add half the habanero chile, a cinnamon stick, and 2 whole cloves. When the vinegar comes to a boil, pour it into the jars and add enough water to the jar to fill (though be sure and leave ¼-inch headroom from the top). Cover and refrigerate. Will be ready in a couple of days. Will last refrigerated for 1 month.

NOTE: When you work with habanero chiles, it's advisable to wear gloves, as they're extremely hot. And please note that these pickles can pack some heat—if you prefer less, don't use the entire half of the habanero in each jar.

CHIPOTLE KETCHUP

ABOUT A PINT

When I was younger, we used to go to a dance hall where bands would serenade a room that was filled with dancers gliding across the floor doing the Texas two-step. Unfortunately, every time a kind gentleman offered to teach me this classic dance, my lack of finesse turned it into the Texas three-step. But I didn't mind, and after a clumsy yet fun evening, my friends and I would laugh about my performance over baskets of fries dipped into ketchup we'd jazzed up with hot sauce.

These days, I'm still not a good dancer, but instead of spooning hot sauce into bottled ketchup, I make from scratch a batch of ketchup fired up with chipotles. It's a cinch to make, and if you've never made ketchup before, you're in for a treat.

1 medium-size sweet onion, diced
1 tablespoon olive oil
1 28-ounce can of whole tomatoes
½ cup apple cider vinegar
¼ cup brown sugar
1 teaspoon molasses
½ teaspoon ground cinnamon
½ teaspoon ground cloves
1 teaspoon celery seeds
3 canned chipotle chiles in adobo
Salt, to taste

SPECIAL EQUIPMENT
1 pint-size jar with lid and band

1. Sterilize the jar and lid in either a pot of boiling water or dishwasher.

2. Over medium-low heat, cook the diced onions in the olive oil in a medium-size pot until the onions start to brown.

3. Add the tomatoes and their juice to the pot, crushing the tomatoes with the back of a spoon. Stir in the vinegar, brown sugar, molasses, cinnamon, clove, celery seeds, and chipotle chiles. Bring to a boil and then simmer for an hour, stirring occasionally. Taste and adjust seasonings, adding salt to taste.

4. After an hour, puree the mixture then continue to cook on low heat until it reaches the desired thickness. Pour the ketchup into the sterile jar, leaving a bit of headspace. Cover with the lid and fasten with the ring. Allow to cool and then refrigerate. Will last for 1 month in the refrigerator.

JALAPEÑO RELISH

1 PINT

I've never been much of a fan of pickle relish. I think it's because pickle relish is most often made with sweet pickles, which I find cloying. If I'm going to dress something up with a condiment, I want some tang and some heat. Relish and I are not good friends.

But one day while driving through West Texas, I took a pit stop at a gas station. I'm usually more prone to get tacos instead of hot dogs when I stop to fill the tank, but as I looked at the array of condiments on the counter, something caught my eye. There was a bright green, chunky topping labeled JALAPEÑO RELISH. Now, this I had to try!

OK, I won't lie—it was a bit sweet. But it was also savory and bright—the one thing I'd always missed in pickle relish. And it was also hot! Finally I'd found a relish that I could like. And no, I don't think it's too much of an overstatement to say that this discovery may have changed my life.

I've since figured out how to whip up my own jalapeño relish, and it's probably one of the easiest things to make. You take the chiles along with some aromatics, spices, and vinegar and blend them in a food processor until well combined. If you grow chile peppers it's a terrific way to use up your garden's bounty, though you can certainly use store-bought chiles as well. And what to do with it? Well, I like to put it on my hot dogs, dollop some into tacos, spoon some into my beans, or mix it with mayonnaise for a spicy dipping sauce. Anytime you'd use sweet relish, you can substitute jalapeño relish instead.

½ pound jalapeño chiles, stems and seeds removed, chopped
1 ripe plum tomato, chopped
¼ medium yellow onion, chopped
4 cloves garlic, cut into quarters
¼ teaspoon ground cumin
½ cup chopped cilantro
¼ cup apple cider vinegar
1 teaspoon granulated sugar
1 teaspoon lime juice
Salt, to taste

SPECIAL EQUIPMENT
2 half-pint-size jars with lids and bands

1. Place the jalapeños, tomato, onion, garlic, cumin, cilantro, vinegar, sugar, and lime juice in a food processor and process until finely minced. Add salt to taste.

2. Pour relish into sterilized jars, cover, and refrigerate, waiting at least 4 hours before serving. Will last for 1 month in the refrigerator.

CHOW CHOW

2 PINTS

1 pound green tomatoes, finely diced (about 3)

4 cups green cabbage (about ¼ of a head), finely shredded and chopped

½ large yellow onion, diced

4 cloves garlic, minced

1 red bell pepper, stem and seeds removed, diced

4 jalapeño chiles, stems and seeds removed, diced

¼ cup kosher salt, plus more to taste

2 cups apple cider vinegar

1 tablespoon dry mustard

½ teaspoon mustard seed

½ teaspoon celery seed

½ teaspoon cumin seed

½ teaspoon turmeric

¼ teaspoon ground cinnamon

2 tablespoons brown sugar

SPECIAL EQUIPMENT

2 pint-size jars or 1 quart-size jar with lids and bands

When my mom told me that she was in possession of all of Great-Grandma Blanche's recipes, I asked, "Is there a recipe for chow chow?" In my great-grandma's letters, she talks about making chow chow, and I was curious how she made hers.

If you're not familiar with chow chow, it's a tangy, crunchy relish that's made with green tomatoes, cabbage, and peppers. Some people make their chow chow sweet, but I keep mine on the piquant and savory side. To use chow chow, you can spoon some into a bowl of beans, spread it on sausage, or even top off a taco. Its flavor goes a long way in brightening up rich, heavy dishes.

1. Combine the green tomatoes, chopped cabbage, onions, garlic, red bell pepper, and jalapeños in a large bowl. Sprinkle with ¼ cup of kosher salt and fill the bowl with water to cover the vegetables. Cover and refrigerate the vegetables at least 4 hours.

2. Sterilize the jars and lids in either a pot of boiling water or dishwasher.

3. In a large pot, bring to a boil the vinegar, dry mustard, mustard seed, celery seed, cumin seed, turmeric, cinnamon, and brown sugar. Drain the vegetables from the brine (but do not rinse) and add to the pot. Turn the heat down to low and simmer for 10 minutes uncovered, stirring occasionally. Add more salt if you feel it's necessary.

4. Pack the cooked chow chow into the jars, cover with the lids, and fasten with the rings. Place in the refrigerator and allow it to sit overnight before using, though it just gets better with age. It will keep in the refrigerator for a month.

STRAWBERRY GUAJILLO JAM

2 PINTS

Spring marks the arrival of bluebonnets, Texas's state flower. From late March until May, this dark blue lupine blankets roadsides, hills, pastures, and even people's yards. During the season, as you drive through the state you'll see bluebonnet patches filled with people taking photos of their families—that annual shot is a Texas tradition.

Strawberries also arrive at this time of year. My grandma has strawberries at her farm, but I don't often make it home in time to eat them. Strawberry jam, however, is a great way to preserve these berries when they're at their peak. I make mine with a chopped guajillo chile, as it has a hint of berries and not too much heat. The guajillo's accent is subtle, but I find it adds a depth not found in regular strawberry jams.

2 pounds strawberries, hulled and quartered

2 cups granulated sugar

1 dried guajillo chile, stem and seeds removed

½ cup lime juice

SPECIAL EQUIPMENT

2 pint-size jars or 4 half-pint-size jars with lids and bands

1. Toss the strawberries in a pot with the sugar and let stand for 4 hours until soft and juicy.

2. Place a plate in the freezer. Dice the dried guajillo chile and add it to the strawberry pot along with the lime juice and ¼ cup of water. Bring pot to a boil and then turn the heat down to low and simmer for 30 minutes, stirring occasionally. Meanwhile, sterilize the jars and lids in either a pot of boiling water or dishwasher.

3. After 30 minutes, take the plate out of the freezer and place a spoonful of the jam on the plate. After a minute, tilt the plate, and if the jam doesn't run then it's ready. If it does run, cook it for 5 more minutes and test again. Continue to test until it doesn't run.

4. Pour jam into hot jars, leaving a bit of headspace. Cover with lids and fasten with rings. Allow to cool and then refrigerate. I find that it can last for a few months in the refrigerator.

TOMATILLO JALAPEÑO JAM

1 PINT

½ pound tomatillos, husks removed, chopped

2 jalapeño chiles, seeds and stems removed, finely diced

½ cup apple cider vinegar

1½ cups granulated sugar

¼ teaspoon ground cloves

¼ teaspoon ground allspice

½ teaspoon ground cinnamon

½ cup lime juice

2 teaspoons lime zest

SPECIAL EQUIPMENT:

1 pint-size jar or 2 half-pint-size jars

At festive gatherings when I was young, while the grown-ups held serious discussions about whether the Cowboys were going to make it to the Super Bowl, I'd spend my time hanging out at the food table, as that was more interesting to me. And nestled between the candied pecans and a crock of chile con queso, you'd always find a block of cream cheese that was draped in a shocking green jelly. This wasn't just any jelly—it was jalapeño jelly, a preserve both hot and sweet.

I decided to revisit jalapeño jelly, but opted to use tomatillos in mine, due to their natural pectin. I also decided not to use food coloring, as I find the natural shade of the chiles and tomatillos attractive as it is.

OK, so I admit that this is not the jalapeño jam you grew up with, but is that so bad? You'll still love pairing it with crackers and cream cheese, spreading it on biscuits, or using it as a topping on toast. If you've never had a pepper jam I urge you to try this—its easy elegance will both impress your guests and make for nice gifts.

1. Sterilize the jars and lids in either a pot of boiling water or dishwasher.

2. In a pot, add the tomatillos, jalapeño, vinegar, sugar, ground cloves, ground allspice, ground cinnamon, lime juice, lime zest, and ½ cup of water. Bring to a boil and then turn the heat down to low and simmer, stirring often, for 45 minutes or until it's thick and syrupy.

3. Pour the jam into the jars, then cover with the lids and fasten with the ring. Let it cool and then refrigerate. The jam will become more solid after a few hours in the refrigerator and will last for a month, refrigerated.

SALSAS, SAUCES, AND GRAVIES

3

One of the first things I learned when I moved to New York City is that Texan condiments aren't found in the Northeast.

Take our ubiquitous cream gravy. This simple sauce that's made from milk, flour, pan drippings, and a hearty dose of black pepper is poured over everything in Texas. We use it to moisten biscuits, coat chicken-fried steak, and jazz up rice. But when I moved to New York City and ordered gravy, what was served was always brown beef gravy; my preferred cream gravy was not to be found.

Then there are our flavorful, fiery salsas. Every Tex-Mex table will be set with bowls of red (and often green) salsas before you've even placed your order for iced tea. And sure, salsa has become more prevalent across the United States over the years, but it's only in Texas and the Southwest that I've found the variety of salsas on offer, many made from native fruits and vegetables. When I moved to New York, the only commercial salsas I could find were tepid affairs made in Vermont or Connecticut, which did little to satisfy my heat-craving palate.

I soon learned that if I wanted my preferred condiments with my Texan dishes, I'd simply have to make them myself.

Coming up with gravy recipes wasn't that difficult for me. As with most other Texan families, we've been making gravies almost every day for as long as I can remember. My grandma recalls her mother making red-eye gravy after frying up slices of home-cured hams; it went well with both the meat and a biscuit.

And it seems almost every night I'd watch Mom sprinkle some flour into a cast-iron skillet and then whisk in milk to make gravy for our supper. They gave me their recipes, and I was satisfied. Making salsas, however, proved to be more of a challenge.

My uncle Richard was the first person I knew who actually made salsa on a regular basis. Being a Texan of a certain age, he calls it hot sauce, which is what everyone, myself included, called it before the term *salsa* became more popular. Now, you may think that it's a little strange that not everyone makes homemade salsa, but in Texas there's such a wide availability of the good stuff for sale, you don't have to make it from scratch. Trust me though—if you do take the little bit of effort, you'll discover that it's a whole lot better.

My first trip home from Texas, I cornered Richard in the kitchen and insisted that he teach me how to make salsa. He graciously obliged me, albeit when I ended up putting my own spin on it, he conceded that I had crafted my own creation. At first I was disappointed that I hadn't made his recipe, as it's probably one of my all-time favorites. But when I thought about it, I realized that if I had indeed made my own version, then I could probably create a host of other varieties as well. I haven't bought a jar of salsa from the store since.

Some may consider condiments a crutch for making less-than-palatable food a bit livelier. Perhaps this is true in other places, but I've found that the gravies, sauces, and salsas on offer at the Texan table are as vital a component of the meal as the main event.

CREAM GRAVY

4 SERVINGS

2 tablespoons pan drippings, bacon grease, or vegetable oil
2 tablespoons all-purpose flour
1½ cups whole milk
Salt and black pepper, to taste

One of the hallmarks of Texan food is cream gravy. This thick, peppery, creamy sauce is poured over everything. It's a simple concoction, made from pan drippings, flour, milk, and cracked black pepper. But while it may appear plain, it's infinitely delicious. Sometimes it goes by the name country gravy or white gravy, but in Texas we call it cream gravy.

The history of cream gravy goes back hundreds of years. People of limited means didn't have the ingredients to make complex meat-stock gravies, but there was always flour, milk, and pepper on hand to add to the pan drippings. My grandma tells me that during the Great Depression, they ate it all the time, pouring it over everything, as it was a great way to stretch a meal. And apparently my great-grandma Blanche even whipped up batches from her bottomless can of bacon grease to feed her dog.

To craft cream gravy is a cinch. It's best cooked with pan drippings, but you can also do it from scratch with either vegetable oil or bacon grease. And while cracked black pepper is the traditional seasoning, you can tart it up with chipotles, jalapeños, cayenne, or chile powder.

1. In a skillet on medium heat, combine fat with flour. Continuously stir, cooking on medium for a couple of minutes until a dark roux is formed.

2. Add milk slowly to skillet and mix with the roux, using either a whisk or wooden spoon (be sure to press out any lumps). Turn the heat down to low and continue stirring until mixture is thickened, a couple more minutes. Add salt and black pepper to taste. If gravy is too thick, you can thin it by adding either more milk or water, a tablespoon at a time.

SAWMILL GRAVY

4 SERVINGS

¼ pound breakfast sausage
2 tablespoons all-purpose flour
1½ cups whole milk
Salt and black pepper, to taste

After basic cream gravy, sawmill gravy is the most common gravy found in Texas. Some people claim that cream gravy and sawmill gravy are the same thing, but in my experience, sawmill gravy is made with sausage.

To make this gravy, you simply fry up crumbled sausage, usually Breakfast Sausage (page 66), and then make the gravy from the sausage drippings, adding the cooked sausage for a final flourish. It goes best over biscuits, rice, or grits, though I have known some people to spoon it over eggs and even their chicken-fried steak as well.

1. In a skillet on medium heat, cook the sausage until browned. With a slotted spoon, remove sausage from the skillet and place on a plate. Drain the oil from the pan, reserving 2 tablespoons in the skillet.

2. Combine fat with flour in a hot skillet, and while stirring, cook on medium for a couple of minutes until a dark roux is formed. Add milk slowly to skillet and mix with the roux, using either a whisk or wooden spoon (be sure to press out any lumps). Turn the heat down to low and continue stirring until mixture is thickened, a couple more minutes.

3. Stir in cooked sausage and add salt and black pepper to taste. If gravy is too thick, you can thin it by adding either more milk or water, a tablespoon at a time. Pour over biscuits, rice, grits, toast, or eggs.

CHIPOTLE AND BACON CREAM GRAVY

4 SERVINGS

When you're feeling a little wild, try this variation on cream gravy that's a bit fiery and smoky from the addition of chipotle chiles and bacon.

4 slices of bacon
2 tablespoons all-purpose flour
1½ cups whole milk
2 canned chipotle chiles in adobo, minced
Salt and black pepper, to taste

1. In a skillet on medium heat, cook the bacon until crisp. Drain bacon on paper towels and reserve 2 tablespoons of bacon grease in the skillet. When bacon has cooled, cut into ½-inch pieces.

2. Combine bacon fat with flour in the hot skillet, and while continuously stirring, cook on medium for a couple of minutes until a dark roux is formed.

3. Add milk slowly to skillet and mix with the roux, using either a whisk or wooden spoon (be sure to press out any lumps). Turn the heat down to low and continue stirring until mixture is thickened, a couple more minutes.

4. Stir in bacon and chipotle chiles, and add salt and black pepper to taste. If gravy is too thick, you can thin it by adding either more milk or water, a tablespoon at a time. Pour over biscuits, rice, grits, toast, or eggs. Also makes a fine dipping sauce for fried chicken livers and chicken-fried steak.

RED-EYE GRAVY

4 SERVINGS

Red-eye gravy is an old southern favorite that was a popular condiment at my grandmother's home when she was growing up in Melissa, Texas. Its preparation is very similar to cream gravy, as it is made with pan drippings. But instead of adding milk to form the gravy, coffee and water are added.

Red-eye gravy is traditionally made after frying up a slice of country ham, though you can make it with bacon drippings as well. Some might find it bitter, but that's nothing a little brown sugar can't fix. I enjoy pouring it over biscuits, but it's also mighty fine spooned over eggs, rice, and grits.

¼ cup bacon or ham pan drippings
½ cup brewed coffee
½ cup water
1 teaspoon brown sugar
Salt and black pepper, to taste

In a skillet, heat the bacon or ham drippings. Stir in the coffee, water, and brown sugar and blend until a thin gravy is formed. Add salt and black pepper to taste. Pour over biscuits, grits, or eggs.

COFFEE-CHIPOTLE BARBECUE SAUCE

2 CUPS

1 tablespoon bacon grease or vegetable oil

¼ medium yellow onion, diced

2 cloves garlic, minced

1 or 2 canned chipotle chiles in adobo, minced

½ cup ketchup

¼ cup tomato paste

¼ cup apple cider vinegar

2 tablespoons lemon juice

¼ cup molasses

1 tablespoon Worcestershire sauce

1 cup brewed coffee

½ tablespoon black pepper

1 teaspoon dry mustard powder

Pinch of ground nutmeg

Pinch of ground clove

1 teaspoon smoked paprika

Salt, to taste

Many Texans will tell you that proper barbecue needs no sauce. "Let the meat speak for itself!" they'll say. I agree. There's nothing finer than a well-smoked, succulent slab of beef, and smothering it in sauce would just be an insult to the meat.

There are times, however, when your meat may not be as juicy and flavorful as you want it to be. In times such as this, a good barbecue sauce will be a salvation.

Texans also like a tomato-based sauce, but we're inclined to make it our own by adding some heat and the bittersweet notes found in molasses. This is my barbecue sauce, which has not only plenty of fire but also smoke from chipotle chiles and smoked paprika. I also tone down the sweetness even further by stirring in a cup of brewed coffee, which has long been a key ingredient in Texan barbecue sauces.

I like to serve this slathered on my Coffee-Chipotle Oven Brisket (page 189), but it also goes well with chicken, ribs, or spooned into a pot of pinto beans.

1. Heat the bacon grease in a sauce pot on medium and cook the onion for 10 minutes or until translucent. Add the garlic and cook for another minute.

2. Stir into the pot the chipotle chile, ketchup, tomato paste, vinegar, lemon juice, molasses, Worcestershire sauce, coffee, black pepper, mustard powder, nutmeg, clove, and smoked paprika. Turn down the heat to low and cook for 30 minutes, stirring occasionally. Add salt to taste. If it's too thick, add a bit of water to make it thinner. Will keep for 1 month in the refrigerator.

JALAPEÑO BUTTERMILK DRESSING

ABOUT 1 CUP

Texans love their buttermilk dressing. We slather it on our salads, pour it over our pizza, and serve it with our fried okra.

Buttermilk dressing has long been a popular staple in a Texan's larder. Its presence harks back to a time when dairy was ubiquitous and cheap, so it made sense to craft a dressing out of buttermilk rather than vegetable oil, which was scarce.

In the 1960s, buttermilk dressing became branded by a food company as ranch dressing, but I prefer to call it by its proper name, especially as the stuff you buy in a bottle has almost no relationship to what you can make at home. And yes, buttermilk is indeed the star.

This creamy dressing has plenty of heat from fresh jalapeños, but don't worry, as the fire is quelled by the buttermilk, mayonnaise, and sour cream. I'm prone to toss this with cabbage and radishes for a slaw or use it as a sauce for fried treats such as okra or shrimp, but I know many people who find that it also works as a dipping sauce for tortilla chips, which definitely works for me.

2 fresh jalapeño chiles, stems and seeds removed, chopped
1 clove garlic
¼ cup cilantro
¼ cup fresh parsley
¼ teaspoon ground cumin
¼ teaspoon paprika
¼ teaspoon lime zest
¼ cup buttermilk
½ cup sour cream
½ cup mayonnaise
Salt and black pepper, to taste

1. In a blender, combine the jalapeños, garlic, cilantro, parsley, cumin, paprika, lime zest, and buttermilk. Blend until it's a green puree.

2. Pour the jalapeño puree into a bowl and gently stir in the sour cream and mayonnaise. Add salt and black pepper to taste.

GUACAMOLE

2 TO 4 SERVINGS

2 ripe Hass avocados, peeled and pitted

2 cloves garlic, crushed

1 serrano chile, seeds and stem removed, diced

½ cup chopped cilantro

1 tablespoon lime juice

Salt, to taste

My mom used to make a batch of guacamole every day, which is where I believe I acquired my taste for this creamy condiment. We'd spread it on top of nachos, spoon it on chalupas, dollop it into tacos, or simply eat it with a basket of crisp tortilla chips.

There are many ways to make guacamole. For instance, some people make complicated guacamoles stuffed with ingredients such as tomatoes and pomegranate seeds, while others go so far as to include mayonnaise. I, however, like to keep it simple.

Guacamole is all about freshness, and while you want the avocado to be the star, the other ingredients need to be heard as well. And nothing is louder than the fire of fresh chiles, the tang of lime juice, and the bite of fresh garlic.

1. Scoop out the flesh from the avocado into a bowl. Add the garlic, serrano chile, cilantro, lime juice, and salt.

2. Mash the ingredients together either with a fork in a bowl or in a Mexican mortar and pestle (*molcajete*) until desired consistency. If you're using a *molcajete*, there's no need to crush the garlic. And you can add another serrano chile if you like it extra hot.

HABANERO SALSA

ABOUT 1½ CUPS

I once stopped at a taco truck in Dallas that had the most glorious bright orange salsa on offer along with the usual red and green. I'm quite partial to the color orange, so I loaded this salsa on my taco, knowing full well what was to follow. Yep, my mouth exploded with fire. This was a habanero salsa.

If you've never had the pleasure of eating a habanero chile, it's a lantern-shaped pepper that packs a ton of heat, almost five times the amount of heat found in a jalapeño. But what makes me love habaneros even more is the chile's fruity notes, which counter the bright heat. Sure, it's fiery, but it's a flavorful fire.

One thing that helps with the heat is the pairing of habaneros with sweet carrots. And once you throw in some tomatoes, spices, and aromatics, you have a creamy, luscious salsa that adds life to anything you choose to adorn it with, be it a taco, a tortilla chip, or even a plate of baked fish.

1 teaspoon vegetable oil

1 carrot, peeled and cut into slices

⅛ medium yellow onion, chopped

2 cloves garlic

½ cup crushed canned tomatoes

1 habanero chile, seeds and stem removed, chopped

¼ teaspoon dried oregano

¼ teaspoon ground cumin

½ cup chicken broth

Salt, to taste

1. In a large skillet on medium heat, warm up the oil. Add the sliced carrots and chopped onions to the skillet. Stirring occasionally, cook until the onions turn translucent and the carrots begin to lighten. With a slotted spoon, transfer carrots and onions to a blender.

2. Add to the blender the garlic, tomatoes, habanero chile, oregano, cumin, and chicken broth. On high speed, puree until smooth, which may take a minute. Taste and add salt and adjust seasonings. Will last in the refrigerator for 1 week.

PICO DE GALLO

2 CUPS

1 pound ripe plum tomatoes, diced

1 clove garlic, minced

¼ medium yellow onion, diced

¼ cup chopped cilantro

2 jalapeño chiles, stems and seeds removed, diced

¼ teaspoon ground cumin

2 tablespoons lime juice

½ tablespoon olive oil

Salt, to taste

Most of my other salsa recipes will taste good with canned tomatoes or tomatillos, but it's impossible to make an excellent pico de gallo unless the ingredients are fresh, ripe, and in season. It's a salsa fresca, which is why I make this only in the summer and early fall.

Pico de gallo in Spanish means "rooster's beak," and there are several schools of thought about why this salsa is so named. Some say it's because the bite of the peppers is like a rooster's bite. Perhaps, but this salsa isn't known for its fire as much as, say, a salsa made with habaneros. Others say the name stems from the Spanish verb picar, which means "to chop," an explanation that makes the most sense to me, as that's exactly what you do in order to create this chunky salsa.

Chopped tomatoes, peppers, onions, garlic, and cilantro are tossed together to make this salsa. Because I want the tomatoes to dominate my pico, I finely mince my peppers, onions, and garlic so they aren't fighting for attention in my mouth. And while it may be a bit untraditional, I also add a smidge of olive oil to bring all the flavors together. Pico de gallo is a versatile condiment. You can use it on top of anything—chips, fish tacos, scrambled eggs—but I often eat it as a simple summer salad, too.

1. Mix together the tomatoes, garlic, onion, cilantro, jalapeños, cumin, lime juice, and olive oil. Taste and add salt.

2. Place in the refrigerator and let it sit for half an hour before serving. Will last for 3 days in the refrigerator.

WATERMELON SALSA

2 CUPS

No summer outdoor feast is complete without big wedges of watermelon piled high on the picnic table. When my grandpa was growing up on his North Texas farm in Sedalia, watermelon season was his favorite. He said that nothing was finer than walking among the many rows of melons and slicing into one picked straight from the vine.

Eating a melon wedge with just a sprinkle of salt may be the best way to savor this fruit, though I find it works in other applications as well, such as this watermelon salsa. In New York, tomatoes take a long time to come to market, so I'll often make this red salsa to tide me over until the tomatoes arrive.

Much like a pico de gallo, this is a cubed-fruit salsa that's served fresh and cold. The sweetness of the watermelon is complemented by the bite of radishes and heat of serrano chiles. If you're feeling fancy, a sprinkle of Cotija cheese adds a salty, creamy finish. It goes well with tortilla chips, fish, and chicken dishes, though you can also serve it as a side dish. And while I tend to use only the red-fleshed variety, this salsa is also good if made with cantaloupe and honeydew melons.

2 cups peeled, diced watermelon
2 radishes, finely diced
¼ small red onion, diced
1 serrano chile, seeds and stems
   removed, diced
¼ cup chopped cilantro
2 tablespoons lime juice
¼ teaspoon ground cumin
Salt to taste
Cotija cheese, for serving

1. Toss together the watermelon, radishes, red onions, serrano chile, cilantro, lime juice, and cumin. Taste and add salt.

2. Place in the refrigerator and let it sit for half an hour before serving. Serve with chips, with chicken and pork dishes, or even as a side dish with a sprinkle of Cotija cheese. Will keep in the refrigerator for 3 days.

SALSA FUEGO

ABOUT 1½ CUPS

2 dried pasilla chiles, stems and
  seeds removed
1 pound plum tomatoes
Salt, to taste
2 cloves garlic
¼ medium yellow onion
1 canned chipotle chile in adobo
½ cup cilantro

I first encountered salsa fuego at Taco Cabana, a Texan fast-food chain that specializes in tacos and other Tex-Mex dishes. One of the things that catapults Taco Cabana above the ranks of other fast-food joints is their extensive salsa bar loaded with freshly chopped cilantro, diced onions, sliced jalapeños, pico de gallo, a mild red salsa, a tart green salsa, and my favorite, the salsa fuego.

For years, the method for making this dark, smoky salsa at home had eluded me. And since you don't see this salsa outside of Texas (I'm not sure of its Mexican provenance, but in Texas it's most commonly found in San Antonio), I knew that if I wanted it, I would have to persevere until I cracked its code.

One day, however, a fortunate accident occurred. I was roasting plum tomatoes under the broiler and forgot about them. After half an hour, when my apartment was beginning to take on a charred smell, I remembered that I had something in the oven. I reached in to pull out the baking sheet, and as can be expected, what was before me was black, shriveled fruit.

I was about to throw the blackened tomatoes away when I noticed a certain scent coming from them. It was a deep, familiar smell that was not at all unpleasant. It took me a second and then I realized—it was the aroma of my beloved salsa fuego. I threw the tomatoes into the blender along with some chiles, garlic, and cilantro and made a puree. After one bite, I realized that I'd finally cracked the salsa fuego code.

This is a robust salsa, which I like to pair with beef dishes. It's also great with refried beans and breakfast tacos, and as a dipping sauce for tortilla chips.

1. In a dry skillet heated on high, toast the pasilla chiles on each side for about 10 seconds or just until they start to puff. Fill the skillet with enough water to cover chiles. Leave the

{CONTINUED}

heat on until the water begins to boil and then turn off the heat and let the chiles soak until soft, about 30 minutes. Discard the soaking water and rinse the chiles once rehydrated.

2. While the chiles are soaking, cut the tomatoes in half, lengthwise, and place seed-side-up on a foil-lined sheet. Sprinkle with salt and place under the broiler for 20 minutes. They should be black. With tongs, gently turn the tomatoes over; add the garlic cloves and onion to the sheet and place back under the broiler for 5 more minutes.

3. Scoop blackened tomatoes, garlic, and onion into a blender. Add the soaked pasilla chiles, chipotle chile, cilantro, and 1 cup of water. Blend until smooth. Add salt to taste. Serve with tortilla chips or tacos. Will last for 1 week in the refrigerator.

NOTE: Don't worry if tomatoes aren't in season, as the cooking process will bring out enough flavor. And feel free to add more water if the salsa is too thick for your liking. For more flavor, you can substitute chicken broth for the water.

HOUSTON-STYLE GREEN SALSA

ABOUT 2 CUPS

When I was nine, we moved to Houston from Dallas. The first time we went to a Mexican restaurant, I was in for a big shock—on Houston Mexican menus there were Tex-Mex dishes I'd never seen in Dallas, such as enchiladas verdes. Also, being close to the Gulf, fish tacos were popular, as were tacos al carbon and a sizzling skillet of fajitas. But most striking to me was that alongside the usual bowl of red salsa on the table there was also a bowl of green.

Being young and leery of all things green, I was reluctant to try it at first. But after my first bite of this creamy, tangy mix of avocados, cilantro, garlic, and tomatillos, I knew that I was going to love my new home. I was hooked.

I once found a recipe in the *Houston Chronicle* for what was purported to be the Ninfa's version of the salsa, and I adapted it and posted it on my Web site. It called for sour cream and green tomatoes, along with the other usual ingredients. While I do admit it's delicious, I came up with an even simpler recipe that's not only healthier but even tastier.

This version of green salsa gets its creaminess from only the avocados, and since you're not adding sour cream, the flavors are brighter. I've added lime juice, which not only adds some tang but also keeps the salsa from turning brown, as avocados are known to do.

¾ pound small tomatillos, husks removed, or one 11-ounce can of whole tomatillos, drained
1 avocado, peeled and pitted
1 or 2 serrano chiles, stems and seeds removed, roughly chopped
4 cloves garlic, chopped
1 tablespoon lime juice
¼ cup cilantro
Salt, to taste

1. If using fresh tomatillos, on high heat, bring a pot of water to boiling and cook tomatillos until soft, about 5 minutes.

2. Add the tomatillos to a blender along with the avocado, serrano chiles, garlic, lime juice, and cilantro. Blend until smooth and then add salt to taste.

UNCLE RICHARD'S HOT SAUCE

3½ CUPS

The first salsa I ever made was my uncle's—a simple tomato-based affair, made with tomatoes, jalapeños, onions, and cilantro. He also throws in a generous dose of chili powder, his secret ingredient, which gives it a Tex-Mex kick. It's an old family favorite that we slather on everything—from turkey leftovers at Thanksgiving to hamburgers on the Fourth of July. It's also a fine dipping sauce for tortilla chips.

When I first moved to New York, I was missing this salsa something fierce. I asked my uncle for the recipe, but he admitted that he didn't have one; if I wanted to figure out how to make it, I'd just have to watch and learn. I took diligent notes, but when I presented him with my interpretation at a family gathering, he took a bite, shook his head, and said, "This is nothing like my salsa! What have you done?"

But I chose to ignore him—he can be very particular, after all. And I must have done something right, because the bowl was soon empty. So even though this salsa may not be exactly like my uncle's, it's still bright, spicy, and refreshing. And that's the beauty of salsa—it's flexible enough that when you make it you can make it your own.

1 28-ounce can of crushed tomatoes
1 medium yellow onion, quartered
2 cloves garlic
½ cup cilantro
1 tablespoon chili powder
½ tablespoon ground cumin
¼ to ½ cup pickled jalapeño chile slices
2 tablespoons lemon juice
Salt, to taste

1. Place the tomatoes, onion, garlic, cilantro, chili powder, cumin, jalapeños, and lemon juice into a blender and blend until smooth.

2. Taste and adjust seasonings and add salt to taste. Will last in the refrigerator for 1 week.

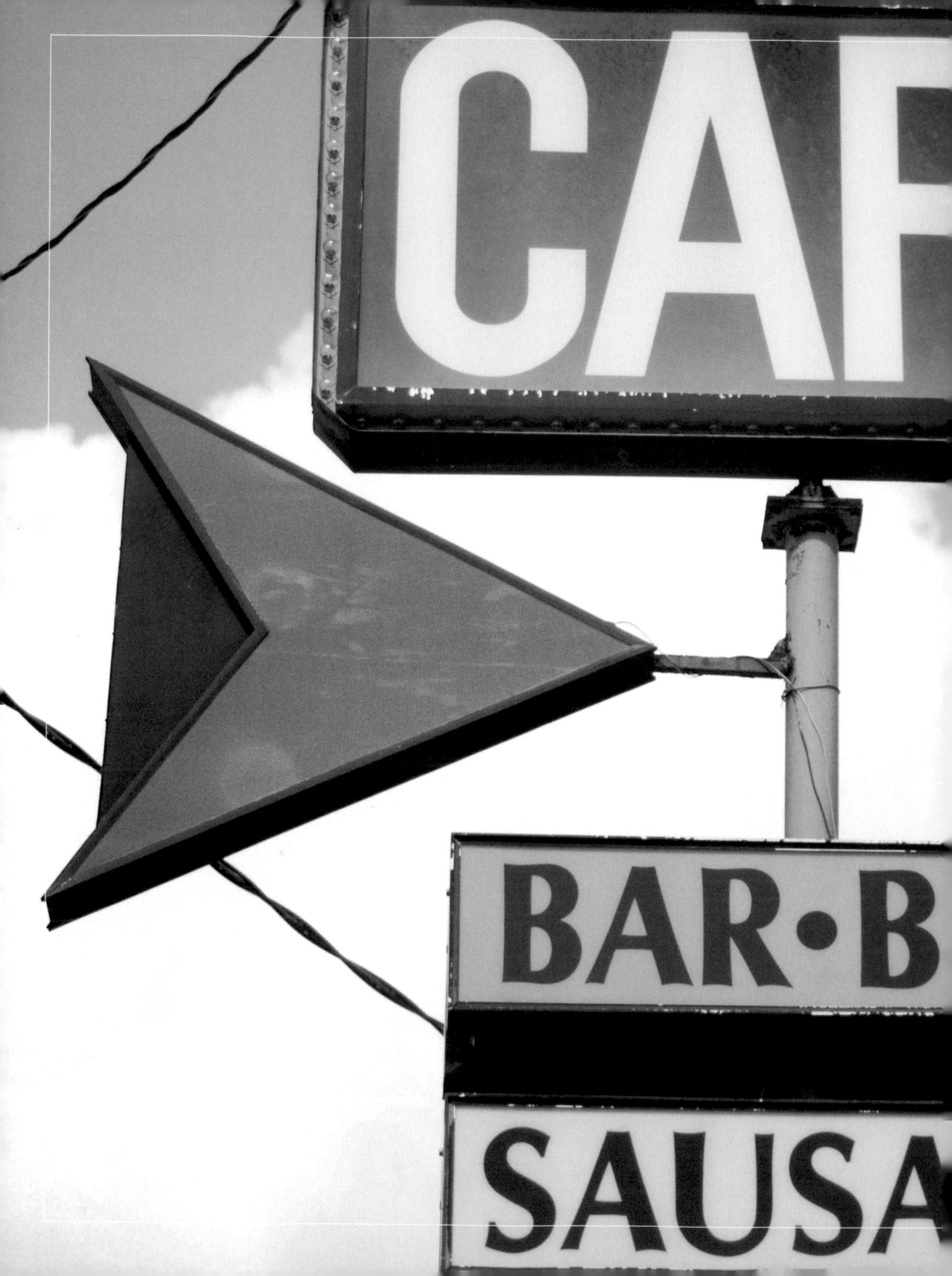
CAF
BAR•B
SAUSA

4

MORNING FOOD

I was walking down Broadway one day when I noticed that some people were giving me a thumbs-up sign or a wide, toothy grin as I passed them on the street. Now, Texas is known for the hidey wave—a greeting you give to friends and strangers alike when you pass them on the road. But New York City? Being overly friendly to strangers probably means that you're not quite right in the head.

I was beginning to suspect that I had something wrong with my face when a woman ran up to me and said, "I miss Texas so much. And I love your shirt!"

I looked down and saw that I was wearing my Kerbey Lane T-shirt, a shirt I'd picked up at the Austin restaurant chain before I had left Texas. This restaurant was famous for its breakfast, so on the shirt was an illustration of a tall stack of pancakes underneath the restaurant's logo.

The woman and I talked about Austin and Texas food, and after comparing notes decided that breakfast in Texas is indeed a very special meal. Sure, there are many fine breakfasts to be found all over the

world, but what makes breakfast in Texas special are the dishes that you will find only there.

Take the breakfast taco, which is one of Texas's most popular morning offerings. It's a simple dish comprised of a tortilla (usually flour) stuffed with eggs and the protein of your choice. Finding a breakfast taco is not difficult, and all over Texas you'll see people gathering at carts, taquerias, and even gas stations so they can grab a breakfast taco or two before hitting the road and beginning their day.

Then there are migas, a Texan classic that scrambles eggs with fried corn tortillas, a savory dish that's best served with a stack of warm flour tortillas and refried beans. We also enjoy breakfast casseroles, which are perfect for feeding a crowd on busy holiday mornings.

Texans love their breakfast. And whether we're standing at a taco truck or sitting at home in front of a tall stack of pancakes, Texans definitely know how to start the day right.

I wish I still had my Kerbey Lane T-shirt, but it was lost in one of my apartment moves. But with these recipes, I no longer need it to remind me of how fine that first meal of the day in Texas can be.

BREAKFAST SAUSAGE

2 POUNDS

2 pounds ground pork, at least
20 percent fat

1 tablespoon dried sage

2 teaspoons dried marjoram

2 teaspoons dried thyme

2 teaspoons red pepper flakes

½ teaspoon cayenne

1 teaspoon brown sugar

½ teaspoon kosher salt

½ teaspoon black pepper

Texans like their breakfast sausage to come in the form of patties, not links (though we seldom say *patty*, as it's just assumed when you have sausage in the morning that's what it'll be). My grandfather once told me that when he was a boy, his job on hog-butchering day was to make the sausage.

Hog-butchering day was an annual event held in January, where the neighboring farmers in the North Texas community of Sedalia would bring their hogs to my grandpa's farm, and they'd work together at the difficult task of slaying, skinning, draining, cleaning, and butchering. At the end of the day, when my great-grandpa could be found outside the barn standing over a kettle rendering lard, my grandpa would go into the smokehouse, grind some pork shoulder, and mix it with herbs, salt, and pepper to make sausage. He didn't follow a recipe, adding the flavors by memory instead. As he worked he'd fry up small pieces of the sausage to adjust his seasonings until it tasted just right. When it was done, he'd stuff it into clean socks for storage. I asked him if he could give me an approximate recipe, and this is what he shared.

While making your own sausage may sound like a daunting task, breakfast sausage is a cinch: you don't have to work with casing, and there's no aging involved. Instead, it's just a simple mixture of ground pork and spices, ready to be formed into patties and cooked immediately.

Breakfast sausage may just be one of the most versatile meats to have on hand. Of course, you can fry it up and serve it with eggs. Or you can place some in a biscuit for a tasty breakfast sandwich. You can crumble it into cream gravy, throw it into breakfast tacos, and I've even been known to use it on top of my pizza. Once you get the hang of making your own, you may never eat store-bought breakfast sausage again.

1. With your hands or a spoon, mix together the pork, sage, marjoram, thyme, red pepper flakes, cayenne, brown sugar, salt, and black pepper.

2. Heat a skillet on medium heat and cook a small spoonful of the sausage a couple of minutes on each side. Taste and adjust seasonings.

3. Once you're satisfied with the flavor balance, form the sausage into patties and fry 6 minutes on each side. The sausage will keep in the refrigerator for a week. It can also be frozen uncooked for 6 months.

NOTE: If you don't grind your own meat (you can do this either with a grinder or in a food processor), make sure that your preground pork has at least 20 percent fat, otherwise the sausage will be too dry.

BISCUITS AND GRAVY

4 SERVINGS

I went to school in Spain my junior year of college. It was a wonderful experience, and I became fluent not only in Spanish but in Spanish cuisine as well. Growing up in Texas close to Mexico, I was already familiar with the language. The food, however, was decidedly not familiar. I loved what I ate, but after a while I began to pine for Texas food something awful. So after the last semester, when I returned home, my first order of business was to stuff myself with all the foods that I had missed while away.

Soon after I got back, my friend Kevin invited me over for dinner. An excellent home cook, he likes to create elaborate feasts. When I arrived, he swept his arm across his kitchen and said, "Fainster, I will cook for you anything that you want." I didn't have to think long before making a decision. And my choice? Biscuits and gravy. "Are you sure?" he said. I was sure. Of course, biscuits and gravy are traditionally served at breakfast, but as there were no biscuits in Spain and there certainly wasn't cream gravy, it was what I wanted for dinner that night. And who better to make biscuits and gravy than an excellent cook who's well versed in both city and country cuisine. Kevin whipped up a batch of biscuits, fried up some sausage, and then stirred flour and milk into the pan drippings to make a gravy. We sliced the biscuits in half, drowned them in gravy, and dug into a simple but wonderful feast. It was a fine welcome back to Texas.

8 Biscuits (page 282)
Sawmill Gravy (page 44)

Slice the biscuits in half and place on a plate. Cover the biscuits with Sawmill Gravy.

BREAKFAST TACOS

4 TACOS

1 tablespoon unsalted butter

4 large eggs, beaten

4 pieces of bacon, cooked and sliced

Salt and black pepper, to taste

4 flour tortillas

1 cup refried beans, heated

1 cup grated longhorn cheddar cheese (4 ounces)

Salsa

Whenever I fly home to Texas, the first thing I do when I get off the plane is head out for Tex-Mex. I've been living outside the state so long, the question is no longer even posed—whoever is picking me up at the airport knows where to take me. If it's midday or later, we'll go to a proper sit-down place. If it's early morning, however, we'll hit a taco truck for breakfast tacos.

I don't know why breakfast tacos are not more popular outside the state. I see places selling breakfast burritos, but they're always in that overstuffed, football-size California style, which, despite my having a hearty appetite, is just a bit much for breaking the fast.

A breakfast taco is a regular eight-inch flour tortilla (always flour tortillas, never corn) stuffed with scrambled eggs, cheese, and breakfast meat.

The brilliance of breakfast tacos is their portability. They easily fit in your hand and your mouth, with all your breakfast needs contained in one neat, little package. While I don't advocate eating and driving, these are up to the task, though they are equally delicious in a more proper, sit-down forum.

As you drive throughout Texas, the different types of breakfast tacos reflect that area's culinary strengths. For instance, if you grab a breakfast taco in the Hill Country, chances are one of the meat options will be spicy smoked hot links. If you're in Houston, shrimp may be on offer. North Texas breakfast tacos tend to be filled with ingredients more identified with country cooking, such as chopped-up sausage patties or bacon. But no matter what you stuff into your breakfast taco, it's always delicious and wonderful.

The variations are endless, so I'm providing a basic recipe, which you can experiment with and change to your heart's desire.

{CONTINUED}

1. Heat a large skillet, preferably cast-iron, on medium-high, and melt the tablespoon unsalted butter. When butter is melted, add the eggs and cooked bacon to the skillet and gently scramble for about 3 minutes or until done to your liking. Taste and add salt and black pepper.

2. Heat up the flour tortillas either in a skillet or by laying them on top of a gas burner turned on to a low flame. When a tortilla starts to puff (about 20 seconds) turn it over and cook for another 20 seconds.

3. Take a tortilla and spread ¼ cup of refried beans in the center of the tortilla. Add a quarter of the scrambled eggs and top with ¼ cup of cheese and salsa. Fold in the bottom 1 inch of the tortilla and then roll from left to right until self-contained.

NOTE: This is a basic recipe, which you can experiment with and change to your heart's desire. The variations on breakfast tacos are endless—you can also add breakfast sausage, chorizo, Mexican fried potatoes, or leftover brisket.

BREAKFAST RELLENO

4 SERVINGS

A friend of mine in North Texas was recently bragging about her favorite breakfast joint, so I asked her what made it so special. She rattled off the usual Texan breakfast specialties—a fine list of dishes, sure, but nothing to get too excited about. But then she said two words: *breakfast relleno*. Now, this sounded interesting!

I've long been a fan of stuffed chile peppers but never thought to serve them in the morning. What a terrific idea! If you're a fan of the stuffed-pepper genre, I think you'll enjoy this, as roasted poblano chiles go so well with eggs. And when you add cheese, salsa, and chorizo, you have yourself a fine breakfast that is definitely worth bragging about.

4 large poblano chiles
8 large eggs
½ teaspoon ground cumin
¼ teaspoon cayenne
1 teaspoon lard or vegetable oil
½ pound Mexican chorizo, removed from casing
¼ medium yellow onion, diced
2 cloves garlic, minced
1 jalapeño chile, seeds and stems removed, diced
¼ cup chopped cilantro
Salt and black pepper, to taste
1 cup grated cheddar cheese (4 ounces)
Salsa, for serving

1. Roast the poblano chiles under the broiler until blackened, about 5 minutes per side. Place chiles in a paper sack or plastic food-storage bag, close it tight, and let the chiles steam for 20 minutes. Take the chiles out of the bag and rub off the skin. With a sharp knife, cut a slit into each chile on one side, from just under the base of the stem down to the tip. Gently pry them open and remove the seeds.

2. To make the filling, beat together the eggs with the cumin and cayenne and set aside. Heat the lard or vegetable oil in a large skillet on medium heat and add the chorizo. While occasionally stirring, cook the chorizo until it starts to brown, about 5 minutes.

(CONTINUED)

3. Leaving the chorizo in the skillet, add the onions, and while occasionally stirring, cook the onions until translucent, about 5 minutes. Add the garlic and cook for 30 seconds. Pour in the beaten eggs and then sprinkle on top of the eggs the diced jalapeño and cilantro.

4. Let the eggs cook untouched for 1 minute so the bottom can set. Then gently stir the eggs a couple of times and let them cook until they are your preferred doneness. Add salt and black pepper to taste.

5. Turn on the broiler and grease a baking sheet. To assemble the rellenos, stuff each chile with ¼ of the egg mixture, and top with ¼ cup of grated cheese. Place chiles on the sheet under the broiler for a couple of minutes or until the cheese has melted. Serve with salsa.

NOTE: For crunch, you can add some crushed fried tortillas on top before placing under the broiler.

HUEVOS RANCHEROS

4 SERVINGS

I like to think of huevos rancheros as a breakfast tostada—as satisfying as a taco but with a presentation that makes it a great weekend dish to share with friends and family.

1. In a dry skillet heated on high, toast the guajillo chiles on each side for about 10 seconds or just until they start to puff. Fill the skillet with enough water to cover the chiles. Leave the heat on until the water begins to boil and then turn off the heat and let the chiles soak until soft, about 30 minutes. Once hydrated, discard the soaking water and rinse the chiles. Add them to a blender, along with the crushed tomatoes, serrano chiles, yellow onion, garlic, cilantro, cumin, allspice, and lime juice. Pulse until a rough puree forms. Taste and add salt.

2. In a pot heated on medium low, add the 1 tablespoon of oil and pour in the salsa along with 1 cup of water. Cook, stirring occasionally, for 20 minutes.

3. To make the fried tortillas, in a large skillet, heat ½ inch of oil on medium heat. When it reaches 300 degrees, fry the tortillas on each side until crisp and lightly browned, about 1 minute. Drain the fried tortillas on paper towels. Remove all but 1 tablespoon of the oil from the skillet and then fry the eggs two at a time (or however many will fit).

4. To assemble, place 2 fried tortillas on a plate, spoon on each tortilla some of the sauce, and top with a fried egg. Garnish with sliced jalapeño.

FOR THE RANCHERO SALSA

4 dried guajillo chiles, stems and seeds removed
1 14-ounce can of crushed tomatoes
1 or 2 serrano chiles, stems and seeds removed, diced
½ medium yellow onion
4 cloves garlic
¼ cup chopped cilantro
½ teaspoon ground cumin
Small pinch of ground allspice
2 tablespoons lime juice
Salt, to taste
1 tablespoon oil

FOR THE EGGS

Oil, for frying
8 corn tortillas
8 large eggs
Salt and black pepper, to taste
1 jalapeño chile, stem and seeds removed, sliced into thin rounds

MIGAS

4 SERVINGS

Oil, for frying

4 corn tortillas cut into strips

½ medium yellow onion, diced

4 jalapeño chiles, seeds and stems
    removed, diced

8 eggs

¼ cup whole milk or half-and-half

½ teaspoon kosher salt, plus more
    to taste

½ teaspoon black pepper, plus
    more, to taste

½ teaspoon ground cumin

¼ cup chopped cilantro

2 cloves garlic, minced

1 cup grated cheddar cheese or
    Monterey Jack cheese (4 ounces)

Salsa, for serving

Warmed-up tortillas, for serving

If you've ever had breakfast in Austin, chances are you've had a plate of migas. This dish of eggs scrambled with fried corn tortilla strips, salsa, and cheese is ubiquitous in some of the Texas capital city's most popular breakfast spots.

This dish is designed to use up old stale tortillas, though if you have only fresh ones the end result will not suffer. You can use any kind of salsa you have on hand as well—migas taste just as good with a green salsa as with a red. While cheese is a must, you can also jazz these up with crumbled Mexican chorizo, chopped poblanos, onions, or anything else.

1. In a large skillet, preferably a cast-iron skillet, heat up ½ inch of vegetable oil on medium-high until it reaches a temperature of 300 degrees. Place tortilla strips into skillet, cooking until crisp for about 3 minutes, turning once. Remove tortilla strips with a slotted spoon and place on a paper-towel-lined plate.

2. Drain the oil from the skillet, leaving 2 tablespoons, and turn the heat down to medium. Add the onions and jalapeños to the skillet, cooking while occasionally stirring until the onions are translucent, about 5 minutes. While the onions and chiles are cooking, whisk the eggs in a bowl with the milk, salt, black pepper, cumin, and cilantro.

3. After the onions and chiles are cooked, add the garlic to the skillet and cook for 30 more seconds. Add the egg mixture and the tortilla strips to the skillet, and let the eggs sit for about a minute or until set on the bottom. Stir gently. Sprinkle cheese on top of the eggs and continue to stir gently until the cheese has melted. Add salt and black pepper to taste. Serve eggs with salsa and tortillas.

MEXICAN FRIED POTATOES

4 SERVINGS

I'm a big fan of breakfast potatoes, and if they're studded with eye-opening jalapeños, smoky paprika, and tangy vinegar, all the better. I like to serve them on the plate with scrambled eggs, or stuffed into a tortilla with chorizo and refried beans. And while my preferred time to eat them is in the morning, they taste just as good any time of the day.

1. In a large skillet, preferably a cast-iron skillet, heat the oil on medium-low heat. When warm, add the potatoes and ½ teaspoon kosher salt, and while stirring occasionally, cook uncovered for 10 minutes.

2. Stir in the onions and cook for 2 more minutes then stir in the jalapeño, garlic, tomatoes, cumin, and smoked paprika. Cook for 30 more seconds and then turn the heat to low and cook covered for 15 minutes.

3. Remove the cover and stir, scraping up any potatoes that may be stuck to the bottom. Cook uncovered for 10 minutes or until the potatoes are your preferred texture. Stir in the vinegar and the chopped cilantro, add pepper, taste and adjust seasonings.

2 tablespoons vegetable oil or bacon grease

2 pounds Russet potatoes, peeled and cut into ¼-inch cubes

½ teaspoon kosher salt, plus more to taste

¼ medium yellow onion, diced

1 jalapeño chile, seeds and stems removed, diced

4 cloves garlic, minced

½ cup crushed canned tomatoes, drained

½ teaspoon ground cumin

¼ teaspoon smoked paprika

2 teaspoons white vinegar

¼ cup chopped cilantro

Black pepper, to taste

GRANDPA'S PANCAKES

2 cups all-purpose flour

1 tablespoon whole wheat flour

1 tablespoon baking powder

½ teaspoon kosher salt

2 tablespoons granulated sugar

1 large egg

1½ cups whole milk

¼ cup vegetable oil

1 tablespoon unsalted butter

½ cup pecans

When I was little, I spent a lot of time at my grandparents' house in the Dallas neighborhood of Oak Cliff. Sundays through Fridays, my grandmother ruled the kitchen. But on Saturdays, the stove belonged to Grandpa. Every Saturday morning, you'd walk into their house, and the smell of Grandpa's pancakes would greet you with an invitation to sit at the table and dig into a stack.

My grandpa was a busy man. During the week, he spent his days as the head psychologist at the Dallas VA hospital. He also pursued photography with a passion, winning awards at the Texas State Fair for his photos of wildlife and people. Besides photography, he was an avid home-movie maker, and his footage of President John F. Kennedy's arrival at Love Field on that sad day in Dallas has been included in documentaries and museum exhibits on the subject.

On weekends, however, Grandpa took a break and made us pancakes so he could relax and reconnect with his family. He liked to doll his pancakes up with sweet crunchy pecans picked from our family farm. And when they were in season, he'd throw in some juicy blueberries as well. But honestly, I could eat these pancakes plain; they were so fluffy and moist, no adornment was necessary.

His pancake recipe is pretty simple, but because they were made with both love and expertise, they are still the best pancakes I've ever had. And while it doesn't matter when you eat them, Grandpa's recipe card notes: "Mighty good on Saturday morning!"

1. Mix together the flours, baking powder, salt, and sugar. Beat together the egg, milk, and vegetable oil and add to the flour mixture.

2. Heat a skillet on medium and melt the butter. Pour ¼ cup of the batter into the skillet and cook for a couple of minutes on one side (until edges are brown and bubbles form in the batter). Flip and cook on the other side a couple more minutes. Continue for the rest of the batter.

PECAN COFFEE CAKE (MICKEY CAKE)

8 SERVINGS

One of my favorite books when I was young was Maurice Sendak's *In the Night Kitchen*, a tale about a little boy named Mickey who hangs out with three giant bakers in an outdoor kitchen in a place that looks much like New York City. As an adult, I'm a bit puzzled by the narrative, but my three-year-old mind found it fantastic.

In the story, Mickey and the bakers bake a cake for breakfast, so my mom took to calling our Sunday-morning coffee cake Mickey Cake after this favorite book. Mom's coffee cake is tender, airy, and soft. But light texture aside, the main reason why I include this coffee cake is that I'm pretty sure *In the Night Kitchen* influenced not only my desire to live in New York City but also my love of cooking. A most significant coffee cake indeed!

1. Preheat the oven to 400 degrees.

2. In a large ovenproof skillet, preferably a cast-iron skillet, melt on low heat 4 tablespoons of unsalted butter. Remove from heat. Mix together the brown sugar, cinnamon, and chopped pecans and sprinkle over melted butter. In a large bowl, mix together the flour, sugar, baking powder, and salt.

3. Beat together the egg, milk, oil, and vanilla. Pour egg mixture into the dry ingredients and stir until a thick batter has formed. Pour this batter into the skillet, spreading evenly over the butter mixture. For the topping, combine the flour, softened butter, brown sugar, and cinnamon, and sprinkle over the cake batter. Bake uncovered for 20 to 25 minutes or until an inserted knife pulls out clean.

FOR THE CAKE
4 tablespoons unsalted butter
¼ cup brown sugar
½ teaspoon ground cinnamon
½ cup pecans, roughly chopped
1½ cups all-purpose flour
½ cup granulated sugar
2 teaspoons baking powder
½ teaspoon kosher salt
1 large egg
¾ cup milk
¼ cup vegetable oil
1 teaspoon vanilla extract

FOR THE TOPPING
2 tablespoons all-purpose flour
4 tablespoons unsalted butter, softened
¼ cup brown sugar
½ teaspoon ground cinnamon

APPETIZERS

L isa, why are there toothpicks everywhere?" said my mom.

I was busted.

My parents had gone away for the weekend and had shuttled my little brother off to my grandparents. This meant that I had the whole house to myself, a fine occurrence when you're seventeen years old. Now, I was a relatively good girl, so when my friends and I decided to have a party (against my parents' stern command to not let anyone come over while they were away), we decided it would be a tasteful dinner party instead of the usual wild shindigs that other high school kids had.

We didn't have much experience with cooking, but one thing we did know from our parents' experience was that while the main dishes served would be important, the true test of an excellent party was the bounty and reception of the appetizers on hand. So to prepare, we focused most of our time on creating foods we felt were sophisticated starters, such as cream cheese–stuffed jalapeños, sausage biscuits, and slender stalks of celery filled with pimento cheese. But to add a bit more pizzazz and class, I decided to stick a toothpick in each small bite. It was a most impressive final flourish, but sadly, this is what caught me out in the end.

When my parents came home, my mom started seeing toothpicks in strange places—next to the washing machine, embedded in the couch cushions, around the stove, on the bookcases, and under the rug. She'd pick them up and scratch her head, as we weren't big on using toothpicks in my family. For a day or so I was able to pretend ignorance, but it didn't take her long to figure out that I'd had a party and yes, I was grounded for a very long time. (As the jig was up, I then pointed out to her the spot on the

ceiling where we'd had a little accident while mixing cream cheese in the blender without a lid. She was not amused.) But I didn't mind too much. To me, the party had been a success—everyone loved the finger foods, which made my friends and me feel like accomplished adults.

If there's one thing that Texans know how to do, it's how to throw a gathering. We don't need many excuses to come together in fellowship, be it at a potluck after church, a game-day party celebrating the hometown team, a backyard barbecue on the Fourth of July, or at an open house after a loved one's funeral. And when we do get together, you can be assured there will be lots of finger foods, dips, and snacks on hand to keep everyone well fed as they move about and visit with friends and family.

While some of our snacks, such as a pecan-crusted cheese log or queso cookies, may seem more tailored to the holiday season, Texans get together throughout the year, and for most of us there's no seasonal limitation on good food. We'll sit on a patio and dip our tortilla chips into a warm bowl of chile con queso even when the temperature is in the triple digits. And you'll find that summertime picnic staple, deviled eggs, are equally welcome at the Thanksgiving table.

When it comes to finger foods, the only limit Texans have is how much to eat so you can save room in your belly for the main event. Though heck, if you wanted to, you could probably get away with serving enough chorizo empanadas, black bean dip, and fried jalapeño pickles that your guests might not even question if there's more food to come.

Just know that if you do choose to stick toothpicks into Texan finger foods, it's a good idea to be thorough when you clean up after the party.

BLACK BEAN DIP

3 CUPS

4 cups Austin-Style Black Beans
(page 124), or 2 15-ounce cans
of black beans, drained

2 cloves garlic

2 to 4 canned chipotle chiles in
adobo

1 cup chopped cilantro

2 teaspoons ground cumin

¼ teaspoon cayenne

2 teaspoons lime juice

2 teaspoons vegetable oil or bacon
grease

½ cup grated Monterey Jack cheese
(2 ounces)

Salt, to taste

My senior year at Austin College was when I first began to experiment with cooking. My housemates and I had gone off the meal plan, so if we were going to eat, we needed to fend for ourselves. Sure, we consumed lots of Whataburgers and chicken-fried steaks from City Limits, but most of our meals were created in the kitchen.

My friend Laura shared with us this recipe for black bean dip. We were having a party and wanted to create some finger foods for our guests. Back in 1991, black beans were still considered slightly exotic up in Sherman, Texas, not to mention that bean dip usually came in a can (along with a bag of Fritos, naturally), so making a bean dip from scratch made us feel as though we'd arrived.

Now, this dip is a snap to make. And sure, bean dips made from all sorts of beans are readily available in jars (and cans) these days. But if you've never made a bean dip from scratch, I highly recommend you give this a try. Not only do you get to control both the spice and the heat, but you also serve it warm, all of which makes it much better than any bean dip you can buy at the store.

1. Place in a blender the black beans, garlic, chipotle chiles, cilantro, cumin, cayenne, and lime juice. Blend until a smooth paste is formed.

2. In a pot, heat the oil on medium-low heat. Add the black bean puree and cook while stirring for 2 minutes. Fold in the Monterey Jack cheese and cook until melted. Add salt to taste. Serve immediately with tortilla chips.

NOTE: You can substitute pinto beans or black-eyed peas for the black beans, if you prefer.

BLUEBONNET
AMARILLO
LUBBOCK
WICHITA FALLS
TEXARKANA
DALLAS
LONGVIEW
TYLER
ABILENE
FORT WORTH
ODESSA
EL PASO
WACO
SAN ANGELO
AUSTIN
BEAUMONT
PORT ARTHUR
HOUSTON
GALVESTON
SAN ANTONIO
Texas
LAREDO
CORPUS CHRISTI
BROWNSVILLE

CHIPOTLE PIMENTO CHEESE

2 CUPS

1 cup freshly grated cheddar cheese
(4 ounces)

1 cup freshly grated Monterey Jack
cheese (4 ounces)

1 teaspoon grated yellow onion

1 garlic clove, minced

½ cup mayonnaise

¼ cup jarred sweet pimentos, diced

1 canned chipotle chile in adobo,
diced

½ cup chopped cilantro

¼ teaspoon ground cumin

1 teaspoon lime juice

Salt and black pepper, to taste

I can't remember a time when there wasn't a tub of pimento cheese in my refrigerator. This creamy combination of cheese, mayonnaise, and pickled red peppers known as pimentos (though spelled *pimiento* by those not from the South) is quite versatile. It works well as a dip for chips, as a filling for celery, or as a spread for a sandwich. And as it's a comforting crowd pleaser, you'll find it welcomed not only at celebrations but even after a funeral.

When my grandfather died, his church prepared for the family a whole host of dishes, including, yep, pimento cheese. After the funeral, Uncle Richard and I sat at the table, telling stories about my grandpa while dipping celery into the creamy pimento cheese. As we neared the end of the bowl, we got into a bit of an argument over who would get the last bite. But before our squabbling got too much out of hand, my cousin solved our problem by taking the last bite for himself. The family laughed at the absurdity of our fight, and indeed, that bowl of pimento cheese had brought us a bit of comic relief and joy on an otherwise sad day.

Now, you certainly don't have to wait for a funeral to make pimento cheese, as it's appropriate anytime. People love to argue about how best to make it, and there may be purists who scoff at my inclusion of chipotle chiles, lime juice, and cilantro. I don't mind—it just leaves more for those of us who like it spicy.

1. In a large bowl, mix together the cheddar cheese and the Monterey Jack cheese, onion, garlic, mayonnaise, pimentos, chipotle, cilantro, cumin, and lime juice. Taste and add salt and black pepper as needed.

2. Chill for one hour before serving. Serve with tortilla chips, crackers, or celery sticks. Also makes a fine filling for a whole, hollowed-out jalapeño. Will last a week in the refrigerator.

CHORIZO EMPANADAS

ABOUT 16

When I lived in Spain, I ate empanadas all the time. But it wasn't until 1995 in Austin that I had my first savory empanada back home.

My boss was having a luncheon at her Hill Country bed-and-breakfast. To get to the party, I hitched a ride from Austin with my friends Nanette and Tony. A new empanada joint had opened in town, and everyone had been raving about it. Ordinarily we'd stop and grab breakfast tacos to tide us over in the morning, but we decided try the empanadas instead.

I hadn't eaten empanadas since returning from Spain, and I was curious to see how their Mexican counterpart would taste. I ordered a chorizo empanada, and what I found was a flaky pastry wrapped around a savory, spicy filling of fiery Mexican chorizo mixed with creamy cheese and juicy sliced olives. It was fantastic and a fine way to begin what ended up being a glorious Hill Country day.

I like to offer these as appetizers, but they could certainly serve as a main course as well. Their hearty nature makes them perfect for cold weather, but I find that they're also terrific in the summer served with cold drinks.

1. To make the crust, mix together the cream cheese and butter until smooth. Stir in the flour and salt until a smooth dough is formed. Wrap in plastic wrap and refrigerate for 30 minutes.

2. Meanwhile, heat the vegetable oil in a large skillet, preferably a cast-iron skillet, on medium-low heat. Crumble the chorizo into the skillet. While occasionally stirring, cook the chorizo until it's done, about 7 to 10 minutes.

FOR THE CRUST
8 ounces cream cheese, room temperature
½ cup unsalted butter, room temperature (1 stick)
1½ cups all-purpose flour
½ teaspoon kosher salt

FOR THE FILLING
1 teaspoon vegetable oil
1 pound Mexican chorizo, removed from its casing
½ cup grated Monterey Jack cheese (2 ounces)
¼ cup pitted black olives, sliced
1 clove garlic, minced
1 jalapeño chile, seeds and stems removed, diced (if your chorizo is extra spicy, feel free to forgo the chile pepper)
2 tablespoons chopped cilantro
¼ teaspoon ground cumin
Salt and black pepper, to taste

FOR THE EMPANADA
1 large egg
2 tablespoons milk
Sesame seeds for sprinkling
Salsa, for dipping

{CONTINUED}

3. Drain the excess fat and in a bowl mix the cooked chorizo with the grated Monterey Jack cheese, black olives, garlic, diced jalapeño, cilantro, and cumin. Taste and add salt and black pepper.

4. To make the empanadas, preheat the oven to 375 degrees and lightly grease a baking sheet. Take the dough out of the refrigerator and roll it out on a floured surface until it's ⅛ inch thick. Cut into 5-inch rounds and then gather the scraps, roll out again and cut more 5-inch rounds until all the dough has been used.

5. Place 2 teaspoons of the filling in the center of each dough circle and fold the dough to the other side so it forms a half-moon shape. Crimp the edges with a fork to seal.

6. For the topping, whisk together the egg and milk. Brush this on top of the empanadas and then sprinkle the empanadas with sesame seeds. Bake for 25 minutes or until top is browned. Serve with salsa on the side for dipping.

NOTE: Some people like to add chopped dried fruit and nuts to their empanadas, so feel free to do so for a more complex flavor. I'd add about ¼ cup of each.

QUESO COOKIES

ABOUT 36 COOKIES

Every self-respecting Texan hostess has made a batch of these spicy cheese cookies, especially during the holidays. They're a snap to make and yet provide endless enjoyment, especially to those who've never had them before.

The dough comes together like a pie-crust dough—all crumbles until that magic moment when suddenly it's moist and supple enough to shape into a ball. And after fifteen minutes in the oven, you'll have a warm basket filled with these crisp, cheesy treats.

1 cup unsalted butter, softened (2 sticks)

2 cups grated sharp white cheddar cheese (8 ounces)

2 cups all-purpose flour

1 jalapeño chile, seeds and stem removed, diced

½ teaspoon kosher salt

½ teaspoon cayenne

¼ teaspoon ground cumin

1. Preheat the oven to 350 degrees and lightly grease a baking sheet.

2. Mix the butter and cheese together. Add the flour, jalapeño, salt, cayenne, and cumin. Stir until it forms a ball. Take a pinch of the dough at a time, shaping it into marble size, and place it on the sheet. Press with a fork.

3. Bake for 20 minutes. Cool and then serve. Will last in an airtight container for 1 week.

SMOKY DEVILED EGGS

4 TO 6 SERVINGS

6 large hard-cooked eggs, peeled and cut in half lengthwise

1 teaspoon lime juice

2 teaspoons chopped cilantro

2 tablespoons yellow prepared mustard

¼ cup mayonnaise

½ teaspoon ground cumin

¼ teaspoon smoked paprika, plus more for garnish

¼ teaspoon chipotle powder

1 clove garlic, minced

Salt, to taste

My grandma called to tell me that she had found the funeral-food card from my great-grandpa's funeral. I asked what the good people of Melissa, Texas, had brought to my great-grandpa's funeral. She laughed and said that every other entry was for a plate of deviled eggs.

Deviled eggs have long had a reputation for being a funeral food. I reckon it's their portability and soft, familiar texture that make them popular during times of grief. But I have to say that these qualities make them a welcome snack at other times as well. Whether you pack them along for a picnic, pass a plate around during a big game, or have a tray on offer before your backyard barbecue, you'll find that people will always respond with enthusiasm. And on second thought, maybe that's why they're such a popular funeral food—deviled eggs will always make people smile.

My deviled eggs are on the simpler end of the spectrum, although lime juice, smoked paprika, and garlic give them a lift beyond the classic mustard and mayonnaise combination.

1. Scoop the yolks out from the eggs into a bowl and mash until smooth.

2. Stir in the lime juice, cilantro, mustard, mayonnaise, ground cumin, smoked paprika, chipotle powder, and garlic. Mix until well combined. Taste and add salt and adjust seasonings.

3. Scoop or pipe mixture into halved eggs and sprinkle with additional smoked paprika if you like.

NOTE: These will last in the refrigerator for a couple of days, so they can be made ahead.

CHILE CON QUESO

In Texas we have a special place in our hearts for Velveeta, especially when it's melted with a can of tomatoes, such as Ro-Tel, a brand of canned tomatoes spiced up with green chiles. We call that concoction chile con queso, or just "queso" for short.

Now, don't get me wrong—I love the processed-cheese version of queso. But I was curious if it was possible to make tasty queso with real cheese. It took much trial and error, but one day when making a cheese sauce for pasta, I realized it was simply a mild version of queso. I threw in some tomatoes and a few sliced serrano chiles, grabbed a bag of chips, and soon I was eating a darn fine bowl of queso.

Don't expect this to taste *exactly* like the Velveeta version—but I find that it's just as good. To keep it warm, simply use a slow cooker or a hot plate.

2 tablespoons unsalted butter

½ medium yellow onion, diced

2 serrano chiles, seeds and stems removed, diced

1 jalapeño chile, seeds and stems removed, diced

2 cloves garlic, minced

2 tablespoons all-purpose flour

1 cup whole milk

½ cup chopped cilantro

1 cup canned diced tomatoes

3 cups grated cheddar cheese (12 ounces)

3 cups grated Monterey Jack cheese (12 ounces)

½ cup sour cream

Salt, to taste

Tortilla chips, for serving

1. Melt the butter in a saucepan on medium-low heat. Add the onions, serrano chiles, and jalapeño and cook for about 5 minutes or until the onions are translucent. Add the garlic and cook for another 30 seconds. Whisk the flour into the pan and cook for about 30 seconds.

2. Pour the milk into the pan and, while whisking, cook until the sauce is thick, about 3 minutes. Stir in the cilantro and tomatoes.

3. Turn the heat down to low, and ¼ cup at a time, slowly stir in the grated cheese until it's completely melted. Repeat until all the cheddar and Monterey Jack cheese has been added. Stir in the sour cream and add salt to taste. Serve with tortilla chips.

EL PASO CHILE CON QUESO

2 TO 4 SERVINGS

2 Hatch or Anaheim green chiles

1 or 2 jalapeño chiles

2 tablespoons unsalted butter

¼ medium yellow onion, diced

2 cloves garlic, diced

¼ cup half-and-half

2 cups grated asadero, Monterey
   Jack, or Muenster cheese, or
   any combination of the three
   (8 ounces)

¼ cup chopped cilantro

Salt, to taste

Tortillas, for serving

The West Texas city of El Paso is one of my favorite places. Sure, it's beautiful, as rugged mountains and big sky surround this high desert city. But it's also the cowboy boot capital of Texas, and I've bought most of my boots there.

The food in El Paso is also outstanding—especially the chile con queso, which is influenced by the city's proximity to Northern Mexico. Instead of the processed cheese mixed with chiles found in other places, El Paso chile con queso is roasted green chiles folded into creamy melted Mexican cheese.

Its thick texture lends itself to being spooned into warm tortillas, though you can eat it with chips.

1. Roast the Hatch or Anaheim chiles under the broiler until blackened, about 5 minutes per side. Place the chiles in a paper sack or plastic food-storage bag, close it tightly, and let the chiles steam for 20 minutes. While the chiles are steaming in the bag, place the jalapeños under the broiler and cook for 10 minutes, or until blackened, turning once.

2. After the Hatch or Anaheim chiles have steamed, remove the chiles from the bag and rub off the skin (you don't need to remove the skin from the jalapeños). Remove the stems and seeds from all of the chiles, and slice into thin, long strips.

3. In a large skillet, heat the butter on medium-low heat. Add the onions and cook for 5 minutes, stirring occasionally. Add the garlic and cook for 30 more seconds. Pour the half-and-half into the skillet and then add the chile strips. Turn the heat down to low, and a little at a time, add the grated cheese, stirring until it's melted. Stir in the cilantro and add salt to taste. Serve immediately with warm corn or flour tortillas.

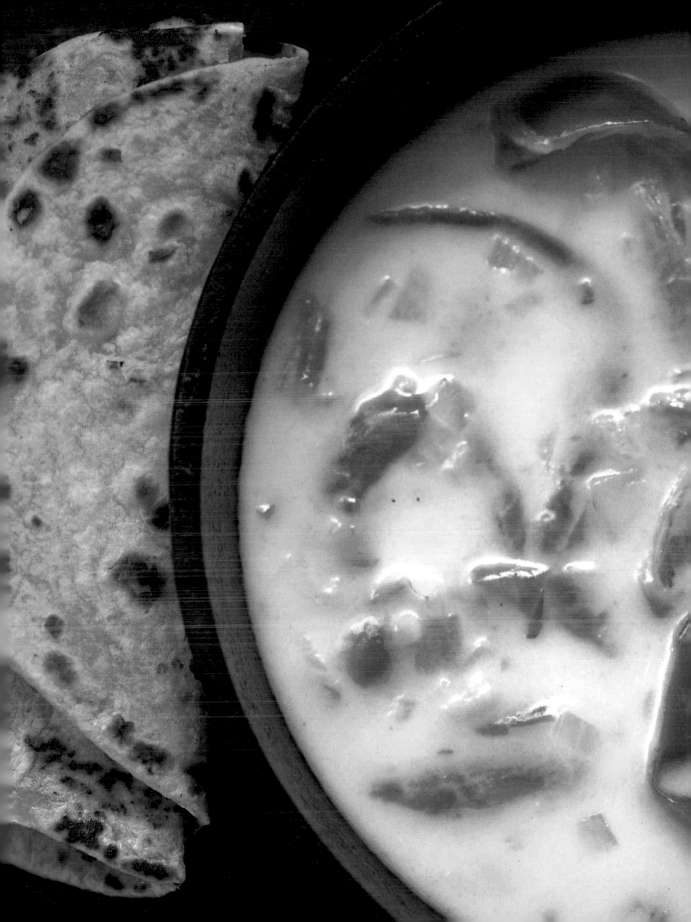

QUESO FLAMEADO

4 SERVINGS

1 poblano chile
¼ pound Mexican chorizo,
  removed from its casing
3 cups grated asadero cheese or
  Muenster cheese (12 ounces)
1 cup grated Monterey Jack cheese
  (4 ounces)
Tortillas, for serving

Queso flameado, which you might know as queso fundido, is a bubbling dish of melted white cheese, such as Monterey Jack or asadero, that's mixed with chiles and chunks of chorizo. It's rich and thick, which makes it perfect for spooning into a soft, warm tortilla.

The name translates to "flaming cheese," and when I was in college, I worked at a restaurant that did indeed set the dish on fire before serving. We servers would pour high-proof alcohol over the dish, strike a match, and wave it until the queso flameado burst into blue flames that danced across the cheese. It was a fine presentation, but you don't have to be that dramatic to make queso flameado, as it's just as good when baked in the oven. You just throw some cheese, roasted poblanos, and cooked chorizo into a skillet, heat it up for a few minutes, and soon you have an oozing, satisfying snack or dinner.

1. Roast the poblano chile under the broiler until blackened, about 5 minutes per side. Place chile in a paper sack or plastic food-storage bag, close it tight, and let the chile steam for 20 minutes. Take the chile out of the bag, rub off the skin, remove the stem and seeds, and cut into strips.

2. Preheat the oven to 350 degrees.

3. Crumble the chorizo into a medium-size cast-iron skillet heated on medium. Cook, occasionally stirring, until it's lightly browned, about 5 minutes. Turn off the heat; add to the skillet the grated cheeses and poblano chile strips. Place the skillet into the oven and cook for 15 minutes or until bubbling. Spoon out the melted queso flameado onto tortillas. Serve immediately.

PROPER TEXAS NACHOS

4 TO 6 SERVINGS

My dad once asked where I fell on the nacho spectrum. Did I prefer a pile of chips with some toppings slopped on willy-nilly, or did I prefer each individual nacho toasted with a tasteful spread of longhorn cheddar cheese and a sliced jalapeño? I was shocked that he even had to ask.

For me and for every Texan, there is only one kind of nacho: the latter. Nachos are simple and elegant. Each nacho is its own entity (and that is key), with just enough toppings to give it flavor and a bit of heft, but not enough to make it saggy or soggy. Anything else is an imposter!

If you've never made nachos the proper way, people will be surprised and find them exotic. That's OK. But what they'll really discover is that a true nacho is a joy to eat and is a sophisticated snack that can stand on its own.

6 corn tortillas
Vegetable oil, for frying
Salt, to taste
½ cup refried beans (optional)
1½ cups grated cheddar cheese (6 ounces)
24 pickled jalapeño chile slices
Guacamole, sour cream, and salsa, for serving

1. Preheat the oven to 375 degrees.

2. Cut the tortillas into quarters. Heat ½ inch of oil in an iron skillet until it reaches 350 degrees. In batches, fry the quartered tortillas for 1 to 2 minutes on each side (until golden brown) and then remove. Drain on a paper towel and sprinkle lightly with salt.

3. Once the chips have been made, top each with 1 teaspoon of refried beans (if using), 1 tablespoon of cheddar cheese, and 1 pickled jalapeño. Bake for 5 minutes or until cheese is melted. Serve with guacamole, sour cream, and salsa.

NOTE: If you don't feel like making your own chips (though you should, as they taste better), tortilla chips from a bag work, too.

FRIED GREEN TOMATOES

4 SERVINGS

1 cup all-purpose flour

½ teaspoon ground cumin

½ teaspoon cayenne

1 teaspoon kosher salt plus more to
taste

1 teaspoon black pepper plus more
to taste

1 pound green tomatoes, cut
into slices (about 6 per tomato,
depending on how thick you like
them)

1 large egg

½ cup buttermilk

2 cups cornmeal

Vegetable oil, for frying

Jalapeño Buttermilk Dressing, for
serving (page 49)

A green tomato is simply an unripe tomato. And because it's not quite done growing, it's still firm, with little juice. This makes it difficult to eat uncooked, but once you dredge it in cornmeal and fry it for a spell, it becomes more soft and succulent, which makes for a crunchy, tangy treat. I like to dip my fried green tomatoes into hot sauce or buttermilk dressing, though they're also good unadorned. Whether to use a fork or your hands is totally up to you.

1. In a large plastic food-storage bag, mix together the flour, cumin, cayenne, salt, and black pepper. Place the green tomato slices in the bag and shake until they are well coated.

2. Mix together the egg with the buttermilk. Place the cornmeal on a plate.

3. In batches, dip the flour-coated tomatoes into the egg mixture and then lightly dredge in the cornmeal. Place cornmeal-coated tomatoes on a large plate or sheet. Repeat until all the tomatoes are coated.

4. In a large, heavy skillet heat ½ inch of oil on medium heat until it reaches 350 degrees. Cook the tomatoes for 2 minutes, turning once. Depending on the size of your skillet, you will probably have to do several batches. Drain on paper towels. Serve with Jalapeño Buttermilk Dressing.

NOTE: You should use your green tomatoes as soon as you get them, as they can start to ripen and turn red after a few days.

CHORIZO-STUFFED JALAPEÑOS

4 SERVINGS

We love our jalapeños in Texas and never miss a chance to eat them. When I was young, one of my favorite snacks was to hollow out a jalapeño and stuff it with cream cheese. As an adult, I've taken that simple dish a bit further by adding some tangy goat cheese and succulent, spicy chorizo to my filling as well. These are always a welcome party food, though I've been known to make a meal out of them. And since they're baked, I can tell myself that they're a spot healthier than the battered and fried versions often served.

12 medium jalapeño chiles

¼ pound chorizo, cooked and drained of excess fat

8 ounces cream cheese, room temperature

2 ounces goat cheese, room temperature

1 tablespoon chopped cilantro

1 teaspoon dried oregano

1 teaspoon ground cumin

2 cloves garlic, minced

¼ teaspoon cayenne

1 teaspoon lime zest

Salt, to taste

1. Preheat the broiler and line a baking sheet with foil.

2. Take each jalapeño and cut in half, lengthwise. With a knife or small spoon scoop out the seeds and white pith and discard.

3. Mix together the cooked chorizo, cream cheese, goat cheese, cilantro, oregano, cumin, garlic, cayenne, and lime zest. Adjust seasonings and add salt to taste.

4. Fill each of the jalapeño halves with about 2 teaspoons of the cheese filling. Place stuffed jalapeños on the sheet and place under the broiler for 8 to 10 minutes or until brown and bubbling.

NOTE: You can vary this by replacing the chorizo with cooked bacon or leftover brisket. And pimento cheese makes for a fine filling as well. For extra decadence, try wrapping them in bacon before baking as well.

FRIED PICKLED JALAPEÑOS

1 cup all-purpose flour

1 teaspoon kosher salt plus more to taste

1 teaspoon black pepper plus more to taste

1½ cups sliced pickled jalapeño chiles

1 large egg

½ cup buttermilk

2 cups finely crushed saltines

½ teaspoon ground cumin

Vegetable oil, for frying

Jalapeño Buttermilk Dressing (page 49), for serving

Fried pickled jalapeños are a common appetizer in Central Texas roadside cafés. Now, if a fried pickle sounds strange to you, don't be scared; you'd be surprised at how well the crunch complements the fiery tang. Once you start eating them, I'll be surprised if you want to stop.

1. In a large plastic food-storage bag, mix together the flour, salt, and black pepper. Place the sliced pickled jalapeños in the bag and shake until they are well coated.

2. Mix together the egg with the buttermilk. Place the crushed saltines on a plate and mix in the cumin.

3. In batches, dip the flour-coated jalapeños into the egg-buttermilk mixture and then lightly dredge in the saltines. Place cracker-coated pickles on a large plate or sheet. Repeat until all the jalapeños are coated.

4. In a large, heavy skillet heat ½ inch of oil on medium heat until it reaches 350 degrees. Cook the pickles for 1 minute, turning once. Depending on the size of your skillet, you will probably have to do several batches. Drain on paper towels. Serve with Jalapeño Buttermilk Dressing.

NOTE: You can make these with sliced fresh jalapeños as well.

Great for Soups, Salads
Gravies and Casseroles
©2005 ... FOOD... INC

7 48159 11753 7

L550753

ROQUEFORT AND PECAN CHEESE LOG

12 SERVINGS

When my grandmother suggested we make a cheese log back when I was eight years old, I was surprised that you could make something like that from scratch. Even though all the ingredients are natural, there's something sort of unnatural-looking about it, if you know what I mean. To my uneducated eyes, a cheese ball seemed highly engineered, not something you could craft with your own two hands.

I was wrong, of course, and discovered that it's surprisingly simple. Cream cheese mixed with some Worcestershire sauce, a bit of garlic, a handful of nuts, and the cheese of your choice are the basic ingredients for a whole host of cheese balls and logs. And the best bit is that they taste delicious, look festive, and have that retro appeal that makes people smile.

8 ounces cream cheese

3 ounces Roquefort cheese (or any other soft and creamy blue cheese)

2 tablespoons Worcestershire sauce

1 clove garlic, minced

¼ teaspoon cayenne

1 cup crushed pecans

Crackers, for serving

1. Mix the cream cheese, Roquefort cheese, Worcestershire sauce, garlic, and cayenne until well blended. Roll into a long tube shape and then roll in crushed pecans.

2. Refrigerate until firm, about an hour. Serve with crackers.

SAUSAGE BALLS

36 SAUSAGE BALLS

2 cups all-purpose flour

1 teaspoon baking powder

½ teaspoon kosher salt

½ teaspoon black pepper

¼ teaspoon cayenne

4 tablespoons unsalted butter

2 tablespoons whole milk

1 pound uncooked breakfast
   sausage

2 cups grated sharp cheddar
   cheese (8 ounces)

At just about every potluck and party you'll find a large plate of these meaty, cheesy treats. I call them sausage balls, though you might also know them as sausage biscuits. I always figured that everyone grew up with these, but when we served them here in New York to a group of northerners, at first they were a bit wary of the appetizer's lumpy appearance. Of course, that all changed once they took a bite; the plate was cleaned in record time.

Now, the recipe I grew up with called for these to be made with boxed biscuit mix. But I've discovered that's not necessary, as it's no more difficult to make them with just flour and baking powder. Plus, the flavor of these balls comes from the quality of the sausage and cheese. I like to use Breakfast Sausage (page 66) or Mexican Red or Green Chorizo (pages 213 and 215) in my balls and sharp cheddar for the cheese. But the fun with these is that you can use any sausage or cheese that you like—making each batch tailored to your taste.

1. Preheat the oven to 350 degrees and grease a baking sheet.

2. In a large bowl, mix together the flour, baking powder, salt, black pepper, and cayenne. Work the butter into the flour mixture with your hands or a pastry blender until it resembles pea-size crumbs. Stir in the milk.

3. With your hands, mix the sausage and cheese into the flour until well blended. Shape the dough into 1-inch-size balls and place on sheet. Bake for 15 minutes or until browned.

NOTE: If you don't finish the batch, these will keep in the refrigerator for a couple of days, and they also freeze well.

CHIPOTLE-CINNAMON SPICED PECANS

4 CUPS

Candied pecans are a holiday tradition in Texas. Our state nut is in season, and it's the rare home you'll visit that doesn't have a tin or bowl filled with these available for snacking. You'll find them accompanying predinner drinks, though they're just as welcome alongside your dessert buffet. They're usually flavored with only sugar and cinnamon, but I've added cumin and chipotle powder to give them a bit of smoke, fire, and spice—flavors that are always welcome in the middle of winter. Don't eat these nuts only in the cold months—I find that they're an excellent treat anytime.

4 tablespoons unsalted butter
4 cups raw pecan halves
1 tablespoon brown sugar
1 teaspoon ground cinnamon
½ teaspoon chipotle powder
¼ teaspoon ground cumin
Salt, to taste

1. Preheat the oven to 350 degrees and line a baking sheet with parchment paper or foil.

2. Melt the butter in a skillet on low heat. Add the pecans and stir until they are covered in the butter. Add the brown sugar, cinnamon, chipotle powder, and cumin and stir to coat.

3. Spread the pecans on the sheet in one layer. Place in the oven and bake for 15 minutes or until darker in color and fragrant. Salt to taste.

CHILIS, SOUPS, AND STEWS

"ow, observe closely: this is the secret ingredient," said Uncle Richard as he poured in a serving of masa harina into his bubbling pot of chili.

It was an early December day, and I was at home in New York, watching my family celebrate Thanksgiving on a video they had made for me. I hadn't been able to go home to Texas for the holiday that year, and so they had recorded the festivities for me so I wouldn't feel left out of the family's fun.

The night before Thanksgiving, my uncle had made chili. He's a Dallas-based filmmaker, but like everyone in my family, he's a passionate home cook—a quality I attribute to my family's making time in the kitchen about fellowship as well as good food. So watching him on video prepare this iconic Texan dish was comforting, as he made it the same way everyone in my family cooks it—with lots of beef, chiles, and a dash of masa harina to thicken the gravy.

When I was growing up, cold nights at my house meant we'd be served supper in a bowl, whether it came from a pot of soupy beans or a pot of meaty chili. Texans are known for making both very well, though it's common knowledge that the two are to remain separate, as most Texans will tell you that there is no place for beans in your bowl of chili.

I'm not sure of the origin of this belief, though I once heard a theory posited that adding beans to a bowl of chili disservices both—the two are strong enough to stand alone. I adhere to this belief, though I do have to admit that when I was in junior high, a northerner who had moved to Texas served her version of chili with beans at a church supper, and I was a bit fascinated by this combination. I spent the next year insisting that my chili have beans (let's just say this was my form of rebellion), so my mom indulged

me and would serve me a bowl of beans on the side to add to my chili; the rest of my family abstained.

But this brief dalliance with beans in my chili didn't last long. By the time I moved to New York in my twenties, I was once again steadfast in my belief that beans did not belong. This, however, sometimes made for an uncomfortable evening with non-Texan friends. I'd serve them my chili, and they'd poke around with their spoons and say, "Isn't there something missing? Where are the beans?" (And if they were from the Midwest, they'd wonder where the pasta was, as well.) So as my mom had done for me, I'd offer a bowl of beans on the side so they could add them if they wished. But I always urged them to try my chili as it stood, so they could taste and understand how Texans prefer their state dish.

My first observation that Texas-style chili might not be available everywhere was on a trip to Washington, D.C., when I was nine. We were visiting my cousin David and his wife, Pat, a military couple who had left Texas to work at the Pentagon. My parents had brought him a grocery bag filled with all the fixings you'd need to make a decent pot of chili, which I thought was a strange gift. But it all made sense when we got off the plane and handed David the bag. He smiled and said, "It's been too long since I've had proper chili. Thank you. This is the best gift ever."

Today, chili ingredients such as dried ancho chiles are more widely available, and I've learned to make a proper Texan chili in New York. I've also been made privy to my mom's fantastic bean recipes, along with other Texan classics such as chicken and dumplings, carne guisada, and tortilla soup. So if you're craving a comfortable meal that's served in a bowl, with a little time and a big pot you too can make these dishes, which will warm you right up and make you feel closer to home.

JALAPEÑO PINTO BEANS

1 pound pinto beans

1 medium yellow onion, cut in half

4 cloves garlic

1 jalapeño chile, seeds and stems removed, cut in half lengthwise

¼ cup white vinegar or jalapeño pickle juice

Salt, to taste

Beans were a big part of my diet growing up. At least once a week, we'd have pinto beans for supper. As my mom has said: "Pinto beans are close to a perfect food." Mom would slow-cook the beans all day with garlic, onions, spices, and her secret ingredient—jalapeño juice—which gave her beans a fantastic flavor.

I enjoy making a pot on Sunday afternoons, which makes for a satisfying Sunday supper. Leftovers are also welcome for easy lunches or quick mid-week dinners, especially since this dish is even better the next day.

1. Rinse and sort through the beans, removing any stones and shriveled beans.

2. Place the beans in a large pot and cover with 1 inch of water. Bring to a boil and then cook for 15 minutes.

3. Drain and rinse the beans and then return them to the pot. Cover the beans with 2 inches of clean water.

4. Add to the pot the onion, garlic, and jalapeño. Bring pot to a boil and then turn the heat down to low. Simmer covered for anywhere from 4 to 6 hours or until beans are tender. (The time needed to cook will depend on the freshness of the beans.) Once beans are tender, stir in the vinegar or jalapeño juice and salt to taste and cook for 10 more minutes.

NOTE: You can add a slab of salt pork to the pot, if you like.

VARIATION

To make these into borracho beans, stir in a bottle of beer 10 minutes before serving.

FRIJOLES A LA CHARRA

4 TO 8 SERVINGS

I used to get upset when I'd go to a Mexican restaurant, order a combination plate, and find a small bowl of soupy charra beans on the plate instead of the usual refried beans.

Then one day, something changed: the frijoles a la charra that came with my tacos al carbon were probably one of the finest bowls of beans I'd ever had. They were bright with tomatoes, fiery with jalapeños, and smoky from the good bacon.

This is a very close approximation of those beans. I fry up the bacon and then add tomatoes, jalapeños, and chipotles to the skillet. I then add cilantro and make a puree that gets stirred into the bean pot. While you can forgo this step, I enjoy the velvety texture it gives to the bean broth.

You can serve these with any Tex-Mex dish, such as Tacos al Carbon, Small-Apartment Style (page 169), West Texas Stacked Enchiladas (page 161), or just make a meal out of them with some Green Chile Rice (page 277) and fresh Corn Tortillas (page 297).

4 slices of bacon, chopped into
    1-inch pieces
1 pound tomatoes, chopped, or one
    14-ounce can of diced tomatoes
    with sauce
2 jalapeño chiles, seeds and stem
    removed, chopped
2 canned chipotle chiles in adobo,
    chopped
1 cup chopped cilantro
4 cups cooked Jalapeño Pinto Beans
    (page 122) and its cooking liquid,
    or 2 15-ounce cans of pinto beans
Salt, to taste

1. Cook the bacon in a skillet until crisp. Add tomatoes, jalapeños, chipotles, and cilantro to the skillet and cook on medium for 10 minutes.

2. Let the tomato-bacon mixture cool. Add 1 cup of bean juice (or water) and then puree. Stir puree into beans and then turn the heat down to low and simmer together uncovered for 20 minutes. Add salt to taste.

3. Alternatively, if you prefer a chunkier texture, you could skip the puree step and add the tomato-bacon mixture straight to the bean pot.

AUSTIN-STYLE BLACK BEANS

1 pound dried black beans
1 tablespoon vegetable oil
1 medium yellow onion, diced
1 carrot, diced
4 cloves garlic, minced
2 canned chipotle chiles in adobo, chopped
½ cup chopped cilantro, divided
½ teaspoon ground cumin
1 tablespoon tomato paste
¼ cup lime juice
Salt, to taste

It was in Austin that I first saw black beans served on a Tex-Mex plate, instead of the usual refried pinto beans found elsewhere throughout the state. This makes sense, as Austin is a colorful and quirky town. Here is my basic black bean recipe, which is vegetarian, but still has a rich smoky flavor that comes from chipotles instead of the usual ham hocks or bacon.

1. Rinse and sort through the beans, removing any stones and shriveled beans

2. Place the beans in a large pot and cover with 1 inch of water. Bring to a boil and then cook for 15 minutes.

3. Drain and rinse the beans in a colander in the sink.

4. Return the empty pot to the stove and on medium-low heat, warm the vegetable oil. Add the onions and carrots to the pot and while occasionally stirring, cook until the onions are translucent and the carrots are lighter, about 8 minutes. Add the garlic to the pot and cook for 30 more seconds.

5. Return the beans to the pot, along with the chipotle chiles and ¼ cup of cilantro. Cover with 2 inches of water, bring to a boil, and then turn the heat down to low and simmer uncovered for 1½ hours.

6. After 1½ hours, add the remaining cilantro, cumin, tomato paste, and lime juice. Taste and add salt. Cook uncovered for 30 more minutes or until beans are tender (the ultimate cooking time will depend on the freshness of your beans). When done, smash a few beans against the side of the pot with a spoon to thicken the broth. Stir the pot and serve.

AVOCADO SOUP

4 SERVINGS

On those sultry summer days when I don't feel like spending much time in the kitchen, I often whip up a batch of this avocado soup. Creamy avocados are brightened with cumin, ginger, lime juice, and buttermilk, with a hint of heat from serrano chiles and sweetness from coconut milk. Little time and effort go into creating this simple, refreshing soup, yet when served with a garnish of cilantro, it can appear as elegant as a four-star dish.

2 cups chicken broth
1 cup canned coconut milk
½ cup chopped cilantro, plus extra for garnish
1 serrano chile, stems and seeds removed, diced
1 teaspoon ground ginger
1 teaspoon ground cumin
2 teaspoons lime juice
2 avocados, peeled and pitted
½ cup buttermilk
Salt and black pepper, to taste

1. Bring to a boil the chicken broth, coconut milk, cilantro, serrano chile, ginger, cumin, and lime juice. Turn the heat down to low and simmer for 5 minutes. Turn off the heat and let it cool for 10 minutes.

2. In a blender, puree the chicken broth mixture, avocado, and buttermilk. Add salt and black pepper to taste. Can serve warm or cool, topped with chopped cilantro.

SMOKY TORTILLA SOUP

6 TO 8 SERVINGS

Tortilla soup is probably one of the most ubiquitous soups in Texas, and yet you'll find that no two recipes are alike. I like to make mine smoky, which I achieve by adding chipotle chiles and smoked paprika. I also prefer my tortilla soup without additional chicken, as I find the combination of broth, chips, cheese, and avocados more than filling. Yet there are those who might question this, so feel free to serve it with shredded chicken if you like.

1. In a dry skillet heated on high, toast the pasilla chiles on each side for about 10 seconds or just until they start to puff. Fill the skillet with enough water to cover chiles. Leave the heat on until the water begins to boil and then turn off the heat and let the chiles soak until soft, about 30 minutes.

2. Heat ½ cup of the vegetable oil in a large skillet on medium heat until a candy thermometer reads 350 degrees. Slice the tortillas into strips ¼ inch thick. Add tortilla strips to the hot oil and cook until crisp, about a minute. Drain tortillas on paper towels.

3. If using fresh tomatoes, cut in half and place on a greased sheet under the broiler, along with the onion quarters and garlic cloves. Cook the tomatoes, onions, and garlic on each side for 5 minutes or until black spots begin to appear. (If using canned tomatoes, broil only the onions and garlic.)

{CONTINUED}

2 dried pasilla chiles, stems and seeds removed

½ cup plus 1 teaspoon vegetable oil

6 corn tortillas, preferably stale

1 pound plum tomatoes, or 1 14-ounce can of diced tomatoes, preferably fire roasted, drained

1 medium yellow onion, cut into quarters

6 cloves garlic

2 canned chipotle chiles in adobo

2 teaspoons ground cumin

2 teaspoons dried oregano

¼ teaspoon ground cloves

½ cup chopped cilantro

6 cups chicken broth

½ teaspoon Worcestershire sauce

2 teaspoons smoked paprika

2 tablespoons lime juice

Salt, to taste

2 cups cooked, shredded chicken meat (optional)

GARNISHES

2 cups grated Monterey Jack cheese (8 ounces)

1 avocado, peeled, pitted, and diced

¼ cup Cotija cheese, crumbled

¼ cup chopped cilantro

4. Place the tomatoes, onions, and garlic into a blender. When the pasilla chiles are hydrated, drain and rinse and also add to the blender along with the chipotle chiles, cumin, oregano, cloves, cilantro, ½ cup of the fried tortilla strips, and ½ cup of water. Blend on high until smooth.

5. In a large pot, heat 1 teaspoon of vegetable oil on medium heat and add the tomatoe puree. Cook, stirring occasionally, for 5 minutes until it thickens and gets darker. Note that it will probably pop and squirt.

6. Add the chicken broth and Worcestershire sauce. Bring to a boil and then turn the heat down to low and simmer for 30 minutes.

7. Stir in the smoked paprika, lime juice, salt to taste, and the chicken meat if you're using it, and simmer for another 10 minutes.

8. Before serving the soup, place the remaining tortilla strips and grated Monterey Jack cheese into 4 or 6 bowls. Top with the soup and serve immediately. Serve with the avocado, Cotija cheese, and cilantro for garnish.

NOTE: If you can't find pasilla chiles, you can add one more canned chipotle chile; you can substitute dried ancho chiles, as these tend to be more available; or you can use 1 tablespoon of chili powder.

CORN CHOWDER WITH ROASTED JALAPEÑOS AND BACON

6 TO 8 SERVINGS

When corn is in season, I can't get enough of this sweet, crunchy crop. I'll make my Ancho Cream Corn (page 269) or my Mexican Corn (Elote en Vaso) (page 257), but one of my favorite preparations is this corn chowder, fired up with a bit of jalapeño and made tangy with a bit of lime. I think it's the bacon that really brings all the flavors together and makes this a hearty soup that can be eaten either warm or cold.

Now, if you don't have fresh corn, don't fret, as it's fine when made with frozen. There are plenty of other flavors that give goodness to this dish. And be sure to make enough for leftovers, as this soup only gets better the next day.

1 jalapeño chile
¼ pound thick-cut bacon, diced
½ medium yellow onion, diced
4 cups corn kernels, frozen or fresh (about 6 cobs shucked)
3 cloves garlic, chopped
4 cups chicken broth
½ teaspoon ground cumin
¼ teaspoon nutmeg
¼ teaspoon cayenne
¼ cup chopped cilantro, plus some for garnishing
¼ cup lime juice
1 cup half-and-half
Salt and black pepper, to taste
Cilantro and tortilla chips, for serving

1. Cook the jalapeño under the broiler, turning once, until it's blackened, about 10 minutes. Once it's cool, leaving on the charred skin, remove the stem and seeds and finely dice.

2. In a large skillet, sauté the bacon on medium heat until crisp and the fat has been rendered, about 5 minutes. Remove bacon from skillet and place on a plate lined with a paper towel. Pour out the bacon grease, leaving 2 tablespoons in the skillet. (You can store the remaining bacon grease in the refrigerator and use it with another recipe.) Add the diced onion to the skillet and cook on medium heat until translucent, about 5 minutes. Add the corn and cook for 3 minutes. Add the garlic and cook for 30 more seconds.

(CONTINUED)

$3.$ Turn off the heat and take out ½ cup of the cooked corn mixture. Add the rest to a blender with 1 cup of chicken broth. Blend on high until a smooth puree has formed.

$4.$ Pour pureed corn into a large pot. Add to the pot the diced jalapeño, remaining chicken broth, cumin, nutmeg, cayenne, cilantro, cooked bacon, the set-aside corn kernel mixture, and lime juice. Bring to a boil and then turn the heat down to low and simmer for 5 minutes. Stir in the half-and-half and add salt and black pepper to taste. Serve either warm or cold with a cilantro garnish and tortilla chips.

GREEN CHILE CHOWDER

6 TO 8 SERVINGS

4 poblano chiles

2 jalapeño chiles

1 tablespoon unsalted butter

1 medium yellow onion, diced

2 cloves garlic, minced

2 pounds Russet potatoes, peeled
and diced

4 cups chicken or vegetable broth

½ cup cilantro

½ teaspoon ground cumin

1½ cups whole milk

1 cup half-and-half

Salt and black pepper, to taste

2 tablespoons lime juice

Grated Monterey Jack cheese,
tortilla chips, and chopped
cilantro, for serving

This recipe for green chile chowder was adapted from *Seasoned with Sun*, the Junior League of El Paso's cookbook. From the original recipe I increased the numbers of chiles, threw in some cumin, cilantro, garlic, and lime juice, and lightened it up by omitting a butter-and-flour roux. I find that this soup is quite versatile. Served warm with cheese melted on top, it staves off the cold. Served chilled with a squirt of lime and tortilla chips, it's light and refreshing.

1. Roast the poblano chiles and jalapeños under the broiler until blackened, about 5 minutes per side. Place the poblano chiles in a paper sack or plastic food-storage bag, close it tightly, and let the chiles steam. Meanwhile, remove stems and seeds from the jalapeños and dice. After 20 minutes, take the poblanos out of the bag and rub off the skin. Remove seeds and stems and then dice the poblano chiles.

2. In a large pot, heat the butter on medium until it's melted. Add the diced onions and cook for 10 minutes or just until they're about to brown. Add the garlic and cook for 30 more seconds. Add to the pot the diced poblano and jalapeño chiles, the potatoes, chicken broth, cilantro, and cumin. Bring to a boil and then turn the heat down to low and simmer for 20 minutes or until the potatoes are tender.

3. Scoop out 2 cups of the soup and set aside. Puree the rest of the soup until smooth and then mix the smooth with the chunky. Add the milk and half-and-half to the soup and cook until warm. Add salt and black pepper to taste. Squeeze in the lime juice and serve either warm or chilled, with grated Monterey Jack cheese, tortilla chips, and extra cilantro.

CALABACITAS
(SQUASH AND PORK STEW)

6 TO 8 SERVINGS

In Houston, tacos are about as hard to find as mosquitoes, but there's one taqueria that's well worth a crosstown drive as it serves something not often found: calabacitas.

Calabacitas is a stewed dish comprised of yellow summer squash, zucchini, and pork. It's usually made with tomatoes, but I like the version served at Houston's Taqueria Laredo because it adds tangy tomatillos to its broth instead.

This one-pot dish only gets better the longer it cooks, but if you're in a hurry you can have it ready in just a little over an hour. I like to spoon it into warm corn tortillas, but it's also great simply served in a bowl with chips or poured over rice.

1 tablespoon vegetable oil
2 to 3 pounds boneless pork shoulder, trimmed of excess fat and cut into 1-inch cubes
1 medium yellow onion, diced
4 cloves garlic, minced
4 serrano chiles, chopped
½ cup chopped cilantro
½ pound fresh tomatillos, husks removed, and quartered
1 tablespoon ground cumin
1 teaspoon dried oregano
1 pound zucchini, diced
1 pound yellow squash, diced
1 cup corn (fresh or frozen)
1 cup chicken or vegetable broth
Salt and black pepper, to taste
2 tablespoons lime juice
Tortillas, for serving

1. In a large pot or Dutch oven, heat the oil on medium and brown the pork until light brown on all sides, about 15 minutes. (You may have to do this in batches.)

2. Remove pork from pot. Add the onions to the pot and cook until they just begin to brown, about 10 minutes. Add the garlic and cook for 30 more seconds.

3. Place the pork back in the pot and add the serrano chiles, cilantro, tomatillos, cumin, oregano, zucchini, yellow squash, corn, and broth. Bring to a boil, turn the heat down to low, and simmer for 30 minutes. Remove the lid and then simmer for 30 more minutes. Add salt and black pepper to taste. Stir in the lime juice and serve with tortillas.

SOPA DE FIDEO

6 SERVINGS

When you think of the Rio Grande Valley, pasta may not be the first thing that comes to mind. But for many South Texans, pasta found in the form of sopa de fideo is a big bowl of comfort. I often hear homesick Texans from this part of the state lament how they can't find that ubiquitous yellow box of fideo, which can inexpensively feed a crowd.

If you're unfamiliar with this dish, it's a soup with a tomato and chile base that's made thick with cooked fideo, a thin, short pasta that's also known as vermicelli. As with all comfort dishes, how your grandmother made it is probably your favorite version, and there are infinite variations to the basic formula. Some people like to add ground beef, while others may add chopped vegetables. Here is my basic recipe, but feel free to embellish as you see fit. And on a cold day or when you're feeling a bit under the weather, I reckon you'll agree that tucking into a bowl of sopa de fideo is comforting indeed.

4 dried guajillo chiles, stems and seeds removed
2 teaspoons vegetable oil, divided
½ medium yellow onion, finely diced
4 cloves garlic, chopped
1 cup canned crushed tomatoes
8 cups chicken broth or vegetable broth
½ teaspoon chili powder
1 teaspoon ground cumin
¼ teaspoon ground allspice
¼ teaspoon cayenne
8 ounces fideo pasta or angel hair pasta broken into 1-inch pieces
Salt and black pepper, to taste
1 lime, cut into wedges
¼ cup chopped cilantro

1. In a dry skillet heated on high, toast the guajillo chiles on each side for about 10 seconds or just until they start to puff. Fill the skillet with enough water to cover chiles. Leave the heat on until the water begins to boil and then turn off the heat and let the chiles soak until soft, about 30 minutes. Once hydrated, discard the soaking water, rinse the chiles, and place in a blender.

2. While the chiles are soaking, heat 1 teaspoon of oil in a large pot set on medium heat. Add the diced onions to the pot and while occasionally stirring, cook the onions until translucent, about 5 minutes. Add the garlic and cook for 30 more seconds.

(CONTINUED)

3. Scrape the onions and garlic along with any oil into the blender. Add the tomatoes, 1 cup of broth, chili powder, cumin, allspice, and cayenne. Puree until smooth.

4. In the same pot you used to cook the onions and garlic, add the remaining teaspoon of oil and set on medium heat. Add the fideo or angel hair pasta and cook for 2 minutes while stirring.

5. Pour into the pot the chile and tomato puree and add the rest of the broth. Bring the pot to a boil on high heat and then cook until the pasta is tender, about 10 minutes. Add salt and black pepper to taste, and serve with lime wedges and cilantro for garnishes.

SEVEN-CHILE TEXAS CHILI

6 TO 8 SERVINGS

People often ask if my chili is authentic Texas chili. I'll say yes, because I'm a Texan and it's the chili I grew up eating. Though defining what is authentic Texas chili can be difficult. The term *chili* comes from chile con carne, which translates to peppers with meat. That's what I make, with the addition of some spices and aromatics. Some could say, however, that my chili isn't the *most* traditional Texas chili, and there has been some grumbling.

Some people have grumbled because there's cinnamon and chocolate in my chili, though these flavors are commonly found in Mexican cuisine. Some people have grumbled because there aren't tomatoes in my chili, though I don't think that cowboys on the range had access to tomatoes all the time. And some people have grumbled because I don't use chili powder, though using fresh chiles will trump chili powder any day.

Feel free to experiment, however, with your own chili. It's hard to mess up chili, as the longer it cooks, the more the flavors both deepen and blend in a complex dish where the sum of the bowl is greater than its parts. Even if you take some liberties with my chili, I will insist that you leave the beans out of the pot. Please feel free to serve them on the side for those who do like beans. But as I once read, serving the two separately shows the utmost respect for *both* dishes, as combining them only lessens both the beans and the chile con carne. And we wouldn't want to do that!

1. Remove the seeds and stems from the dried chiles. In a dry skillet heated on high, toast the ancho chiles, pasilla chiles, guajillo chiles, chipotle chiles, and chiles de arbol on each side for about 10 seconds or just until they start to puff. Fill the skillet with enough water to cover chiles. Leave the heat on until the water begins to boil and then turn off the heat and let the chiles soak until soft, about 30 minutes.

(CONTINUED)

6 dried ancho chiles

2 dried pasilla chiles

2 dried guajillo chiles

2 dried chipotle chiles

4 dried chiles de arbol

4 pieces of bacon

4 pounds chuck roast, cut into ¼-inch cubes

1 large onion, diced

6 cloves garlic, minced

1 cup brewed coffee

1 bottle of beer

1 tablespoon ground cumin

1 teaspoon dried oregano

½ teaspoon ground cinnamon

¼ teaspoon ground clove

½ teaspoon ground allspice

½ teaspoon cayenne

½ teaspoon grated Mexican hot chocolate

1 teaspoon kosher salt, plus more to taste

4 dried pequin chiles

2 tablespoons masa harina

Grated cheddar and chopped onions, for serving

$2.$ Meanwhile, in a large, heavy pot such as a Dutch oven, fry the bacon on medium heat. When it's done, remove from the pan and drain on a paper-towel-lined plate. Leave the bacon grease in the pot, and on medium heat, cook the beef on each side until lightly browned, about 10 minutes. (You may have to do this in batches.)

$3.$ Remove the browned beef from the pot. Leaving the heat on, add the diced onions to the pot and cook until translucent, about 5 minutes. Add the garlic and cook for another 30 seconds. Add the beef back into the pot, crumble in the bacon, and add the coffee, beer, cumin, oregano, cinnamon, clove, allspice, cayenne, chocolate, 3 cups of water, and salt. Turn the heat up to high.

$4.$ While the pot is coming to a boil, make the chile puree. Drain and rinse the chiles then place them in a blender along with the pequin chiles (you don't need to presoak these little chiles) and 1 cup of fresh water. Puree until nice and smooth and then pour the chile puree into the pot.

$5.$ When the chili begins to boil, turn the heat down to low and simmer uncovered for 5 hours, stirring occasionally. Taste it once an hour and adjust seasonings. If it starts to get too dry, add more water. After 5 hours, scoop out ¼ cup of broth out of the pot and combine with the masa harina. Pour the masa harina mixture into the pot and stir until the chili is thickened. Let the chili simmer for another 30 minutes or so. When done, serve with cheddar and onions.

NOTE: If you can't find all of these chiles, just use the more readily available anchos and chipotles.

ONE-HOUR TEXAS CHILI

6 TO 8 SERVINGS

6 dried ancho chiles, stems and
seeds removed

2 dried chipotle chiles, stems and
seeds removed

1 tablespoon vegetable oil or
bacon grease

1 medium yellow onion, quartered

4 cloves garlic, chopped

4 dried pequin chiles

1 tablespoon ground cumin

1 teaspoon dried oregano

½ teaspoon ground clove

½ teaspoon ground cinnamon

2 pounds beef, coarsely ground
(you can ask your butcher to do
this)

Salt and black pepper, to taste

2 teaspoons masa harina (optional,
but will thicken chili if needed)

2 tablespoons lime juice

When I make my Seven-Chile Texas Chili, it's an all-day affair. But sometimes you don't have the time or the patience to wait for a hearty bowl of red. And for those times I offer my One-Hour Texas Chili, which is still a flavorful, meaty dish.

The main difference between this chili and my Seven-Chile Texas Chili is that for this I use ground beef, preferably the rougher chili-chuck grind. Ground beef takes less time to cook, and in my experience, the longer it sits on a stove, the more mealy it gets—it's perfect for a quick chili. There are still plenty of chiles and spices, however, to give this chili a complex flavor.

I make this on weeknights when I'm looking for a quick meal. I also find that this chili is a fine accompaniment to hot dogs and for that Texan treat known as Frito pie.

1. In a large skillet, preferably a cast-iron skillet, heat the dried ancho and chipotle chiles on medium-high heat about a minute on each side. Turn off the heat, fill the skillet with water, and let the chiles soak until rehydrated, about 30 minutes.

2. In a large pot or Dutch oven, heat 1 tablespoon of vegetable oil over medium heat. Add the onion quarters, stirring occasionally until they start to brown, about 10 minutes. Throw in the garlic and cook for 30 more seconds. Place cooked onions and garlic into a blender.

3. Drain the chiles from the soaking water and add them to the blender along with the pequin chiles (you don't need to presoak these little chiles). Add the cumin, oregano, clove, cinnamon, and 1 cup of water. Blend until smooth.

4. Form the ground beef into little balls about the size of a marble. In the same large pot, on medium, cook the meat, stirring occasionally until lightly browned on each side, about 10 minutes. Add the chile puree and 4 cups of water, heat on high until boiling, then turn the heat down to low and simmer uncovered for 45 minutes, stirring occasionally.

5. After 45 minutes, adjust seasonings and add salt and black pepper to taste. Also, if the chili isn't thick enough, slowly stir in the masa harina. Add the lime juice and then cook for 15 more minutes.

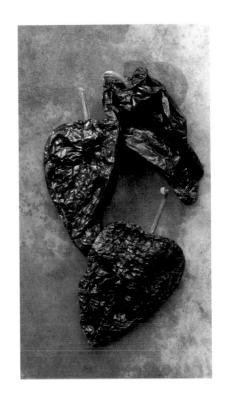

NOTE: If you can't find dried chipotle chiles, substitute canned chipotle chiles and forgo the soaking step.

VARIATION

FRITO PIE

4 SERVINGS

Once you have a batch of one-hour chili, why not make a Frito pie? If you are a deprived soul that has never eaten a Frito pie, then you have a treat in store. It's simply a pile of Fritos topped with chili, cheese, diced onions, and sometimes, if you're feeling flush, pickled jalapeños and sour cream. In Texas, it's a mainstay at Friday-night football games, county fairs, school cafeteria lunches, church youth group suppers, and yes, even at home.

4 cups Fritos
4 cups One-Hour Texas Chili
1 cup grated cheddar cheese
  (8 ounces)
¼ cup diced onions

For each Frito pie, ladle 1 cup of chili over 1 cup of Fritos. Top with ¼ cup of grated cheddar and 1 tablespoon diced onions. If you want to be supertraditional, you can rip open a small package of Fritos and then proceed with the recipe.

CARNE GUISADA

6 TO 8 SERVINGS

Carne guisada, which translates as "stewed meat," is a slow-simmered stew that varies across the state. Sometimes you'll see carne guisada as a group of distinct cubes floating in a rich sauce. Other times you'll see carne guisada where the stew has cooked so long it's hard to tell where the meat ends and the gravy begins. My carne guisada tends to fall into the latter category.

Carne guisada can be a meal in itself, served in a bowl with tortilla chips. It's also wonderful nestled between refried beans and rice. I like to wrap it up in flour tortillas for tacos, and the leftovers are a hearty topping on a pile of scrambled eggs.

4 pounds chuck or bottom round beef, cut into 1-inch cubes

2 tablespoons lard, bacon grease, or vegetable oil, divided

1 medium yellow onion, diced

½ bell pepper, stems and seeds removed, diced

2 jalapeño chiles, stems and seeds removed, diced

2 serrano chiles, stems and seeds removed, diced

5 cloves garlic, minced

1 pound fresh plum tomatoes, diced, or 1 14-ounce can of diced tomatoes, preferably fire-roasted, drained

1 tablespoon ground cumin

1 tablespoon chili powder

1 teaspoon dried oregano

½ cup chopped cilantro

1 bay leaf

1 bottle of dark Mexican beer

Salt and black pepper, to taste

1. In a large pot or a Dutch oven, brown the beef on medium-high heat in 1 tablespoon of the lard, bacon grease, or vegetable oil. You may have to do this in batches.

2. Remove the beef from the pot, add the final 1 tablespoon of lard, and cook on medium-low heat the diced onions, bell pepper, jalapeños, and serrano chiles for about 10 minutes or until the onions start to brown. Add the garlic and cook for another 30 seconds.

3. Add the browned beef back to the pot, along with the tomatoes, cumin, chili powder, oregano, cilantro, bay leaf, and beer. Add 2 cups of water as well. Turn the heat up to high and bring to a boil and then turn the heat down to low. Simmer uncovered for 2 to 4 hours, depending on how tender you want your meat. Add salt and pepper to taste.

GREEN CHILE POSOLE WITH BLACK BEANS

1 poblano chile

½ pound fresh tomatillos, husked, or 1 11-ounce can of tomatillos, drained

2 serrano chiles, stems and seeds removed, chopped

½ medium yellow onion, chopped

4 cloves garlic, chopped

1 cup chopped cilantro

½ cup chopped parsley

½ cup fresh spinach leaves

1 teaspoon ground cumin

1 teaspoon dried oregano

¼ teaspoon ground allspice

6 cups chicken or vegetable broth, divided

2 15-ounce cans of hominy, drained

2 cups Austin-Style Black Beans, drained (page 124), or 1 15-ounce can of black beans, drained

2 tablespoons lime juice

¼ cup half-and-half (optional)

Salt, to taste

Grated Monterey Jack cheese, for serving

In far West Texas, posole is a hearty soup that's served to celebrate the New Year. The eponymous ingredient of this dish is posole, which is a puffed corn kernel that's been treated with the mineral lime. Posole, which in English is known as hominy, has a soft, chewy texture with a toasted corn flavor that is very similar to a corn tortilla. As such, posole goes well with chiles, both red and green. I like to make my posole into a green stew, as I find the combination of roasted poblano, serrano chiles, cilantro, parsley, and spinach bright and lively.

1. Roast the poblano chile under the broiler until blackened, about 5 minutes per side. Place chile in a paper sack or plastic food-storage bag, close it tightly, and let the chile steam for 20 minutes. Take the chile out of the bag and rub off the skin. Remove stem and seeds and place in a blender.

2. If using fresh tomatillos, on high heat, bring a pot of water to a boil, add the tomatillos, and cook until soft, about 5 minutes. (If using canned, skip this step.) Add the tomatillos to the blender along with the serrano chiles, onions, garlic, cilantro, parsley, spinach, cumin, oregano, allspice, and 2 cups of the chicken broth. Blend until smooth.

3. In a pot, pour the puree and add the rest of the chicken broth, the hominy, and the black beans. Bring to a boil and then turn the heat down to low and simmer uncovered for 30 minutes. Before serving, stir in the lime juice and the half-and-half, if using. Adjust seasonings and add salt to taste. Serve with grated Monterey Jack cheese.

TEX-MEX 7 CLASSICS

After I graduated from Austin College, my best friend, Alex, and I took a road trip to California. She had grown up in Arlington, Texas, but after her parents moved to the Sacramento area our senior year, she decided to join them postgraduation in their new California home.

I'd always wanted to see the West, and when she invited me to make the journey from Texas to California, I couldn't refuse. When we began the trip, our initial plan was to hit New Mexico by evening of the first day. But it was slow going as Alex said her good-byes. Heck, it seemed that in every town she knew somebody she wanted to hug one last time before she moved away from the state.

When we were an hour or so from the Texas-New Mexico border, Alex steered the car off the highway and pulled up to a Tex-Mex café. We'd already eaten quite a bit that day, and since I was anxious to arrive in New Mexico, I said, "What gives?" She said she was hungry for cheese enchiladas and she didn't care what I thought—we were going to stop.

Now, I would never refuse a plate of cheese enchiladas, but I have to admit that enjoying yet another meal in Texas didn't seem necessary to me. I would be returning to Texas after our trip, so a plate of enchiladas was just another plate of food (albeit very good food). But when I think about it, I believe that Alex was pretty smart. Her instincts told her that she had to have that one last platter, as it would probably be a while before she'd see Texas and Tex-Mex again. For her, that meal was yet another good-bye to a good Texan friend.

After living so long away from Texas myself, I now know exactly how she felt. Whenever I return home, my first and last meals during my visits are always Tex-Mex. Upon landing—no matter the time of day—I drive to the nearest Mexican restaurant or taco stand to get my fix. My family's always thought this was a bit odd, especially when I'll arrive on, say,

Christmas morning and there's a full holiday feast awaiting me in a few hours. But I don't care; I'll insist that we stop so I can grab a taco; it's an itch that must be scratched.

What is it about Tex-Mex that tugs at my heart? I'm sure part of it is rooted in a longing for a time when there was nothing more pressing than spending a lazy afternoon in a Tex-Mex greasy spoon, a place where the basket of chips and bowls of salsa were bottomless; a place where the sizzling-hot platters were overflowing with yellow cheese enchiladas smothered in brown gravy; a place where there was always someone patting out fresh tortillas that would be delivered to your table, still warm to the touch; a place where the sound track was lively music from the border, conjunto and Tejano tunes filled with a bouncing beat propelled by accordions and singers who sang so passionately you didn't need a translator to tell you that the word for *heart* in Spanish was *corazon*.

When I first moved to New York, I spent most of my free time searching for restaurants that captured this feeling, always with little to no success. The enchiladas would be covered in a tepid sauce, the tacos would be wrapped in cold tortillas, and the tamales tasted like they came from a can. It made me sad. But it also pushed me into my kitchen, as I realized that making these dishes myself would be the best way to have that taste of home.

Now, throughout this book I have recipes that are part of the Tex-Mex canon, such as Houston-Style and San Antonio–Style Flour Tortillas (pages 299 and 302), Chile con Queso (page 101), and Pralines (page 346). But the recipes I've chosen for this chapter, such as Cheese Enchiladas with Chile con Carne, Dallas Gas Station Tacos, Gorditas with Picadillo, and Chalupas, I feel deserve their own category.

If you've never cooked Tex-Mex dishes such as enchiladas or flautas at home, don't worry—I've discovered that it's not difficult. And if you add a bit of love and perhaps play some Tejano music while you have fun in the kitchen, I promise that you, too, will feel like you're at a Tex-Mex joint on a lazy afternoon.

CHEESE ENCHILADAS WITH CHILE CON CARNE

4 TO 6 SERVINGS

John Sayles's movie *Lone Star* came out just after I moved to New York City. As I sat in a movie theater on Broadway watching this murder mystery set on the Texas-Mexico border, I cried on more than one occasion as the landscape, the accents, and the people were all so familiar to my homesick self. But the shots that killed me the most were the loving, lingering close-ups of cheese enchilada platters. I reached out my hand—as if to grab the plate on the screen—and said, "I want!" My New Yorker friends looked at me like I was nuts, but I didn't care—most Texans will agree that a plate of cheese enchiladas drowning in savory chile con carne is the essence of Tex-Mex.

While enchiladas are found across the border in Mexico, in Texas we've put our stamp on it by stuffing the enchiladas with yellow cheese and covering it in our state dish—a hearty, beefy chili.

If you ask a Texan what they miss the most, more often than not it's this signature dish. You just can't find it done well at restaurants outside the state, as for some reason this particular combination of flavors is hard to reproduce unless you grew up with the dish and know how it's supposed to taste.

I, however, have figured out a way to make it at home. If you're feeling homesick, I guarantee that after taking one bite of these cheese enchiladas, you'll be instantly transported back to Texas.

FOR THE CHILE CON CARNE

6 dried ancho chiles, stems and
   seeds removed
1 tablespoon vegetable oil or lard
½ medium yellow onion, chopped
2 cloves garlic, chopped
½ tablespoon ground cumin
½ teaspoon dried oregano
¼ teaspoon ground allspice
¼ teaspoon ground cinnamon
¼ pound ground beef
2 cups beef broth
Salt, black pepper, and cayenne,
   to taste

FOR THE ENCHILADAS

1 tablespoon vegetable oil or lard
12 corn tortillas
4 cups grated cheddar cheese
   (16 ounces)
½ medium yellow onion, diced

1. In a dry skillet heated on high, toast the ancho chiles on each side for about 10 seconds or just until they start to puff. Fill the skillet with enough water to cover chiles. Leave the

{CONTINUED}

heat on until the water begins to boil and then turn off the heat and let the chiles soak until soft, about 30 minutes. Once hydrated, discard the soaking water and rinse the chiles. Place in a blender.

2. In a large pot or Dutch oven, heat the vegetable oil or lard, and cook the onions, occasionally stirring, until translucent, about 5 minutes. Add the garlic and cook for 30 more seconds. Place cooked onions and garlic into the blender, along with the cumin, oregano, allspice, cinnamon, and 1 cup of water. Blend until smooth.

3. In the same pot that you used to cook the onions and garlic, on medium heat brown the ground beef, stirring occasionally, about 10 minutes. (If you like, you can drain the extra fat once the meat is browned.) Add the chile puree and the beef broth, heat on high until boiling, and then turn the heat down to low and simmer for 30 minutes, stirring occasionally. After 30 minutes, adjust seasonings and add salt, black pepper, and cayenne to taste.

4. To make the enchiladas, first preheat the oven to 350 degrees and grease a large baking dish. In a skillet, heat up the oil or lard on medium-low heat. One at a time, heat up the tortillas in the hot oil. Keep them wrapped in a cloth or tortilla warmer until all the tortillas are heated.

5. Take a heated tortilla and use tongs to dip it into the sauce. Shake off most of the sauce, but make sure that it's moist enough to be pliable. Lay the tortilla on a plate or clean cooking surface, add ¼ cup of the grated cheese down the center of it, along with a few of the diced onions. Roll the tortilla. Place rolled enchilada in the greased baking dish and repeat with remaining tortillas. Pour sauce over enchiladas and top with remaining grated cheese and diced onions. Bake for 15 minutes or until cheese is lightly browned and bubbling.

SPINACH AND MUSHROOM ENCHILADAS WITH TOMATILLO SALSA

4 TO 6 SERVINGS

The first time I served these spinach enchiladas to a rabid carnivore, he was suspicious: how could a filling comprised of a leafy green be satisfying? He shouldn't have worried. Tender mushrooms and smooth ricotta cheese add weight to the flavorful spinach, while the tart and fiery green salsa keeps these enchiladas from being too rich. As for my meat-eating friend, he returned for both a second and a third helping. My job was done.

1. For the tomatillo salsa, roast the poblano chile under the broiler until blackened, about 5 minutes per side. Place the chile in a paper sack or plastic food-storage bag, close it tight, and let the chile steam for 20 minutes. Take the chile out of the bag and rub off the skin. Remove stem and seeds and chop the chile. Place in a blender.

2. Meanwhile, if using fresh tomatillos, on high heat, bring a pot of water to boil and cook tomatillos until soft, about 5 minutes. Drain cooked tomatillos. (If using canned, skip this step.) Place tomatillos, either cooked or canned, in the blender with the poblano chile. Add the cilantro, garlic, serrano chiles, lime juice, chicken broth, and cumin, and blend until smooth.

TOMATILLO SALSA

1 poblano chile

½ pound fresh tomatillos, husks removed, or 1 11-ounce can of tomatillos, drained

½ cup cilantro

2 cloves garlic

1 or 2 serrano chiles, seeds and stems removed, cut in half

1 teaspoon lime juice

1 cup chicken broth

¼ teaspoon ground cumin

1 teaspoon vegetable oil

Salt and black pepper, to taste

FILLING

1 teaspoon vegetable oil

10 ounces mushrooms, sliced (about 2½ cups)

½ medium yellow onion, diced

2 cloves garlic, minced

1 serrano chile, seeds and stem removed, diced

1 pound fresh spinach, or 10 ounces frozen spinach, thawed

{CONTINUED}

2 cups ricotta cheese

1 tablespoon lime juice

¼ teaspoon cayenne

½ teaspoon ground cumin

¼ teaspoon ground cinnamon

Salt and black pepper, to
taste

FOR THE ENCHILADAS

1 tablespoon vegetable oil or
lard

12 corn tortillas

2 cups Monterey Jack cheese,
grated

3. Heat the oil in a pot on medium low, pour sauce into pot, turn the heat down to low, and simmer for 15 minutes, stirring occasionally. Adjust seasonings and add salt and black pepper to taste.

4. For the filling, heat the oil on medium in a large skillet. Sauté the sliced mushrooms for 5 minutes. Add a pinch of salt and with a slotted spoon remove the mushrooms from the skillet and place in a large bowl. Add to the skillet the onion and cook until translucent, 5 minutes. Add the garlic and serrano chile and cook for another minute. Add the spinach. Stir until it's mixed with the onions, garlic, and serrano chile, cover the skillet, and cook for 5 minutes or until wilted.

5. Remove the lid and season the spinach with salt and black pepper. Drain spinach mixture and add to the bowl with the mushrooms. Stir in the ricotta cheese, lime juice, cayenne, cumin, and cinnamon and mix well. Taste and adjust seasonings.

6. Preheat the oven to 350 degrees and grease a large baking dish. In a skillet heat up the oil or lard on medium-low heat. One at a time, heat up the tortillas in the hot oil. Keep them wrapped in a cloth or tortilla warmer until all the tortillas are heated.

7. Take a heated tortilla and with tongs dip it into the sauce. Shake off most of the salsa, but make sure that it's moist enough to be pliable. Lay the tortilla on a plate or clean cooking surface, add ¼ cup of the filling down the center of it, and then roll the tortilla. Place rolled enchilada in the greased baking dish and repeat with remaining tortillas. Pour salsa over enchiladas and top with grated cheese. Bake for 15 minutes or until cheese is lightly browned and bubbling.

SOUR CREAM
CHICKEN ENCHILADAS

FOR THE CHICKEN

2 pounds boneless, skinless chicken
    breasts
1 teaspoon kosher salt
1 teaspoon black pepper
1 tablespoon olive oil

FOR THE SOUR CREAM SAUCE

2 tablespoons unsalted butter
2 serrano chiles, seeds and stems
    removed, diced
2 cloves garlic, minced
2 tablespoons all-purpose flour
2 cups chicken broth
2 cups sour cream
1 teaspoon ground cumin
Dash of cayenne
¼ cup chopped cilantro
1 pound fresh tomatillos, husks
    removed, and cut in half, or
    1 11-ounce can of tomatillos,
    drained
Salt and black pepper, to taste

When I was in college, on Saturday afternoons a large group of us would celebrate the weekend by going to lunch at a local Tex-Mex restaurant. We'd toast the weekend with tall glasses of iced tea and salty chips dipped in salsa, and as we were in North Texas, most of us would order the house special—sour cream chicken enchiladas.

The sour cream enchiladas were stuffed with shredded chicken that had been spiced with generous amounts of salt and black pepper, a simple blend that still had flavor. The sauce itself was a creamy blend of sour cream and chicken broth. A few pickled jalapeños were added, yet they provided more color than fire, as all that cream mitigated any heat. But what this sauce lacked in piquancy, it made up for in creamy comfort and a taste so smooth I'd always order an extra bowl on the side.

My tastes have changed a bit since then, so I've taken some liberties with the basic sour cream sauce by punching it up with tomatillos for tang and a bit of cayenne for heat. But whether you're a longtime fan of sour cream enchiladas or approaching them for the first time, I don't think you'll be disappointed.

1. Preheat the oven to 350 degrees.

2. Sprinkle the chicken breasts on each side with the salt and black pepper. In a large oven-proof skillet, preferably cast-iron, heat the oil on medium. Add the chicken breasts and cook on each side for 3 minutes. Place the skillet in the oven and bake uncovered for 30 minutes.

3. When the chicken is done, take it out of the oven and let cool, then shred with two forks. Keep the oven on, as you'll be using it again.

4. As the chicken is baking, in a pot melt the butter on medium-low heat. Add the diced serrano chiles and cook until soft, about 3 or 4 minutes. Add the minced garlic and cook for 1 minute.

5. Whisk in the flour and cook for 1 minute. Pour the chicken broth into the pot and whisk, cooking the chicken broth until it has thickened. Stir in the sour cream, cumin, cayenne, and cilantro. Remove from heat.

6. If using fresh tomatillos, place them under the broiler on a foil-lined sheet and cook on each side until blackened, about 4 minutes per side. Place in a blender along with the sour cream sauce and puree until smooth. If using canned tomatillos, skip the broiler step and just place them in the blender with the sour cream sauce and proceed.

7. Grease a large baking dish.

8. To make the enchiladas, heat the vegetable oil or lard in a skillet and cook the corn tortillas on each side a couple of minutes until soft. Wrap in a cloth to keep warm as you continue to cook all 12.

FOR THE ENCHILADAS
1 tablespoon vegetable oil or lard
12 corn tortillas
½ medium yellow onion, diced
2 cups grated Monterey Jack cheese (8 ounces)
½ cup chopped cilantro, for serving

{CONTINUED}

9. To assemble the enchiladas, pour 1 cup of the sour cream sauce in the bottom of a casserole pan. Take each corn tortilla and place ¼ cup of shredded chicken in the middle of it, 1 teaspoon of diced onions, and 1 tablespoon of cheese.

10. Roll the tortillas around the filling and place the rolled tortillas seam side down in the dish. Cover the enchiladas with the remaining sauce and cheese and bake for 25 minutes or until top is brown and bubbling. Serve topped with chopped cilantro.

WEST TEXAS STACKED ENCHILADAS

4 SERVINGS

In most parts of Texas, enchiladas are rolled tortillas stuffed with a filling and covered in sauce. But often in West Texas (and also New Mexico) the filling and sauce are instead layered between flat tortillas. They look a bit different, but the end taste is the same, not to mention stacked enchiladas are a heck of a lot easier to make.

Another feature of stacked enchiladas is the inclusion of a fried egg on top. I don't know how this tradition came about, but it's a brilliant addition. When the yolk mixes with the sauce, its creamy transformation takes the sauce from merely delicious to truly decadent.

I was born and raised a rolled-enchilada girl, but I can appreciate a plate of stacked ones, especially those made with an ancho chile sauce. And if I squint, I can see in the stack the rugged terrain of West Texas, with the egg standing in for clouds and the sun. It's West Texas on a plate.

1. In a dry skillet heated on high, toast the ancho chiles on each side for about 10 seconds or just until they start to puff. Fill the skillet with enough water to cover chiles. Leave the heat on until water begins to boil and then turn off the heat and let the chiles soak until soft, about 30 minutes. Once hydrated, discard the soaking water and rinse the chiles.

2. Put ancho chiles, chipotle chiles, garlic, half of the diced onions, cumin, oregano, allspice, and chicken broth in a blender and puree. It should be thick and smooth.

FOR THE CHILE SAUCE

6 dried ancho chiles, seeds and stems removed

2 canned chipotle chiles in adobo

4 large cloves garlic, chopped

¼ medium yellow onion, chopped

1 teaspoon ground cumin

½ teaspoon oregano

¼ teaspoon ground allspice

2 cups chicken broth or water

1 tablespoon lard or vegetable oil

1 tablespoon all-purpose flour

Salt and black pepper, to taste

FOR THE ENCHILADAS

2 tablespoons lard or vegetable oil, divided

12 corn tortillas

1½ cups grated cheddar cheese (6 ounces)

1½ cups grated Monterey Jack cheese (6 ounces)

¼ medium yellow onion, diced

4 large eggs

(CONTINUED)

3. In a pot, heat 1 tablespoon of lard or oil on low heat and then whisk in the flour. Pour in the sauce, and simmer for 15 minutes, stirring occasionally. Add salt and black pepper to taste, and adjust other seasonings as needed.

4. Preheat the oven to 350 degrees and lightly grease a large baking dish.

5. In a skillet, heat on medium 1 tablespoon of lard or oil. Cook each tortilla for about 30 seconds on each side (or until soft). Keep warm in a towel or a warmer.

6. To assemble the enchiladas, take a tortilla and place it in the baking dish. Drizzle ¼ cup of the sauce on each tortilla and then add ¼ cup of the grated cheeses, mixed, and 1 teaspoon of onions. Add another tortilla, and add same amount of sauce, cheese, and onions. Add a third tortilla, and again top with sauce, cheese, and onions. Repeat until you have four stacks.

7. Bake enchiladas in the oven for 15 minutes or until cheese is melted and bubbling. While enchiladas are cooking, heat the remaining tablespoon of lard or oil in the cast-iron skillet and then fry the eggs two at a time (or however many will fit). To serve, place an enchilada stack on a plate and top with a fried egg.

SOFT CHEESE TACOS

4 TO 6 SERVINGS

The first time I ordered a soft cheese taco plate in Dallas, I assumed that I would get corn or flour tortillas stuffed with shredded cheese, lettuce, and tomatoes. Imagine my surprise when instead I was served what appeared to be cheese enchiladas covered in chile con queso. "I believe you've made a mistake," I said to the waiter. He replied that what was before me was indeed a plate of soft cheese tacos. After one bite, I had to admit I didn't mind at all and decided that I was a big fan of this Dallas Tex-Mex dish.

Soft cheese tacos, much like sour cream enchiladas, are a North Texas Tex-Mex phenomenon. They're creamy and bland with barely a hint of fire, but trust me, if you like queso, you will also find these very good. To create these distinctive tacos, you make a chile con queso sauce that uses chicken broth instead of the usual milk. And while I usually make my Chile con Queso (page 101) with cheddar and Monterey Jack, I find that using American cheese for the sauce is the only way to be truly authentic. In a twist, however, I stuff the tortillas with cheddar, which is another quirk of this dish. Sure, some use only American cheese, but the best soft cheese tacos are a balance of both sharp cheddar cheese and bland American cheese, a combination that adds a hint of complexity. Ultimately, however, soft cheese tacos are a simple plate that don't require too much thought. Not that there's anything wrong with that, as it's still a very satisfying combination of cheese and tortillas.

FOR THE CHILE CON QUESO SAUCE
1 tablespoon unsalted butter
¼ medium yellow onion, finely diced
1 or 2 jalapeño chiles, stems and seeds removed, diced
2 cloves garlic, minced
1 cup chicken broth
1 tablespoon cornstarch
2 cups shredded American cheese (8 ounces)
¼ teaspoon ground cumin
¼ teaspoon cayenne
½ cup canned diced tomatoes, preferably canned tomatoes with green chiles or fire roasted, drained
¼ cup chopped cilantro
Salt, to taste
Milk or half-and-half (optional)

FOR THE CHEESE TACOS
12 corn tortillas
3 cups grated cheddar cheese (12 ounces)

1. To make the chile con queso sauce, in a pot melt the butter on medium-low heat. Add the diced onion and jalapeño, and cook, occasionally stirring, until the onions are translucent, about 5 minutes. Add the garlic to the pot and cook for 30 more seconds.

{CONTINUED}

2. Whisk together the chicken broth and cornstarch and then pour into the pot. While stirring, cook until the sauce begins to thicken, about 2 minutes.

3. Turn the heat down to low and slowly stir in the American cheese, ¼ cup at a time, until all the cheese is completely melted.

4. Stir in the ground cumin, cayenne, diced tomatoes, and cilantro. Adjust seasonings and add salt to taste. If you wish to thin the chile con queso sauce, stir in milk or half-and-half, a tablespoon at a time, until it's the desired consistency. Keep the chile con queso on low heat while you assemble the tacos so it will stay warm.

5. To make the soft cheese tacos, preheat the oven to 375 degrees and pour ½ cup of the chile con queso sauce into the bottom of a greased baking dish.

6. Wrap the corn tortillas in foil and place in the oven for 10 minutes while the oven is preheating. Remove the tortillas from the oven and open the foil (be careful, as there may be hot steam). Take a warm tortilla and, on a clean surface, add ¼ cup of the grated cheddar cheese down the center of the tortilla and then roll the tortilla. Place the rolled soft tacos seam side down in the baking dish. Repeat with remaining tortillas.

7. Cover the baking dish with foil and bake for 10 to 12 minutes or until the cheese in the tortillas has melted. Remove from the oven, remove foil, and pour the remaining chile con queso sauce over the tacos. (If you choose not to use all of the remaining sauce, note that it's excellent with tortilla chips.)

PORK TACOS, DALLAS GAS STATION STYLE

4 TO 6 SERVINGS

Gas station tacos are found all over Texas. It's a wonderful thing—you walk into a gas station, and in the back will be a short-order cook heating up tortillas and stuffing them with all sorts of savory fillings.

I've found, however, that Dallas is the place where gas station tacos are most prevalent. Fuel City, a monster gas station near downtown, gets all the attention. And yes, they make a fine taco. But along South Buckner you'll find a multitude of gas stations selling tacos, and I've started calling this Dallas's gas station taco belt.

The tacos on offer at Dallas gas stations include all the usual fillings such as Picadillo (page 177) and, for the adventurous, tongue. But my favorite filling is the spicy pork these stations offer, a tender piece of meat made flavorful by some time spent in a chile marinade.

Here is my version of this pork filling. Another hallmark of Dallas gas station tacos is that they're always served with a roasted jalapeño; I suggest you do the same.

1. In a dry skillet heated on high, toast the pasilla chiles on each side for about 10 seconds or just until they start to puff. Fill the skillet with enough water to cover chiles. Leave the heat on until water begins to boil and then turn off the heat and let the chiles soak until soft, about 30 minutes.

2. While the pasilla chiles are soaking, rinse the pork and trim the fat. Cut into half-inch-size pieces.

(CONTINUED)

FOR THE PORK

4 dried pasilla chiles, stems and seeds removed
2 pounds pork shoulder
1 canned chipotle chile in adobo
4 cloves garlic, chopped
½ teaspoon dried oregano
½ teaspoon ground cumin
Small pinch of ground cloves
¼ cup orange juice
¼ cup pineapple juice
1 tablespoon white vinegar
2 tablespoons olive oil
Salt, to taste
1 tablespoon vegetable oil

FOR THE TACOS

6 jalapeño chiles
Tortillas, either corn or flour
½ cup chopped cilantro
¼ medium yellow onion, diced
1 lime, cut into wedges
Salsa, for serving

2. Heat on high for 5 minutes a large ovenproof skillet, preferably cast iron, or a grill pan (you may have to cut the steak in half to fit). Also, turn on the broiler in your oven. When the skillet is hot (to test, I throw in a drop of water and it should immediately evaporate), grease the pan with the oil and add the steak. Cook on one side for 2 minutes then turn and cook on the other side for 2 minutes.

3. After it's cooked on both sides, place the green onions, if using, in the skillet with the steak still in it, and place the skillet under the broiler for 2 minutes. Remove the steak from the skillet and let it rest for 10 minutes. If onions aren't charred enough, slide the skillet back under the broiler. After the meat has rested, slice the meat against the grain and roll in fluffy, flour tortillas with green onions on the side. Serve with Houston-Style Green Salsa.

NOTE: I don't have a grill or an outdoor space, but if you want to cook these outside and make them truly al carbon, 5 minutes per side should do the trick.

VARIATION

FAJITAS

1 tablespoon vegetable oil

1 bell pepper, stems and seeds removed, sliced

1 medium yellow onion, cut into slivers

Guacamole (page 50)

Pico de Gallo (page 54)

Flour tortillas

Salsa

Sour cream

This meat will make a fine batch of fajitas. You just need to add these garnishes.

1. In a large cast-iron skillet, heat up the oil on medium heat.

2. Add the bell pepper slices and onion slices and sauté until the onions and peppers are soft, about 10 minutes. Serve the sliced al carbon meat with guacamole, pico de gallo, flour tortillas, salsa, and sour cream.

BEEF FLAUTAS

4 SERVINGS

1 tablespoon vegetable oil or lard

2 pounds chuck roast, cut into 4-inch chunks

1 medium yellow onion, quartered

5 cloves garlic, crushed

2 to 4 jalapeño chiles, seeds and stems removed, diced

1 pound tomatillos, husked and quartered, or canned

2 tablespoons ground cumin

1 cup chopped cilantro, divided

Salt and black pepper, to taste

2 tablespoons lime juice

12 corn tortillas

Vegetable oil for frying

Salsa, chopped cilantro, diced onions, and sour cream, for garnishing

Flauta (which means "flute" in Spanish) is what I grew up calling this fried rolled taco, though in other places you may see them called taquitos or tacos dorado. But no matter what you call them, the key to a good flauta is that it needs to be fresh.

Making these is not difficult—as long as you're brave when confronted with a skillet that is hissing and popping with hot fat. (I wear long sleeves and oven mitts to keep myself safe.) But because of your fearlessness, you will enjoy the best flautas you've ever had.

1. In a large pot or Dutch oven, on medium heat warm up the oil or lard. Add the beef chunks to the pot and brown on each side, about 10 minutes. (You may have to do this in batches.) Add the onions, garlic, jalapeños, tomatillos, cumin, ½ cup of the chopped cilantro, 4 cups of water, salt and black pepper to taste.

2. Bring to a boil and then turn the heat down to low and simmer uncovered for 2 hours until the meat is tender. Remove the beef from the pot, shred it, and then toss it with the lime juice, ¼ cup of the cooking liquid (you can save the rest for another use), and salt and black pepper to taste.

3. Preheat the oven to 350 degrees. Wrap the tortillas in foil and cook in the oven for 10 minutes. Take each warmed tortilla and place 2 tablespoons of the shredded beef into it and roll tightly.

4. Heat ½ inch of vegetable oil in a large skillet, and when the oil is 350 degrees, gently place three flautas into oil, seam side down, and cook on each side until crisp, 45 seconds per side. Serve immediately with salsa, chopped cilantro, onions, and sour cream.

REFRIED BEANS

8 SERVINGS

I won't lie—while I adore enchiladas, tacos, and anything else you may find on a Tex-Mex combination platter, it's the mound of refried beans that makes my heart beat faster. Ever since I can remember, refried beans have been one of my favorite foods. I reckon it's because when I was young and my parents were just beginning their careers, beans graced our table more than any other dish. They are my ultimate comfort food.

Though some may think of beans as a humble food, refried beans' smooth texture and their luscious flavor make them a most satisfying dish. While it may take some effort to give them flavor, it's certainly not difficult. Here's the secret for making the refried beans smooth as velvet: lard. Or if you want to amp up the smoky flavor, add bacon grease. Yes, pork fat is the key to the best refried beans. Of course, if you're a vegetarian, you can fry them in vegetable oil and add enough onions, garlic, and spices to give the refried beans a hearty flavor. But if you want to take a bite and feel like you're sitting on the patio of your favorite Mexican restaurant back home, I highly recommend you try them with lard or bacon grease. You won't be sorry.

4 cups cooked Jalapeño Pinto Beans (page 122)
¼ cup lard, bacon grease, or vegetable oil
¼ medium yellow onion, diced
2 cloves garlic, minced
Salt, to taste

1. In a blender, place the beans along with ¼ cup of their cooking liquid. On low, pulse until a chunky paste is formed.

2. In a large cast-iron skillet, on medium-low heat melt the lard. Add the onions and cook until translucent, stirring occasionally, about 5 minutes. Add the garlic and cook for 30 more seconds. Pour in the bean puree and while stirring cook the beans until the oil is well incorporated and the refried beans are a little darker in color, about 5 minutes. Taste and add salt.

CHALUPAS

Oil, for frying

8 corn tortillas

Salt

2 cups refried beans

1 cup grated cheddar cheese
(4 ounces)

2 cups shredded iceberg lettuce

½ cup canned diced tomatoes,
drained, or 2 fresh plum tomatoes,
diced

¼ medium yellow onion, diced

¼ cup chopped cilantro

Sliced pickled jalapeños

Salsa, for serving

Whenever I think of chalupas, I think of my mom, as they're her favorite Tex-Mex dish. This makes sense, as she adores nachos, and chalupas are essentially one big nacho. Chalupas, which may also be called tostadas, are a whole fried corn tortilla loaded with toppings such as refried beans, cheddar cheese, lettuce, tomatoes, and pickled jalapeños. If you're feeling fancy, you can add some picadillo or shredded chicken, but I find they're just as satisfying in their most basic incarnation.

1. To make the fried tortillas, which are the chalupa base, in a large skillet, heat ½ inch of oil on medium heat. When it reaches 300 degrees, fry the tortillas on each side until crisp and lightly browned, about 1 minute. Drain the fried tortillas on paper towels and lightly salt. If not already warm, in a pot heat up the refried beans.

2. To assemble the chalupas, spread each fried tortilla with ¼ cup of refried beans. Top with cheddar cheese, lettuce, tomatoes, onions, cilantro, and pickled jalapeños. Serve with salsa.

GORDITAS WITH PICADILLO

8 GORDITAS

If you've ever had the pleasure of attending San Antonio's spring festival, known as Fiesta, then you are familiar with this hallmark of San Antonio Tex-Mex cuisine, the gordita.

Gordita, which means "little fat one" in Spanish, is a thick masa pocket that's stuffed with picadillo, beans, and cheese. They are very popular in San Antonio, and you'll find them in West Texas towns as well, though you seldom see them in other places in the state.

Like most Tex-Mex dishes, gorditas have a Mexican counterpart. This makes me happy, as I'll often find them at Mexican restaurants and taco trucks in my New York neighborhood. Texans, however, have made the gordita their own by adding lots of shredded iceberg lettuce and chopped tomatoes.

Ostensibly, gorditas are meant to be eaten with your hands, but I find that they're better served with a knife and fork. That is, unless you don't mind getting picadillo juice on your chin and shirt, which for some can be a badge of honor that says, "I've eaten well today!"

1. In a large skillet, heat the oil and cook the beef and the onion on medium-low heat, stirring occasionally, until beef is lightly browned and onions are translucent, about 5 to 8 minutes. (If you wish, you can drain some of the grease.)

2. Add to the skillet the garlic, jalapeños, chili powder, oregano, cumin, cayenne, cilantro, tomatoes, diced potato, salt and black pepper. Stir until the spices are well distributed, add ¼ cup of water, turn down heat, and then cover and cook for 30 minutes or until potatoes are tender. Taste and adjust seasonings and stir in the lime juice. Remove from heat.

FOR THE PICADILLO FILLING

1 tablespoon vegetable oil

1 pound of ground beef

½ medium yellow onion, diced

4 cloves garlic, minced

1 or 2 jalapeño chiles, stems and seeds removed, diced

1 tablespoon chili powder

1 tablespoon dried oregano

1 tablespoon ground cumin

¼ teaspoon cayenne

¼ cup chopped cilantro

1 pound plum tomatoes, diced, or 1 14-ounce can of diced tomatoes, preferably fire roasted, drained

1 medium Russet potato, peeled and diced

Salt and black pepper, to taste

2 tablespoons lime juice

FOR THE GORDITAS

1¾ cups masa harina

¼ cup all-purpose flour

1 teaspoon baking powder

½ teaspoon kosher salt

1 tablespoon lard or shortening, room temperature

1½ cups water

Oil, for frying

{CONTINUED}

TO ASSEMBLE
Grated cheddar cheese
Shredded iceberg lettuce
Chopped tomatoes
Salsa to taste

3. To make the gorditas, mix together the masa harina, flour, baking powder, and salt until well combined. Add the lard and water and stir until a soft, smooth ball is formed.

4. Divide the dough into 8 balls. Roll or press out each one until it's 4 inches round. In a greased skillet, cook each gordita on medium for 2 minutes on each side until golden brown. Cool on a rack.

5. Heat 1 inch of oil in a large pot to 300 degrees. One at a time, cook the gorditas in the oil, flipping once, about 2 minutes per side or until it puffs. Remove with a slotted spoon and drain on a paper-towel-lined plate.

6. When cool enough to handle, with a sharp knife split the gordita on the outer edge halfway through to form a pocket. Stuff gorditas with picadillo, grated cheese, lettuce, and tomatoes, and top with salsa.

TAMALES WITH RAJAS

24 TAMALES

When I was a child, whenever we went out to eat at Herrera's in Dallas, I'd always order tamales. I'd have to say that after rice and refried beans, tamales were my first great Tex-Mex love. This is not unusual, as what's not to love about masa dough that's been stuffed and then steamed until it's soft, moist, and tender.

Tamales are eaten all over the state at all times of the year. Though for many, they are considered the quintessential Christmas dish and in December you'll see friends and family gathering to have a tamale-making party, which is known as a tamalada. My family didn't have tamaladas when I was young; we ordered our tamales instead. It wasn't until I moved to New York, actually, that I started making tamales with friends.

Making tamales isn't difficult, although it does take time; I suggest you do this with others, as the work will go by faster. But don't be intimidated by the process, as it's difficult to mess up a batch of tamales. At heart they are a simple dish.

I like to stuff mine with a poblano chile and cheese combination that is known as rajas. You may, however, stuff them with any filling you like, such as Picadillo (page 177), Refried Beans (page 173), or shredded Coffee-Chipotle Oven Brisket (page 189).

24 dried corn husks

4 poblano chiles

1 cup lard or unsalted butter, room temperature

4 cups masa harina

2 cups chicken or vegetable broth

¼ teaspoon cayenne

Salt, to taste

1 pound (2 cups) white cheese, such as asadero or Monterey Jack, grated

1. Place the corn husks in a pan of water and submerge until completely covered. Let soak for 45 minutes or until soft and pliable.

2. Next, roast the poblano chiles under the broiler until blackened, about 5 minutes per side. Place the chiles in a paper sack or plastic food-storage bag, close it tightly, and let the chiles steam for 20 minutes. Take the chiles out of the bag, rub off the skin, remove the stem and seeds, and cut into strips.

(CONTINUED)

3. To make the masa dough, in a mixer beat the lard or butter until fluffy and creamy. Add the masa harina, chicken broth, and cayenne and continue to beat until the dough comes together into a moist paste. Add salt to taste.

4. To form the tamales, take a corn husk, which you'll see has four sides and is in sort of a cone shape. Place the corn husk in front of you, with the pointed end at your right. In the center of the husk, spoon out ¼ cup of the masa and spread it, leaving a clean border around the masa. Place a couple of poblano chile strips in the center of the masa and cover with 1 tablespoon of the grated cheese.

5. Join together the two long sides and then roll the husk until it's about the width of a cigar. Take the narrower, pointed end and fold it about a quarter of the way up the tamale. Alternatively, you can rip strips from a corn husk and, after rolling, tie up each end like it's a package.

6. Place a steamer basket or a colander in a large pot. Add water to the pot just to the base of the basket (don't let the water get into it). Place the tamales in the basket seam side down. Bring the water to a boil and then cover the pot and turn the heat down to low.

7. Check the water level occasionally to make sure there's enough in the pot, and steam tamales for 2 hours. You'll know they're done when the masa pulls cleanly away from the husk.

NOTE: If you like, you can fill these with pork, beef, chicken, or refried beans. You'll need 2 cups of whatever filling you choose to use.

BEEF, PORK, AND FOWL

8

One of the first gatherings I had in New York was a lively chicken-fried-steak dinner. My Texas friends and I were frustrated that we couldn't find it at any restaurant, and we thought it would be terrific to share this dish with our New York friends. Chicken-fried steak—which is a rough cut of beef that's been tenderized, breaded, and fried—is one of our state's edible icons. It's difficult to find a Texan who doesn't love it, and heck, I've even known vegetarians to indulge in chicken-fried steak on the sly.

To make chicken-fried steak, you first have to tenderize the beef. At the party, everyone got into the spirit of pounding the beef flat with a metal mallet. After breading and frying the steaks, we slathered them with cream gravy and sawed off that first bite. The Texans were most satisfied, but some of the New Yorkers didn't quite understand the spirit of the dish.

There was one guest who questioned if perhaps chicken-fried steak would be better if made with filet mignon instead, which goes against everything chicken-fried steak is about. And then there was the guest who was so offended by the dish that she said she'd never forgive me for making her eat a dish that was an insult to both beef and her palate. No matter, this just left more chicken-fried steak for the rest of us.

Texas is cattle country, so naturally we eat a lot of beef. Besides chicken-fried steak, we also adore

brisket, whether it's smoked over post-oak wood low and slow, or cooked in the oven with plenty of aromatics and fiery chiles. And if you have leftovers, you can make that El Paso dish known as salpicón, a bed of lettuce topped with brisket, tomatoes, and avocadoes.

Texans, however, eat more than just beef. Take the hog, for instance. My grandfather used to tell me stories about his community's hog-butchering day, a winter event where everyone would gather at his farm and slaughter hogs so they'd have plenty to eat in the upcoming months. Thick-cut pork chops topped with rice would soon grace the table.

Then there's chicken. My great-grandma Blanche was known for being deft with this bird; it's been said she could wring and pluck one in minutes flat. Popular chicken dishes in Texas include King Ranch Chicken, a comforting dish that uses a cream sauce to bind chicken, tortillas, chiles, and tomatoes. If you need a quick weeknight supper, nothing beats a roasted chicken coated in a mustard-jalapeño sauce. And as Texans are resourceful, we'll eat the chicken livers, too, which are best served battered and fried.

When I moved to New York, everyone told me that the best meat in the world could be found in my new home. Sure, I can find plenty of humanely raised, quality cuts of meat in New York, as we have butchers and farmers' markets that focus on selling meat that's been raised with respect and care. But perhaps it's my family's history or perhaps it's just my personal taste, but nothing tastes quite as good as the beef, pork, or chicken I can get back home.

CHICKEN-FRIED STEAK

4 SERVINGS

All Texans have their favorite chicken-fried steak, and I'm no exception: mine is my dad's. His version was my introduction to the dish, and I was fortunate as a child to be able to eat it at least once a week. I knew dinner was going to be divine if I came home to the smells and sounds of chicken-fried steak frying in the pan. And while I've had hundreds of different chicken-fried steaks since, his is still superior to all others. He is renowned for his recipe and method—a craft he learned from his mother, who learned it from her mother. So not only is his the best, but it's also part of my culinary legacy—a fine inheritance, if I don't say so myself.

Now, before I outline how to make it, a few words of caution. The preparation of chicken-fried steak is a violent, messy, and dangerous affair. Do not be afraid of small chunks of meat flying from your tenderizer and adhering to your walls. Do not be afraid of being covered head to toe in a pastelike mixture of flour, batter, and grease. And do not be afraid of hot oil splattering and some screechy sizzling as you flip the steaks in the skillet. Be patient: in the midst of this bloody battle, this culinary chaos, you will ultimately find both the beauty and order that is a plate of chicken-fried steak served with cream gravy.

If you still have reservations about chicken-fried steak, consider these words from the late *Fort Worth Star-Telegram* columnist Jerry Flemmons: "As splendid and noble as barbecue and Tex-Mex are, both pale before that Great God Beef dish, chicken-fried steak. No single food better defines the Texas character; it has, in fact, become a kind of nutritive metaphor for the romanticized, prairie-hardened personality of Texans." High praise, indeed!

1½ pounds top-round steak
1½ cups all-purpose flour
1 teaspoon kosher salt
1 teaspoon black pepper
½ teaspoon cayenne
3 large eggs, beaten
½ cup whole milk or buttermilk
Lard or vegetable oil, for frying
Cream Gravy (page 42), for serving

1. Cut the top-round steak into four pieces. Pound beef with a meat tenderizer until flattened and almost doubled in size. Sprinkle pieces of beef with salt and black pepper.

{CONTINUED}

2. Place the flour in a large bowl and add salt, black pepper, and cayenne. Taste and adjust seasonings. In another large bowl, mix eggs with milk. Take a piece of the tenderized beef and coat in the flour mixture. Dip the coated beef into the egg mixture and then dip back into the flour again. Repeat for each piece of beef.

3. In a large skillet, preferably cast-iron, heat ½ inch of oil to 300 degrees.

4. Take the pieces of coated beef and gently place into the skillet. There will be a lot of popping and hissing, so be careful. After about 3 or 4 minutes, or when the blood starts bubbling out of the top of the steak, gently turn over the steaks with tongs and cook for 5 more minutes.

5. Remove from skillet and drain on a paper-towel-lined plate. While cooking remaining steaks, you can keep cooked steaks warm in an oven set at 200 degrees. Serve with Cream Gravy.

COFFEE-CHIPOTLE OVEN BRISKET

6 TO 8 SERVINGS

Right up there with proper Tex-Mex and chicken-fried steak, Texas barbecue is something that homesick Texans miss the most. Sure, you'll find barbecue in other parts of the country, but for them *barbecue* means pork; in Texas, it's all about the beef.

Because Texas barbecue is so unique, when others outside the state try to re-create it the results are usually less than satisfactory. Sure, plenty of Texans—both at home and homesick alike—know how to fire up the smoker and go low and slow with a twelve-pound packer cut of brisket. But when you're stuck in the city without an outdoor space and get a hankering for barbecue, sometimes you have to improvise.

I will confess that this baked brisket will probably not completely transport you back to Lockhart, the barbecue capital of Texas, because let's face it—there's no way a few hours in an oven can ever truly approximate the real thing. But this brisket provides a smoky, earthy alternative that is different but still very good.

With hints of smoke from the bacon and chipotle chiles and a crust formed by running the meat under the broiler, this brisket goes well with jalapeño pickles, some cubes of cheddar cheese, a few soda crackers, or slices of thick white bread.

1 teaspoon kosher salt

2 teaspoons black pepper

2 teaspoons chipotle powder

1 teaspoon mustard powder

1 teaspoon ground cumin

1 3- or 4-pound brisket, the flat cut, preferably with a bit of fat still on it

4 slices of bacon

½ medium yellow onion, cut into slivers

4 cloves garlic, cut in half

1 cup Coffee-Chipotle Barbecue Sauce (page 48)

1. Preheat the oven to 325 degrees and line a baking sheet with foil.

2. Mix together the salt, black pepper, chipotle powder, mustard powder, and cumin. Rub both sides of the brisket with the spices. Place brisket on a large sheet of foil, fat side down, and top it with the bacon, onion slivers, and garlic. Wrap the brisket tightly in the foil, and then wrap it with

{CONTINUED}

another piece of foil to ensure that no juices leak out. Place foil-wrapped brisket on foil-lined baking sheet (bacon side up) and cook it for 6 hours.

3. After 6 hours, remove the brisket from the oven and let it sit in the foil for 20 minutes. After it's rested, open up the foil (be careful, as very hot steam will escape) and remove the brisket from the foil. Add 1 tablespoon of the brisket juices to your barbecue sauce.

4. To serve, take off the bacon, onions, and garlic from the brisket (they've done their duty, though if you like you can chop them together to make a bacon-onion jam) and cut slices against the grain. Serve with the barbecue sauce on the side. If you want a bit of a crust, place the brisket under the broiler for 5 minutes before serving.

NOTE: If you prefer not to have barbecue sauce, you can serve it with the pan juices instead.

SALPICÓN (MEXICAN SHREDDED BEEF SALAD)

6 SERVINGS

My first encounter with salpicón was after a long plane ride from New York to El Paso. It was late morning and I was headed to Marfa, a small West Texas town that has achieved some renown for its art scene. In the 1980s the artist Donald Judd converted an old fort into the Chinati Foundation—a multibuilding museum that serves as a showcase for his large-scale minimalist sculptures. This collection, along with the big sky, wide vistas, and the town's adobe architecture, has attracted other artists to open galleries in this town, which is about three hours away from El Paso by car. Marfa's remote location is about as far as you can get from the hustle of New York City, and I like to visit that part of Texas once a year to relax my mind by taking in the scenery and austere atmosphere.

When I flew into El Paso that day, I was anxious to be on my way. But before leaving town I decided to take a break and grab some lunch. I pulled off the highway and stopped at Julio's Café Colonial, a restaurant highly recommended to me by a friend. My plan had been to order cheese enchiladas, as that's usually my first dish upon rearrival in Texas. But as I looked around at the lunchtime crowd, I noticed everyone was eating the same thing—a saladlike dish that appeared to be a bed of lettuce topped with shredded beef, cheese, tomatoes, and avocados.

"What is that?" I asked the server. "It's salpicón," he said. I changed my mind about the enchiladas and ordered that instead, and the spicy beef paired with the crisp lettuce, soft tomatoes, and avocados was just the reintroduction to Texan food that I needed.

Salpicón is refreshing on a warm day, but it's also hearty enough to serve in the colder months, too. Traditionally the beef is served cold or at room temperature, but it can still be warm from the oven as well.

(CONTINUED)

FOR THE FILLING

1 2-pound brisket
1 tablespoon chipotle powder
1 tablespoon ground cumin
Salt and black pepper to taste
4 cloves garlic, chopped
¼ medium yellow onion, cut into slivers

FOR THE DRESSING

2 canned chipotle chiles in adobo, minced
2 cloves garlic, minced
2 tablespoons cilantro, leaves and stems chopped
½ teaspoon ground cumin
Pinch of ground cloves
1 tablespoon lime juice
1 tablespoon red wine vinegar
¼ cup olive oil
Salt, to taste

FOR THE SALAD

1 large head of romaine lettuce, torn into pieces
1 cup grated Monterey Jack cheese (4 ounces)
4 ripe plum tomatoes, diced
2 avocados, peeled, pitted, and diced

1. Preheat the oven to 325 degrees and grease a baking sheet.

2. Take the brisket and season on both sides with chipotle powder, cumin, salt, and black pepper. Place the brisket on a large sheet of foil, fat side up, and top with the garlic and the slivered onions. Wrap the brisket tightly and then wrap it with another piece of foil to ensure that no juices leak out. Place the foil-wrapped brisket on the greased baking sheet (make sure that the fat side is up) and cook for 5 hours.

3. After 5 hours, remove the brisket from the oven and let it rest for 20 minutes still wrapped in foil. After it's rested, gently open up the foil (be careful, as very hot steam will escape). Remove the brisket from the foil and place it in a bowl. Shred the brisket with two forks. Take 1 tablespoon of pan drippings from the foil and stir into the shredded brisket. Add salt and black pepper, to taste.

4. To make the dressing, whisk together the chipotle chiles, garlic, cilantro, cumin, cloves, lime juice, vinegar, olive oil, and salt to taste. Toss the dressing with the shredded beef.

5. To assemble the salad, place the brisket on a bed of romaine lettuce leaves. Garnish with cheese, tomatoes, and avocados. It can be served with tortillas or tortilla chips.

NOTE: You can make the brisket and dressing a day ahead and store in the refrigerator until ready to serve.

PASILLA TOMATILLO BRAISED SHORT RIBS

4 TO 6 SERVINGS

Short ribs have a strong flavor, which in this recipe is balanced by the bright acidity of the tomatillos and the smoky, slightly bitter notes of the pasilla chiles. My great-grandpa Gibson—who was head of the Collin County Cattleman's Association—might not have prepared beef in this fashion, but I reckon he would have enjoyed having a plate of these over rice. These short ribs are also terrific in tacos or stuffed into enchiladas.

2 dried pasilla chiles, stems and seeds removed
4 pounds boneless beef short ribs
Salt and black pepper, to taste
1 tablespoon vegetable oil, lard, or bacon grease
1 medium yellow onion, diced
1 pound tomatillos, husks removed, and quartered
6 cloves garlic, minced
2 bottles of beer or 2½ cups beef broth or water
½ teaspoon ground cumin
¼ teaspoon cayenne
1 cup chopped cilantro, divided
2 tablespoons lime juice
Flour tortillas or Red Chile Rice (page 276), for serving

1. In a dry skillet heated on high, toast the pasilla chiles on each side for about 10 seconds or just until they start to puff. Fill the skillet with enough water to cover chiles. Leave the heat on until the water begins to boil and then turn off the heat and let the chiles soak until soft, about 30 minutes. Take the rehydrated chiles and dice.

2. Sprinkle the short ribs with salt and black pepper. In a large pot, heat the vegetable oil, lard, or bacon grease on medium and brown the short ribs for about 3 minutes on each side until browned. Remove the short ribs and throw the onions into the pot. Cook for 5 minutes and then add the tomatillos to the pot and cook for another 2 minutes. Add the garlic, cook for 1 minute, then put the short ribs back into the pot. Pour in the beer and stir in the diced pasilla chiles, cumin, cayenne, and ½ cup of the cilantro. Bring to a boil and then turn the heat down to low and simmer, covered, for 1½ hours.

3. After 1½ hours, remove the lid and stir in the remaining cilantro. Continue to simmer uncovered for another 1½ hours. Before serving, squeeze with lime juice. Serve with flour tortillas or over rice, using the pan juices as a gravy.

TEX-MEX MEAT LOAF WITH A CHIPOTLE-TOMATO GLAZE

12 SERVINGS

There's a gas station in Marfa that sells the best meat loaf sandwiches. And while you may be eating it cold, it's so tender and smooth that temperature is not an issue. But excellent texture aside, my favorite thing about this meat loaf is the spice and heat that it gets from chile peppers. When you take a bite, you know just where you are—within squinting distance of the border in far West Texas.

This meat loaf shares many characteristics with that West Texan dish, though I've added a few flourishes that give it even more of a Tex-Mex border flair. I've replaced some of the beef with chorizo sausage, thrown in some lime juice for tang, and given it a chipotle-tomato glaze on top. There's only one chipotle chile listed in the recipe, which for a Texan's palate may border on the mild, so feel free to bump up the quantity if you wish. If you're concerned that this dish might be too spicy for children, I understand that it's been a big hit with a couple of kids under the age of five.

This pairs very well with Red Chile Rice (page 276) or Mexican Fried Potatoes (page 81). And yes, in case you're wondering, leftovers make for terrific sandwiches the next day—though if you have enough hungry eaters, there might not be any of this Tex-Mex meat loaf left.

1. Preheat the oven to 350 degrees and line a large baking sheet with foil that's been greased.

2. To make the chipotle-tomato glaze, in a blender, puree until smooth the crushed tomatoes, chipotle chile, lime juice, allspice, and garlic. Add salt to taste.

{CONTINUED}

FOR THE CHIPOTLE-TOMATO GLAZE

1 cup crushed canned tomatoes, preferably fire roasted

½ or 1 canned chipotle chile in adobo (depending on how much heat you can handle)

2 tablespoons lime juice

½ teaspoon ground allspice

2 cloves garlic

Salt, to taste

FOR THE MEAT LOAF

½ tablespoon vegetable oil

¼ medium yellow onion, finely diced

2 cloves garlic, finely minced

1½ pounds lean ground beef

½ pound Mexican chorizo, removed from casing

¼ cup chopped cilantro

2 large eggs

1 cup finely ground crackers or tortilla chips or a combination of the two

1 teaspoon dried oregano

1 teaspoon ground cumin

1 teaspoon Worcestershire sauce

1 teaspoon black pepper

1 teaspoon kosher salt

3. To make the meat loaf, heat the oil in a skillet on medium-low heat, and add the onion. Cook uncovered for 5 minutes, stirring occasionally. Add the garlic and cook for 30 more seconds.

4. Slide the cooked onions and garlic into a large bowl. Add to the bowl the ground beef, the chorizo, cilantro, eggs, ground crackers or tortilla chips, oregano, cumin, Worcestershire sauce, black pepper, and salt. With your hands, gently mix all ingredients until well combined.

5. Take the meat and form it into a loaf. Place it on the sheet and take half of the chipotle-tomato glaze and spread it on top of the meat loaf. Place meat loaf in the oven and bake for 50 minutes. Remove from the oven, spread the remaining chipotle-tomato glaze on top, and place back in the oven for about 10 more minutes. Let the cooked meat loaf sit for 15 minutes and then slice with a serrated knife and serve.

NOTE: This recipe can easily be cut in half. If you prefer to bake it in a loaf pan, that's fine. I prefer doing it on the sheet so all sides get browned a bit.

DR PEPPER RIBS

4 SERVINGS

Texans love to cook with soda; these Dr Pepper ribs are no exception. The ribs are coated in a smoky sweet dry rub made with chipotle powder and brown sugar, and then glazed with a barbecue sauce made with a Dr Pepper base.

1. First, make a rub by mixing the salt, black pepper, brown sugar, mustard powder, cayenne, chipotle powder, and ground allspice. Coat the ribs with the rub, cover them with plastic wrap, and place in the refrigerator for at least 4 hours.

2. Preheat the oven to 300 degrees and bring the ribs to room temperature. In a large baking or roasting pan lined with foil, arrange the ribs with the meat side up, pour in ¼ cup of Dr Pepper, cover pan tightly with foil, and place in the oven.

3. Meanwhile, to make the glaze, place in a saucepot the Dr Pepper, ketchup, mustard, apple cider vinegar, molasses, and chipotle powder. Bring to a boil, then turn the heat down to low and simmer for 20 minutes until thick and syrupy.

4. After 1½ hours, take the ribs out of the oven and spread some of the glaze on each side of the racks. Place back in the oven, meat side up, and cook uncovered for 30 minutes. After 30 minutes, take out the ribs and spread more glaze over them, and cook for 30 more minutes or until ribs are desired tenderness. Take the ribs out of the oven, spread more glaze on them, and then cook each side under the broiler for 4 minutes.

FOR THE RIBS
¼ cup kosher salt
¼ cup black pepper
¼ cup brown sugar
4 teaspoons mustard powder
½ teaspoon cayenne
2 teaspoons chipotle powder
½ teaspoon ground allspice
2 racks of St. Louis ribs
¼ cup Dr Pepper (don't use diet)

FOR THE GLAZE
2 cups Dr Pepper (don't use diet)
1 cup ketchup
½ cup yellow prepared mustard
¼ cup apple cider vinegar
2 tablespoons molasses
2 to 4 teaspoons chipotle powder

NOTE: If you have access to Dublin Dr Pepper, which is Dr Pepper made with cane sugar instead of corn syrup, I recommend you use that, as it has a superior flavor.

CARNITAS

Carnitas, which means "little meats" in Spanish, come in several guises. Some people serve it stringy, like pulled pork. Some people serve it in huge chunks, with bits of bone still attached. And some serve it in smaller cubes, perfect for popping in your mouth. Though no matter how it's presented, it's always succulent slow-cooked pork that's tender on the inside and crunchy on the out.

The state of Michoacán, Mexico, is renowned for its carnitas, which they cook in lard. It's a decadent eating experience, as the pork is slick and smooth with just enough texture to keep things interesting.

You can, however, achieve a similar texture by cooking the pork shoulder in water until the liquid has evaporated. Because you haven't trimmed the fat off the pork, after the liquid is gone the pot is filled with rendered pork fat that browns the outside to a caramelized crisp, yielding succulent carnitas that are crisp on the outside and tender on the inside.

3 pounds boneless pork shoulder, cut into 2-inch cubes

½ cup orange juice

¼ cup lime juice

4 cloves garlic

1 teaspoon ground cumin

1 teaspoon kosher salt, plus more to taste

Houston-Style Green Salsa (page 59), tortillas, avocado slices and chopped cilantro, for serving

1. Place the pork in a large Dutch oven or pot; add the orange juice, lime juice, garlic, cumin, salt, and enough water to barely cover the meat. Bring the pot to a boil and then turn the heat down to low and simmer uncovered for 2 hours. Do not touch the meat.

2. After 2 hours, turn the heat up to medium-high, and while occasionally stirring, continue to cook uncovered for about 45 minutes or until all the liquid has evaporated and the pork fat has been rendered.

3. When pork has browned on both sides, it's ready. (There will still be liquid fat in the pan.) Taste and add salt. Serve either cubed or shredded with Houston-Style Green Salsa, tortillas, avocado slices, and chopped cilantro.

FANCY-PANTS KING RANCH CHICKEN CASSEROLE

12 SERVINGS

FOR THE CHICKEN

2 pounds boneless, skinless chicken breasts

2 teaspoons lime juice

2 teaspoons ancho chile powder

1 teaspoon kosher salt

1 tablespoon vegetable oil

FOR THE CASSEROLE

4 tablespoons unsalted butter

½ medium yellow onion, diced

1 red bell pepper, seeds and stems removed, diced

1 poblano pepper, seeds and stems removed, diced

3 cloves garlic, minced

1 teaspoon ground cumin

½ teaspoon cayenne

2 teaspoons ancho chile powder

2 tablespoons all-purpose flour

1 cup chicken broth

½ cup half-and-half

1 10-ounce can of tomatoes with green chiles, drained

½ cup sour cream

2 teaspoons lime juice

½ cup chopped cilantro, divided

1 tablespoon vegetable oil

10 corn tortillas

My grandparents used to gather with friends and play 42. This popular Texan game—which involves bidding and trumps—is similar to bridge, but it's played with dominoes instead of cards. My grandma tried to teach the game to me, but its rules were a bit too complex for me to grasp. But while I couldn't figure out how to play 42, I could *completely* understand why at each of these domino parties, large pans of King Ranch chicken casserole would be served.

King Ranch chicken casserole—a soft, slightly spicy, cheesy mixture of tomatoes, corn tortillas, chicken, cream, and peppers—is one of the most popular casseroles that Texans make. It goes down easy, travels well, and is the ultimate comfort food.

The origin of this dish is a bit murky, but most agree that despite the name, it did not originate at Texas's famed King Ranch. King Ranch chicken is basically an enchilada casserole, but it's creamier than most. And yes, most recipes for it call for canned cream soup. This certainly makes preparation simpler, but it can taste just as good without.

1. Sprinkle the chicken with lime juice, ancho chile powder, and salt. In a skillet heated on medium, warm up the oil and then cook the chicken on each side for 20 minutes, turning once. Shred cooked chicken with two forks. Should yield about 3 cups.

2. To make the casserole, melt the butter in a saucepan on medium and add the onions, red bell pepper, and poblano pepper. Cook for 5 minutes while occasionally stirring.

3. Stir in the garlic, cumin, cayenne, ancho chile powder, and flour, and cook for 1 minute. Stir in the chicken broth and cook on low until the mixture is thickened, a few minutes. Once the broth has thickened, stir in the half-and-half and canned tomatoes, cover the pot, turn the heat down to low, and simmer for about 15 minutes, stirring occasionally.

4. Uncover the pot and stir in the sour cream, lime juice, and ¼ cup of cilantro. Adjust seasonings and add salt and black pepper to taste. Turn off the heat.

5. Preheat the oven to 350 degrees and grease a large baking dish.

6. Heat the vegetable oil in a skillet and cook the corn tortillas on each side a couple of minutes until soft. Wrap in a cloth to keep warm as you continue to cook the rest. Ladle ½ cup of the sauce onto the bottom of the baking dish. Layer half the tortillas along the bottom of the dish on top of the sauce. To make sure the entire dish is evenly covered, you can rip some of the tortillas into strips to fill any gaps. Add half the chicken, half the remaining sauce, the remaining cilantro, and 1½ cups of the grated cheese, mixed. Repeat the layering, topping with a cheese layer. Cook uncovered for 30 minutes or until brown and bubbling.

1½ cups grated cheddar cheese (6 ounces)

1½ cups grated pepper Jack cheese (6 ounces)

Salt and black pepper, to taste

NOTE: If you can't find ancho chile powder, chili powder can be substituted.

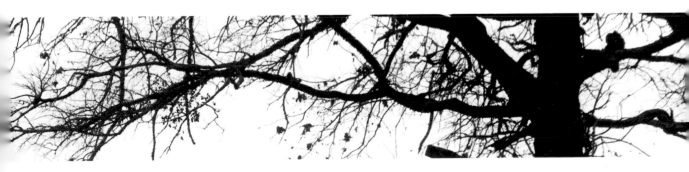

FRIED CHICKEN LIVERS

4 TO 6 SERVINGS

1 pound chicken livers, cut into
  bite-size pieces
1½ cups buttermilk, divided
1 cup all-purpose flour
1 teaspoon kosher salt
1½ teaspoons black pepper
¼ teaspoon cayenne
2 large eggs, beaten
2½ cups saltine cracker crumbs,
  finely ground
Vegetable oil, for frying

Fried chicken livers. I don't know why, but just saying the name gives me a giggle. And if you've ever had the pleasure of eating them, you'll know that eating them is no joke—this is some seriously good food.

Now, if you're ordinarily the sort who doesn't enjoy the mineral, earthy tones of beef liver, do not fear—these have a more delicate flavor. Firm on the inside and crunchy on the outside, fried chicken livers make for either a great snack or a whole meal. I like to just pop them in my mouth unadorned, but they also serve as an excellent vehicle for Jalapeño Buttermilk Dressing (page 49) or Chipotle and Bacon Cream Gravy (page 45).

1. In a large bowl, soak the chicken livers in ½ cup of the buttermilk for 1 hour. Drain and rinse then lightly season the chicken livers with salt and black pepper.

2. In a large plastic food-storage bag, mix together the flour, salt, black pepper, and cayenne. Place the chicken livers in the bag and shake until they are well coated.

3. Mix together the eggs with remaining 1 cup of buttermilk. Place the saltine crumbs on a plate. In batches, dip the flour-coated livers into the egg mixture and then lightly dredge in the saltine crumbs. Place cracker-coated livers on a large plate or sheet. Repeat until all the livers are coated.

4. In a large, heavy skillet heat ½ inch of oil on medium heat until it reaches 350 degrees. Cook the livers for 5 minutes, turning once. Depending on the size of your skillet, you will probably have to do several batches. Drain on paper towels.

JALAPEÑO MUSTARD ROAST CHICKEN

4 SERVINGS

When I shared this chicken with a homesick Texan friend, she took a bite and exclaimed, "This is the best roast chicken!" OK, I don't mean to brag, but that said, I often find that cooking a roast chicken can be a challenge. The white meat takes less time to cook than the dark meat, so by the time the whole bird is done, the white meat is dried out and has the texture of paper. Not good.

But I learned a technique called spatchcocking, which is just a fancy way to say "cut out the backbone and lay that bird flat." The chicken, which is now on a level plane, cooks evenly, so the breasts turn out as tender and succulent as the thighs and legs.

I'm sure this is one reason why my friend enjoyed the chicken, but I do think that the combination of honey, jalapeño, and mustard probably played a large role in creating such a delectable bird. The mustard adds tang and helps the flavors of the jalapeño, lime juice, and garlic stick to the meat, while the honey adds a hint of sweetness.

The best thing about this chicken, however, is what a cinch it is to make. Sure, it takes a while for it to marinate, but once you put it in the oven, you can walk away until it's done—no busting necessary. But you don't have to tell anyone; its simplicity can be our secret.

½ cup yellow prepared mustard

1 or 2 jalapeño chiles, stems and seeds removed, chopped

¼ cup lime juice

6 cloves garlic

½ cup cilantro

½ teaspoon ground ginger

1 teaspoon ground cumin

2 tablespoons honey

Salt, to taste

1 3-to-4-pound chicken

1. In a blender or food processor, mix together the mustard, jalapeño, lime juice, garlic, cilantro, ground ginger, cumin, and honey until well combined. Taste and add salt.

2. Rinse the chicken and remove the giblets (you can save the giblets for another use, if you like). To butterfly the chicken

{CONTINUED}

for more even cooking, remove the spine from the back of the chicken with poultry or kitchen shears, and save for another use.

3. Lightly salt the chicken all over, about 1 or 2 teaspoons. Take the mustard marinade and rub it all over the chicken, gently lifting the skin so you can spread some of it on the meat under the skin. Place the coated chicken in a plastic bag and refrigerate for up to 8 hours.

4. Preheat the oven to 400 degrees and line a sheet with foil.

5. Take the chicken out of the refrigerator and lay it flat, breast side up on the sheet with the legs on the outside. Let it come to room temperature (about 20 minutes) and then cook in the oven for 45 to 50 minutes or when a thermometer inserted in the thigh reads 170 degrees and the juices run clear. Remove from the oven and let it rest for 10 minutes before serving.

PORK CHOPS
WITH SALSA VERDE RICE

4 SERVINGS

My great-grandma Blanche used to make a pork chop dish where you take the chop, place a tablespoon of rice on top of it, pour some tomato sauce over the meat, and bake it covered for an hour. When you take the chop out of the oven, not only do you have a succulent piece of meat, but you also have a serving of rice. It's a wonderful one-pot dish.

I thought it would be fun to give it more of a Tex-Mex flavor profile, so I swapped out the tomatoes for tomatillos, added some jalapeño, and included a bit of cumin, cilantro, and lime juice, as well. This makes for a great weeknight dinner, but it's impressive enough to share with company, too.

½ pound tomatillos, husks removed, cut in half, or 1 11-ounce can of tomatillos, drained
¼ medium yellow onion, cut into slivers, divided
2 cloves garlic
¼ cup cilantro
1 jalapeño chile, seeds and stems removed, roughly chopped
½ teaspoon ground cumin
1 cup chicken broth
2 tablespoons lime juice
1 tablespoon vegetable oil
4 bone-in, thick-cut pork chops (they should be about ½ pound each)
Salt and black pepper, to taste
½ cup rice, soaked in water for 30 minutes and then drained

1. Preheat the oven to 325 degrees.

2. In a blender, mix together the tomatillos, half the slivered onions, garlic, cilantro, jalapeño, cumin, chicken broth, and lime juice. Add salt to taste.

3. In a large ovenproof skillet, preferably a cast-iron skillet, heat the oil on medium heat. Lightly season the pork chops with salt and black pepper and then cook for 6 minutes, turning once.

4. Remove the skillet from heat. On top of each chop, place 2 tablespoons of the soaked rice and the remaining onion slivers. Pour the tomatillo salsa over the chops (it's OK if some of the rice slides off the chops), cover the skillet tightly with foil, and bake for 1 hour. Then remove the skillet from the oven and let rest for 10 minutes. Remove foil and serve chops with the rice and salsa.

WEST TEXAS CARNE ASADO

8 SERVINGS

Out in far West Texas they make a pork dish called carne asado. It's a slow-cooked pot of pork that's flavored by ancho chiles, garlic, and oregano. I first encountered carne asado when I was passing though Odessa and met up with my old college friend Mark for dinner. I asked what the locals ate, and he urged me to order the asado.

Unfortunately, the asado was so popular the restaurant was out of it for the evening, and I was leaving Odessa early the next morning. I was very disappointed that I didn't get to try it. A few days later, however, I found myself in Midland, the sister city of Odessa. And when I stepped into a taqueria to grab some lunch, they had carne asado on the menu. I ordered a taco and indulged, and after one bite, I knew why it was the local favorite.

When I returned to New York, I begged Mark to give me a recipe. And yes, this asado tastes just like the version I had back in West Texas, especially when served with warm flour tortillas and a handful of cilantro.

12 dried ancho chiles, stems and seeds removed

3 pounds boneless pork shoulder, cut into 1-inch cubes

Salt and black pepper, to taste

2 tablespoons lard, bacon grease, or vegetable oil, divided

½ medium yellow onion, roughly chopped

10 cloves garlic, roughly chopped

2 teaspoons dried oregano

1 teaspoon ground cumin

¼ teaspoon ground allspice

1½ cups chicken broth or water

Cotija, lime wedges, and flour tortillas, for serving

1. In a dry skillet heated on high, toast the ancho chiles on each side for about 10 seconds or just until they start to puff. Fill the skillet with enough water to cover the chiles. Leave the heat on until the water begins to boil and then turn off the heat and let the chiles soak until soft, about 30 minutes. Once hydrated, discard the soaking water and rinse the chiles.

2. While the chiles are soaking, sprinkle the pork with salt and black pepper. In a large pot or Dutch oven, heat 1 tablespoon of the lard, bacon grease, or vegetable oil on medium heat and brown the pork on each side. (You may have to do this in batches.)

(CONTINUED)

3. Remove the browned pork from the pan and add the remaining tablespoon of lard, bacon grease, or vegetable oil. While occasionally stirring, cook the onions until translucent, about 5 minutes. Add the garlic and cook for 30 more seconds. Turn off the heat.

4. Place the cooked onion and garlic into the blender along with the drained, soaked chiles, oregano, cumin, allspice, and ½ cup of the chicken broth. Puree until a thick paste is formed. Add salt to taste. Pour the chile paste back into the pot along with the remaining 1 cup of chicken broth. While occasionally stirring, cook the chile sauce for 5 minutes. Don't be alarmed, but it might dramatically bubble and heave.

5. Add the meat back into the pan and cook covered on low heat for 2½ hours, occasionally stirring. After an hour of cooking, taste and adjust seasonings and add water to the pot if it looks too dry. When done, serve in bowls with Cotija cheese sprinkled on top along with warm flour tortillas and lime wedges.

NOTE: Sometimes ancho chiles can be bitter, even after rinsing them of the soaking water. If you feel that the asado is too bitter, add a pinch of ground cinnamon or brown sugar to level the taste.

MEXICAN RED CHORIZO

1 POUND

In Texas, Mexican red chorizo, or simply chorizo as it's usually called, is almost as ubiquitous in the morning as bacon and breakfast sausage, though I also like to stuff it into empanadas (page 95) or swirl it into cheese bread (page 288).

Vinegar and chiles give Mexican red chorizo its distinctive flavor, and it's simple to make, as you don't have to stuff the sausage into a casing. Chorizo tastes better after it has rested for a while, but if you don't want to wait, it's still delicious just after you've made it.

2 dried guajillo chiles, stems and seeds removed
2 dried ancho chiles, stems and seeds removed
2 tablespoons apple cider vinegar
¼ medium yellow onion, chopped
4 cloves garlic, chopped
1 pound ground pork, at least 20 percent fat
¼ teaspoon ground cinnamon
½ teaspoon ground cumin
½ teaspoon paprika
½ teaspoon dried oregano
¼ teaspoon cayenne
2 teaspoons kosher salt

1. In a dry skillet heated on high, toast the guajillo and ancho chiles on each side for about 10 seconds, or until they start to puff. Fill the skillet with enough water to cover the chiles. Leave the heat on until the water begins to boil and then turn off the heat and let the chiles soak until soft, about 30 minutes. Once rehydrated, discard the soaking water and rinse the chiles.

2. Place the chiles and vinegar in a blender, also adding the chopped onions and chopped garlic. Puree until a smooth, bright red paste is formed (add a splash of water or vinegar if it's too dry to blend). It will look like ketchup. Add the chile puree to the ground pork, along with the rest of the spices. Mix well.

3. To test the flavors, pinch off a small piece and fry it in a skillet for a minute or so. Taste and adjust seasonings. You can let it sit for a few hours so the flavors will meld, but I find that it's delicious right after making, too.

4. To prepare, fry in a greased skillet in either crumbles or patties. The sausage will keep in the refrigerator for a week. It can also be frozen, uncooked, for 6 months.

MEXICAN GREEN CHORIZO

1 POUND

Green chorizo, or chorizo verde as it's known in Spanish, is a variety of chorizo that's found in the Pueblo region of Mexico. As red chorizo gets its flavor and color from red chiles such as guajillo and ancho chiles, green chorizo gets its flavor and color from green chiles such as poblano and serrano chiles. So while red chorizo has an earthier flavor profile, green chorizo is brighter and lighter.

If you're wondering what to do with your batch of green chorizo, I use it just as I use red—in tacos, in my Poblano Macaroni and Cheese (page 265), or stuffed into jalapeños (page 111)—but really, the possibilities are limited only by your imagination.

1 poblano chile
2 cloves garlic
1½ cups fresh spinach leaves
½ cup cilantro
2 serrano chiles, stems and seeds removed, sliced
1 teaspoon ground cumin
1 teaspoon dried oregano
¼ teaspoon ground cloves
¼ teaspoon cayenne
2 tablespoons white wine vinegar
1 teaspoon lime zest
1 pound ground pork, at least 20 percent fat
1 teaspoon kosher salt
1 teaspoon black pepper

1. Roast the poblano chile under the broiler until blackened, about 5 minutes per side. Place chile in a paper sack or plastic food-storage bag, close it tightly, and let the chile steam for 20 minutes. Take the chile out of the bag and rub off the skin. Remove stem and seeds and chop the chile.

2. In a blender or food processor, add the poblano, garlic, spinach, cilantro, serrano chiles, cumin, oregano, cloves, cayenne, white wine vinegar, and lime zest. Blend until a green paste is formed. Mix green paste with the ground pork and add salt and black pepper. (I start with 1 teaspoon of each.)

3. Heat a skillet on medium and cook a small spoonful of the pork, a couple of minutes on each side. Taste and adjust seasonings. You can let it sit for a few hours so the flavors will meld, but I find that it's delicious right after making, too.

4. To prepare, fry in a greased skillet in either crumbles or patties. The sausage will keep in the refrigerator for a week. It can also be frozen, uncooked, for 6 months.

9

In the early evenings, you'll often find me walking along the Hudson River. This body of water runs along the western side of Manhattan and can be a peaceful setting for some spectacular sunsets. When I'm in this city of skyscrapers and sidewalks, one of the things I miss most about Texas is the presence of nature. Fortunately, there are parks and rivers in New York that offer small patches of green and blue. And with a little footwork, you can find yourself in the midst of natural beauty.

One day I saw a group of kids on the pier dangling fishing poles into the river. Now, the Hudson isn't known for being the cleanest body of water, and I don't think I'd want to eat anything that came out of it. I can, however, understand the appeal of attempting to connect with nature and forage for your food.

When I was about their age, my friends and I did the same thing. My Houston home was near a golf course that was filled with small ponds. One afternoon we gathered slices of uncooked bacon,

hooks and poles, and made our way to the course. Our aim was to catch fish for that evening's supper.

One of my friends went fishing with his family often and assured us that he was an old pro at the sport, so we let him tell us what to do. He showed us how to thread the raw bacon onto the hook and throw out the line. Then we waited. And waited. And waited. Nobody reeled in a catch, which is probably because there weren't any fish, only golf balls, in that pond.

I've had better success at my grandma's farm. On her land, there's a body of water that's technically known as a reservoir tank but that we call the lake. We keep it stocked with freshwater fish such as crappie, and after digging for worms in the dirt, my grandma, my uncle Richard, and my brother Jacob have been known to row out to the middle of the lake and cast their lines. I have to admit, the one time I joined them, I fell out of the boat, so they prefer that I make my contribution in the kitchen. That's OK, as after a bit of patience and time, they'll catch a few

fish and I'll crust them with pecans and mustard for supper that night.

There are no catfish at the farm, but my grandma talks about how many years ago her brother-in-law, a World War I veteran, would take his boat up to Lake Texoma and catch a mess of them with his bare hands. OK, I may have made that last part up (catching catfish with your hands is a time-honored tradition known as noodling), but he would reel in buckets of these ugly but delectable fish and bring them back home to Melissa. After skinning and filleting the fish, my great-aunt Frances would dip them in cornmeal, and a fine Texas catfish fry would ensue.

Of course, with a large portion of Texas's border formed by the Gulf of Mexico, I've spent a fair amount of time eating what that bountiful body of water yields. We'll take chile-soaked tilapia and wrap it in a flour tortilla for a fine fish taco. Or we'll serve redfish drenched in flavorful butter. But my favorite seafood that comes from the Gulf would have to be shrimp. When I was growing up in Houston, I'd

see, during the summer shrimp season, trucks alongside the road selling that day's catch. We'd stop and buy a few pounds, roll them in crushed crackers, and fry them up for a feast. But shrimp also pair well with crab for a spicy Mexican seafood cocktail known as campechana, and they are also a key ingredient in shrimp and okra gumbo. And if you love butter, shrimp are a wonderful vehicle for a pasilla-chile, garlic butter sauce.

Now, New York is a coastal city, so there are many seafood offerings that remind me of home. In the Bronx, there's the New Fulton Fish Market at Hunts Point, which is the second-largest fish market in the world. You can also find fresh fish at markets across the city. Heck, even seeing those kids fishing off the pier takes me back, so re-creating many of my Texan seafood favorites in New York City hasn't been that difficult a task. But despite New York's seafood bounty, nothing will ever replace the lake at my family's farm or the Gulf of Mexico in my heart.

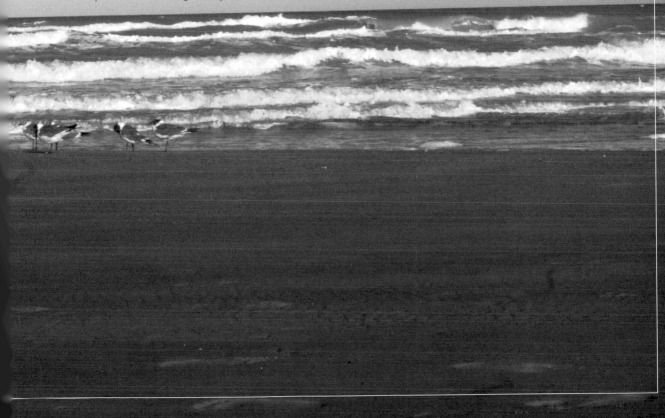

CRAB CAKES WITH CHIPOTLE CHILES AND CORN

4 SERVINGS

I had a friend in college who'd go crab fishing in the Gulf every August with his dad. He'd return with an ice chest filled with boiled crabs that we'd sprinkle with lemon juice, and then we'd slurp the meat out of the shell. If you ask me, fresh crabmeat doesn't need more adornment than that.

But sometimes your access to fresh crab may be limited, so if you have a craving for this sweet meat, you may want to do a little embellishing. I'm a big fan of crab cakes, a Maryland export that made its way to Texas in the early 1980s. For a long time Texans have served deviled crab, which is essentially a similar mixture, but instead of trying up the filling, you stuff it into a hollowed-out crab shell and then bake it.

For my crab cakes, I add corn, which goes well with crab's natural sweetness. I also brighten them up with lime and ginger, while adding a bit of chipotle chile for smoky heat. They make for a fine entree, though you can make them a smaller size for an appetizer.

1 pound fresh crabmeat
½ cup mayonnaise
2 cloves garlic, minced
½ cup corn kernels
1 canned chipotle in adobo, finely diced
½ cup cilantro, diced
¼ teaspoon cayenne
½ teaspoon ground cumin
¼ teaspoon ground ginger
¼ cup lime juice
1 cup finely crushed saltines
Salt and black pepper, to taste
2 tablespoons unsalted butter
Mayonnaise, hot sauce, and limes, for serving

1. Drain the crabmeat and pick out any shell or cartilage.

2. Stir together the mayonnaise, garlic, corn, chipotle, cilantro, cayenne, cumin, ginger, and lime juice until the ingredients are well combined. Add the crabmeat and then stir in the saltine cracker crumbs, adding salt and black pepper to taste. Form into 8 patties and refrigerate for 1 hour.

3. To cook the crab cakes, melt the butter in a skillet set on medium-low heat. Add the crab cakes, cooking for 3 minutes on each side or until each side is golden brown. Serve with mayonnaise, hot sauce, and a squirt of lime.

CAMPECHANA (MEXICAN SEAFOOD COCKTAIL)

4 SERVINGS

1 pound ripe plum tomatoes, diced;
  or 1 14-ounce can of diced
  tomatoes, preferably fire roasted,
  drained, divided

2 canned chipotle chiles in adobo

8 medium pitted green olives,
  diced (about ¼ cup)

4 tablespoons chopped cilantro

⅛ medium yellow onion, diced

1 clove garlic, minced

1 serrano chile, seeds and stem
  removed, diced

¼ teaspoon ground cumin

2 teaspoons lime juice

1 teaspoon olive oil

Salt and black pepper to taste

½ pound large shrimp (21 to
  30 per pound), boiled, peeled,
  and deveined

½ pound lump crabmeat

1 avocado, peeled and pitted,
  diced

Tortilla chips, for serving

When you walk into a restaurant and see that every table has ordered the same dish, you know that it's probably worth ordering as well. That's always been my experience in Houston with Goode Company Seafood's campechana, a Mexican seafood cocktail that's cool and refreshing.

This dish of usually shrimp and crab tossed with avocado, green olives, jalapeños, cilantro, and dressing isn't unique to Goode Company, as you'll find it at most Mexican seafood restaurants and in Mexican coastal cities such as Campeche, which gives the dish its name. But Goode Company's was the first, and it's still my favorite—there's a reason why everyone orders it, though I've found that's it darn easy to make at home.

1. If using fresh tomatoes, place them under the broiler for a couple of minutes on each side until blackened. (If using canned tomatoes, skip this step.) Dice the blackened tomatoes. Place 1½ cups of the tomatoes, fresh or canned, in the blender with the chipotle chiles. Blend until a smooth puree forms. Pour tomato puree into a bowl and stir in the olives, cilantro, onions, garlic, serrano chile, and cumin. Stir in the remaining diced tomatoes.

2. Add the lime juice and olive oil. Stir in the shrimp and crabmeat and refrigerate for 4 hours. Before serving, add the diced avocado. Campechana is traditionally served in ice cream parfait glasses, but any vessel will do. Serve with tortilla chips.

BOILED CRAWFISH

4 SERVINGS

Crawfish boils were a common event for anyone growing up in Houston. This freshwater crustacean is in season during the early part of the year, so you would find yourself feasting on these at Super Bowl parties, Mardi Gras events, or spring gatherings.

The drill was always the same: you'd go to someone's house, and on the back porch they'd have a pot the size of a small child bubbling away in anticipation of receiving the crawfish. Not far away would be a long table covered in newspapers, ready to receive the cooked crawfish along with the potatoes, corn, and sausage sharing the pot.

Sure, eating crawfish is a bit messy, as you use your hands and your mouth to get at the goodness inside the shells. But if you're a fan of lobster or other shellfish and have never experienced a proper crawfish boil, I highly recommend it.

1. First, clean the crawfish by placing them in a bucket or large sink filled with cold water. If there are any with a straight tail, throw them out, as this means they're already dead.

2. While the crawfish are soaking, fill the large pot with water two-thirds up the sides and add the lemons, celery, onion, garlic, mustard seeds, allspice, cloves, cayenne, sea salt, and bay leaves. Bring to a boil then add the potatoes, corn, and andouille sausage. Let the water boil for 10 minutes.

3. Drain the crawfish from the soaking water and then add to the pot. Boil for 10 minutes and then turn off the heat, cover the pot, and let the crawfish sit in the pot for 10 more minutes. Drain the liquid from the pot. Line a table with newspaper and pour out the crawfish, potatoes, corn, and sausage. Serve with hot sauce, melted butter, and lemon wedges.

10 pounds live crawfish

4 lemons cut in half

1 stalk of celery, quartered

1 onion, cut in half

12 cloves garlic, peeled

2 tablespoons mustard seeds

2 tablespoons whole allspice

1 tablespoon whole cloves

2 tablespoons ground cayenne

¼ cup kosher salt

4 bay leaves

8 red potatoes

8 ears of corn, husked and cut in half

½ pound andouille sausage, cut into 1-inch pieces

Hot sauce, melted butter, and lemon wedges, for serving

SPECIAL EQUIPMENT

A tall stockpot that can hold 5 gallons of water

CRAWFISH ROLLS

4 SERVINGS

1 pound crawfish tails
½ cup mayonnaise
1 stalk of celery, finely diced
¼ cup chopped cilantro
1 tablespoon lime juice
¼ teaspoon ground cumin
¼ teaspoon paprika
¼ teaspoon cayenne
Salt and black pepper, to taste
1 tablespoon unsalted butter
4 hot dog buns (preferably top loading, if you can find them)

On the East Coast, the lobster roll, especially in the summer, is ubiquitous. Tender pieces of lobster meat are tossed with a bit of mayonnaise and spooned into a buttered, split hot dog bun. It's both decadent and comforting at the same time.

I always thought that crawfish tasted like miniature lobsters, which makes sense, as they're both crustaceans. So why not make a crawfish roll instead? I've used just the tails in this recipe, as they're easier to find if you don't want to mess with having a whole crawfish boil. I've also added flavors such as cilantro, lime juice, and cumin to make them even more Texan.

If you can find top-loading hot dog buns, I recommend you use those, though it's not required. The crawfish filling also goes well in a hollowed-out tomato or alongside an iceberg lettuce wedge.

1. If your crawfish tails aren't cooked, bring a pot of water to a boil, add the crawfish, and boil for 10 minutes. Drain and rinse with cold water.

2. Toss the cooked crawfish tails with the mayonnaise, celery, cilantro, lime juice, cumin, paprika, and cayenne. Taste and add salt and pepper. Refrigerate for at least 1 hour.

3. To assemble the rolls, heat the butter in a skillet on medium-low heat, flatten the buns, and cook on each side a couple of minutes or until lightly brown. Scoop the crawfish salad into the buns and serve.

NOTE: You can find crawfish tails either fresh or frozen in many seafood departments. If you are unable to find them, frozen langoustine tails are a good substitute.

GUAJILLO-CHILE FISH TACOS WITH CABBAGE SLAW

4 SERVINGS

Fish tacos weren't always a popular Texan dish. Like all tacos, they were originally found in Mexico, primarily in the Baja area on the West Coast, though you could also find versions in the Yucatán. A man named Rick Rubio is said to have brought them to the United States by way of San Diego, California, back in the 1980s. Soon, however, you started seeing them on menus in coastal Texas towns such as Corpus Christi and Houston.

I had my first fish taco at Berryhill in Houston, a restaurant that has been credited with making fish tacos popular in Texas. Their version is the Baja interpretation, which means it's battered and fried. I, however, prefer the marinated version, which is more commonly found in South Texas. I find that this type of fish taco not only has more flavor but is a bit healthier as well, since it isn't fried.

I take mild tilapia and soak it in a tangy, bright guajillo chile paste and then quickly cook it in a skillet. For a bit of crunch, I pair the fish with a creamy cabbage slaw that's given a bit of heat with a serrano chile. Served with warm tortillas, Cotija, and lime, these tacos make for a satisfying meal.

1. In a dry skillet heated on high, toast the guajillo chiles on each side for about 10 seconds, or just until they start to puff. Fill the skillet with enough water to cover the chiles. Leave the heat on until the water begins to boil, then turn off the heat and let the chiles soak until soft, about 30 minutes.

2. Drain the chiles and place in a blender with the garlic, cilantro, cumin, cayenne, ginger, lime juice, and olive oil. Blend until a smooth paste forms. Add salt to taste.

FOR THE FISH

6 dried guajillo chiles, stems and seeds removed
4 cloves garlic
½ cup cilantro
1 teaspoon ground cumin
½ teaspoon cayenne
½ teaspoon ground ginger
¼ cup lime juice
¼ cup olive oil
Salt, to taste
1 pound tilapia fillets
1 tablespoon unsalted butter

FOR THE CABBAGE SLAW

2 cups shredded cabbage
1 teaspoon kosher salt
1 serrano chile, diced
¼ teaspoon ground cumin
¼ cup cilantro
2 tablespoons mayonnaise
2 tablespoons lime juice

FOR THE TACOS

Flour or corn tortillas
Cotija cheese, crumbled
Lime wedges
Salsa

(CONTINUED)

3. Rinse and dry the fish, sprinkle with a bit of salt, and place in a nonreactive container. Cover the fish on all sides with the guajillo chile paste and refrigerate for a couple of hours.

4. While the fish is marinating, you can make the cabbage topping. Toss the shredded cabbage with 1 teaspoon of salt and let it sit unrefrigerated for 1 hour. Drain off the excess liquid and then mix the cabbage with the serrano chile, cumin, cilantro, mayonnaise, and lime juice. Add salt and black pepper to taste and refrigerate.

5. After the fish has marinated, melt the butter in a skillet on medium heat. Shake off any excess marinade and then cook the fillets for 3 minutes on each side. Add salt to taste. Cut the fish into bite-size pieces and place in warm tortillas. Top with the cabbage slaw and serve with Cotija cheese, lime wedges, and salsa.

REDFISH ON THE HALF SHELL

4 SERVINGS

Along the Gulf Coast you'll commonly find redfish, which is also known as reds, red drum, channel bass, or spottail sea bass. Now, you'd think that the fish would be red, considering its name, but instead it usually sports a shiny silver skin. No matter, it's a flavorful meaty fish that is served in a variety of preparations—in tacos or ceviches, roasted, or my favorite, on the half shell.

Redfish on the half shell is an old Texan fish-camp dish, where the fish is cut in half and filleted without removing the skin and scales. The fish is then placed scale side down on the grill, with the scale creating a shell that protects the meat as it cooks. Don't fret if you don't have a grill, as you can create the same great dish in your oven as well. Also, it can be difficult to find redfish sold outside of the South, but I find that red snapper is a wonderful substitute.

4 tablespoons unsalted butter, room temperature
2 cloves garlic, minced
1 tablespoon chopped cilantro
½ teaspoon dried oregano
¼ teaspoon ground ginger
½ teaspoon ground cumin
¼ teaspoon cayenne
2 1-pound redfish cut in half with skin and scales still on, bones removed
Salt and black pepper, to taste
1 lime, cut into 12 thin slices

1. Preheat the oven to 400 degrees and grease a baking sheet.

2. Mix together the butter with the garlic, cilantro, oregano, ginger, cumin, and cayenne.

3. On the greased baking sheet, place the fish fillets scale side down and sprinkle with salt and pepper. Spread over each fillet a tablespoon of the seasoned butter, and top each fillet with 3 lime slices. Cook uncovered for 20 minutes or until fish flakes. Alternatively, you can fire up your grill and cook the fish scale side down and covered for 20 minutes.

4. Serve in its skin-and-scale shell.

PECAN-CRUSTED CRAPPIE

4 SERVINGS

1 pound crappie fillets (or other firm
   white fish such as grouper, perch,
   rainbow trout, or walleye), cut into
   4 pieces
½ teaspoon kosher salt, plus more
   to taste
1 large egg, beaten
1 cup pecans, finely chopped
½ cup sour cream
1 tablespoon yellow or Dijon
   mustard
1 serrano chile, seeds and stems
   removed, finely diced
1 clove garlic, minced
1 teaspoon chopped cilantro
1 teaspoon lime juice

There's a reservoir tank at my grandma's farm, a body of water that we refer to as the lake. Sure, it's not Lake Texoma, but you can take a boat out and go fishing on it. And so my grandma and her neighbors keep the lake well stocked, primarily with a delicious freshwater fish known as crappie.

If you've never had crappie, well, first ignore its name—it's a complete misnomer. This flaky white panfish has a firm texture and a clean flavor. Even people who don't like fish find crappie a pleasure to eat.

Because we have pecans growing on the farm, coating the fish with Texas's state nut is the natural choice. And for added tang, I like to serve the fish with a jalapeño-mustard sauce.

Now, this is where you're going to get angry with me. You can't buy crappie at the store; I've tried. And while yes, for this recipe I recommend crappie because we make this pecan-crusted fish dish at the farm, I believe you'll be just fine making it with other firm, white-fleshed fish such as grouper, perch, rainbow trout, or walleye.

1. Preheat the oven to 400 degrees and lightly grease a baking sheet.

2. Sprinkle salt on both sides of the fish fillets.

3. Place the beaten egg in a bowl and the chopped pecans on a plate. Dip each fillet in the egg and then roll the fish in the chopped pecans. Place each coated fillet on the sheet and bake for 15 to 20 minutes, or until fish flakes.

4. While the fish are baking, mix together the sour cream, mustard, serrano chile, garlic, cilantro, and lime juice. Taste and add salt. Serve mustard sauce with the cooked fish.

SALMON CROQUETTES

2 TO 4 SERVINGS

My grandma likes to check in occasionally and see what I'm making in my small apartment in New York City. One evening, when I told her I was whipping up a batch of salmon croquettes, she informed me that they had been my grandpa's favorite meal.

What? How had I not known this about my grandpa? We certainly ate our fair share of salmon croquettes, as many North Texan folk do—and yes, the salmon always came from a can. But I had no recollection of this about my grandpa, which made my batch of salmon croquettes even more important to me.

As I formed the patties, I asked myself if my grandpa would even recognize these croquettes. See, I had mixed fresh salmon with mashed potatoes and a host of spices such as cumin and ginger; my grandma's salmon croquettes were simply made with canned salmon, egg, and cornmeal. My conclusion? I do believe he would have recognized them and even enjoyed them. And while I was a little bummed that I couldn't share them with him when he was alive, I took pleasure in knowing that it had been his favorite dish.

1 pound salmon fillet
¼ pound Yukon gold potatoes, peeled and cut in half
1 teaspoon vegetable oil
1 jalapeño chile, seeds and stems removed, finely diced
2 cloves garlic, minced
¼ teaspoon ground ginger
½ teaspoon ground cumin
2 tablespoons half-and-half
1 tablespoon lime juice
¼ cup chopped cilantro
1 large egg, beaten
½ cup finely crushed saltines
2 tablespoons unsalted butter
Salt and black pepper, to taste
Hot sauce, limes, and jalapeño tartar sauce (page 241), for serving

1. Preheat the oven to 350 degrees.

2. Place the salmon skin side down in a greased cast-iron skillet or large baking dish. Sprinkle with salt and bake uncovered for 15 minutes. When done, remove the skin from the salmon, place the fish in a large bowl and break it into flakes.

3. Meanwhile, place the potatoes in a pot and cover with 1 inch of cold, salted water. Bring to a boil and then cook until soft, about 10 minutes. Drain the potatoes and then return them to the pot. Turn the heat on medium and gently stir until

(CONTINUED)

all the moisture has evaporated, about 15 seconds. Turn off the heat and leave the potatoes in the pot.

4. In a skillet, heat 1 teaspoon of vegetable oil on medium heat and cook the jalapeño for 2 minutes. Add the garlic and cook for 30 more seconds. Pour the jalapeño and garlic into the potato pot and add the ginger and cumin. Mash until smooth and then stir in the half-and-half. Taste and add salt and black pepper.

5. Add the potatoes to the salmon, along with the lime juice and cilantro. Taste and adjust the seasonings and then mix in the egg. Blend all the ingredients until a thick, wet paste is formed.

6. Place in the refrigerator for at least an hour, as the mixture is very moist, and the colder it is, the easier it will be to form the croquettes. To assemble the salmon croquettes, form into 8 balls and then lightly press until it makes a hockey-puck shape. Sprinkle all sides of each patty with the crushed saltines.

7. To cook the croquettes, melt the butter in a skillet set on medium-low heat. Using a spatula, add the salmon patties to the skillet and cook for 3 minutes on each side or until each side is golden brown. Serve with hot sauce, limes, and/or jalapeño tartar sauce.

NOTE: You can take a shortcut with this recipe if you have leftover cooked salmon or mashed potatoes. You can also substitute panko crumbs for the crushed saltines.

FRIED CATFISH

4 SERVINGS

1 pound catfish fillets, cut into
    inch-wide strips
½ teaspoon kosher salt
½ teaspoon black pepper
2 large eggs
½ cup whole milk
1 cup yellow cornmeal
¼ teaspoon cayenne
Vegetable oil, for frying

After barbecue, fried catfish is the dish of choice when a group of Texans gather to celebrate. Family reunions, wedding receptions, and Fridays (especially during Lent if you're Catholic) are all best served with delectable deep-fried, cornmeal-coated catfish.

In countless small towns across the state it's more ubiquitous than either Tex-Mex or barbecue—chances are, in most places, if there is only one restaurant, it's a catfish joint. That's certainly the case for my grandma. A stone's throw up the road from her farm in the no-stop-sign town of Chambersville is the one-stop-sign town of Weston. It has a gas station, a post office, and one restaurant that specializes in, yep, catfish.

While it's fun to go out for a fish fry, making it at home doesn't take much effort, as fried catfish is a simple affair. Though when served with Cabbage and Radish Slaw (page 255) and a basket of Hush Puppies (page 285), I can't think of a finer feast.

1. Salt and pepper the catfish fillets.

2. Beat eggs and milk together in a bowl. Mix together the cornmeal and the cayenne, and place on a plate.

3. In a large, heavy skillet heat 2 inches of oil on medium heat until it reaches 350 degrees.

4. Dip fillets in egg-milk mixture and then dredge in the cornmeal, covering both sides. Place battered fish into hot oil and cook 4 minutes, turning once. Drain on a paper-towel-lined plate. (You may have to do this in batches, depending on the size of your skillet.) Serve with Jalapeño Relish (page 31) mixed with mayonnaise, Chipotle Ketchup (page 29), or tartar sauce.

FRIED FROG LEGS

4 TO 6 SERVINGS

In the eighth grade, a friend's family opened a restaurant. I asked my friend what kind of food his family restaurant was going to serve, and he said Texan food, like frog legs.

Frog legs? I asked my dad about it, and he said that frog legs were commonly eaten in the Brazos Valley area and around Caddo Lake; this was East Texas food.

When we ate there, I ordered the frog legs. I don't know what I had been expecting, but when they arrived I was a little shocked—they looked like skinny chicken drumsticks. Matter of fact, they tasted like chicken, too.

Now, if you've never had fried frog legs, I urge you to try them, as you may be surprised at how succulent they are. And if you're from East Texas, then you definitely know what a treat they can be.

12 frog legs

1½ cups buttermilk, divided

1 cup all-purpose flour

1 teaspoon kosher salt, plus more
    to taste

1½ teaspoons black pepper, plus
    more to taste

¼ teaspoon cayenne

2 large eggs, beaten

2½ cups saltine cracker crumbs,
    finely ground

Vegetable oil, for frying

Hot sauce

Lemon wedges

1. In a large bowl, soak the frog legs in ½ cup of the buttermilk for 1 hour. Drain and rinse then lightly salt and pepper the frog legs.

2. In a large plastic food-storage bag, mix together the flour, salt, black pepper, and cayenne. Place the frog legs in the bag and shake until they are well coated. Mix together the eggs with remaining 1 cup of buttermilk. Place the saltine crumbs on a plate.

3. In batches, dip the flour-coated frog legs into the eggs and then lightly dredge in the saltine crumbs. Place the cracker-coated frog legs on a large plate or sheet.

4. In a large, heavy skillet heat ½ inch of oil on medium heat until it reaches 350 degrees. Cook the frog legs for 6 minutes, turning once. Drain on paper towels. Serve with hot sauce and lemon wedges.

BEER-STEAMED MUSSELS WITH MEXICAN CHORIZO

4 SERVINGS

2 pounds mussels

2 tablespoons unsalted butter

½ medium yellow onion, diced

6 cloves garlic, minced

½ pound plum tomatoes, diced, or
 1 cup canned diced tomatoes,
 drained

2 serrano chiles, stems and seeds
 removed, diced

½ cup cilantro

¼ pound Mexican Red Chorizo,
 cooked, drained, and crumbled
 (page 213)

¼ cup lime juice

1 tablespoon lime zest

1 teaspoon kosher salt

1 12-ounce bottle of dark Mexican
 beer, such as Negra Modelo

Bread, for serving

"Let's go get seafood!" said my friend Monica. Now, if Monica lived in Houston, I wouldn't have blinked. But she lives in Austin, a Central Texas town not exactly known for its aquatic life. I was hesitant, but she assured me that the restaurant was a real gem.

The place is known for its oysters, but as it was July and oysters were out of season, we opted for the mussels instead. They were meaty and soft, with a briny hint of the sea, and nestled in each shell were a few crumbles of spicy Mexican chorizo.

Inspired, when I returned to New York I decided to re-create the dish. Now, if you've never made mussels before, they are one of the easiest things to prepare. You simply throw all the ingredients into a pot and let it steam. Be sure to have bread on hand, as you'll want to sop up every last drop of the cooking broth.

1. Clean the mussels in cold water, removing the beard (the hairy patch that will be poking through the shell's opening) by pulling on it if it hasn't already been removed.

2. In a large pot or Dutch oven heated on medium-low, melt the butter and add the onions. Cook while stirring occasionally for 5 minutes. Add the garlic and cook for 30 more seconds. Add to the pot the tomatoes, serrano chiles, cilantro, cooked chorizo, lime juice, lime zest, salt, mussels, and beer.

3. Cover the pot and turn the heat up to high and cook until the shells open, about 10 minutes. Use a slotted spoon to transfer steamed mussels into either a large bowl or individual bowls. (Discard any mussels that did not open.) Pour some of the cooking liquid over the mussels and serve with bread, for sopping up the liquid, and an extra bowl to collect the shells.

FRIED SHRIMP

4 SERVINGS

When you visit coastal Texas towns, such as Corpus Christi and Galveston, the site of paper-lined baskets overflowing with fried shrimp will be common. If you can't decide where to eat, just ask a local, as they'll know where you can find the juiciest, freshest, crispest battered and fried shrimp.

I've taken a bit of an untraditional path with my fried shrimp by adding diced serrano chiles to my first flour dredge. Don't be alarmed by this; the chiles will stick to the shrimp and will provide an added burst of flavor as you crunch into the fried morsels.

I like to serve my fried shrimp with a jalapeño tartar sauce I make from my Jalapeño Relish (page 31), but Chipotle Ketchup (page 29) would also be terrific.

1. In a bowl or large plastic food-storage bag, mix together the flour, serrano chile, salt, black pepper, cumin, and lime juice. Toss the shrimp until coated with the flour mixture.

2. Mix together the eggs with the buttermilk. Place the saltine crumbs on a plate and stir in the cayenne.

3. In batches, dip the flour-coated shrimp into the egg mixture and then lightly dredge in the saltine crumbs. Place cracker-coated shrimp on a large plate or sheet. Repeat until all the shrimp are coated.

4. In a large, heavy skillet heat ½ inch of oil on medium heat until it reaches 350 degrees. Cook the shrimp for 2 minutes, turning once. Depending on the size of your skillet, you will probably have to do several batches. Drain on paper towels.

5. To make the jalapeño tartar sauce, mix together the Jalapeño Relish with the mayonnaise. Serve immediately with the fried shrimp.

FOR THE SHRIMP

¼ cup all-purpose flour

1 serrano chile, stems and seeds removed, finely diced

½ teaspoon kosher salt

½ teaspoon black pepper

¼ teaspoon ground cumin

1 teaspoon lime juice

1 pound medium shrimp (31 to 35 per pound), peeled and deveined

2 large eggs

½ cup buttermilk

2 cups finely crushed saltines

¼ teaspoon cayenne

Vegetable oil, for frying

FOR THE JALAPEÑO TARTAR SAUCE

2 tablespoons Jalapeño Relish (page 31)

1 cup mayonnaise

PASILLA GARLIC SHRIMP

4 SERVINGS

2 dried pasilla chiles, stems and
seeds removed
2 pounds large shrimp (21 to 30 per
pound), heads removed
½ cup chopped cilantro
4 cloves garlic, minced
½ teaspoon ground ginger
½ teaspoon ground cumin
¼ teaspoon cayenne
2 tablespoons lime juice
1 tablespoon olive oil
4 tablespoons unsalted butter
(½ a stick)
Salt and black pepper, to taste

In Texas, we often serve a dish called camarones al mojo de ajo, which roughly translates to "shrimp in a garlic sauce." It's a simple preparation—shrimp is bathed in a sauce made with garlic, parsley, and lots of butter. It's a fine way to eat shrimp, but my inclination is that it could be a bit more flavorful and, well, Texan.

To give the dish more depth, I've added the bittersweet fire of pasilla chiles along with earthly cumin and bright ginger. I've also replaced the parsley with cilantro. But don't worry, there's still plenty of garlic and butter, which is why you eat this dish in the first place, as shrimp are a perfect vehicle for this pairing. Serve over rice or grits, or just with a loaf of crusty bread, as you will want to sop up every last bit of this pasilla garlic sauce.

1. In a dry skillet heated on high, toast the pasilla chiles on each side for about 10 seconds or just until they start to puff. Fill the skillet with enough water to cover chiles. Leave the heat on until the water begins to boil, then turn off the heat and let the chiles soak until soft, about 30 minutes.

2. Remove shells from shrimp and place the shells in a pot. Add 4 cups of water, a pinch of salt, and bring to a boil. Turn the heat down to low and simmer for 20 minutes. Remove from the heat and strain out the shells. You now have a simple shrimp stock.

3. Take rehydrated chiles and rinse, discarding the soaking water. Place the chiles, cilantro, garlic, ginger, cumin, cayenne, lime juice, and 1 cup of the shrimp stock in a blender. Blend until a smooth puree is formed.

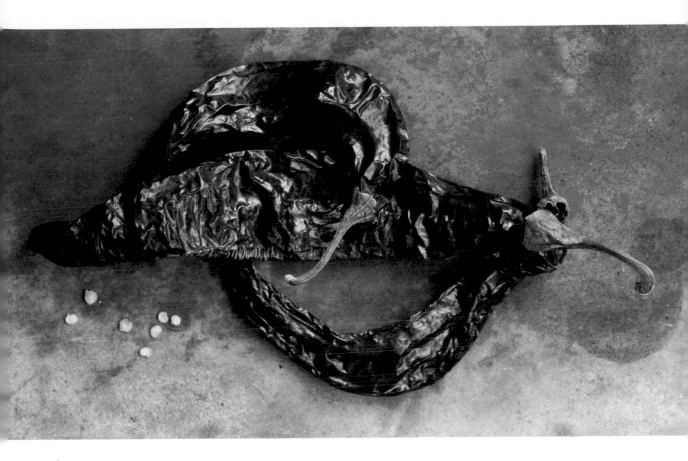

4. In a large skillet, heat the olive oil on medium-low heat; add the chile puree and cook, stirring occasionally, for 10 minutes. Add the butter and 2 tablespoons of the shrimp stock. (You can use the remaining shrimp stock for something else, or freeze it for 6 months.) When the butter has melted, stir until the sauce is well combined and add the shrimp, along with salt and pepper to taste. Cook the shrimp about 3 minutes on each side or until pink. Remove shrimp and drizzle chile butter sauce on top. Serve over rice, grits, or just with a loaf of crusty bread to sop up the sauce.

NOTE: If you can't find pasilla chiles, you may substitute ancho chiles, or in a pinch canned chipotle chiles (the latter will not need to be rehydrated).

SHRIMP AND OKRA GUMBO

8 SERVINGS

Growing up in Houston, I was no stranger to gumbo. The city's close proximity to Louisiana's Cajun country ensured that I knew plenty of kids whose parents often had a big pot of the chunky soup simmering on the stove. After an afternoon of riding bikes, you could walk into one of these kitchens, grab a bowl, and ladle a portion thick with smoky, succulent meats over a pile of rice. During the colder months, gumbo was almost as prevalent as chili in my part of town, and as with our state dish, there are a host of arguments on what constitutes good gumbo.

Some will add tomatoes, while others will cry that this is blasphemy. You have your garlic lovers versus your garlic haters, and then there are those who insist on boiled eggs. I could continue, but the one argument that I find most intriguing is the okra argument.

I have Cajun friends who swear that okra doesn't belong in the pot, mainly because they don't like its taste and texture. But considering that the word *gumbo* stems from the West African Bantu word *quingombo*, which means "okra," I reckon that okra's place in gumbo is a must. Now, if you don't like okra, let me assure you that its mucilaginous qualities add a certain smooth viscosity to the final dish, and it helps thicken the broth. Though if it's not in season, you can add some filé powder (ground sassafras root) to gumbo to add heft to the broth instead.

This is my recipe for gumbo, which may not be anything like how you make it. But that's what's fun about making gumbo, so please feel free to add anything you want.

2 pounds small (41 to 50 per pound) shrimp, unpeeled

1 cup vegetable oil plus 1 tablespoon

1 cup all-purpose flour

1 medium yellow onion, diced

2 pounds okra, cut into slices

1 green bell pepper, stem and seeds removed, diced

2 ribs of celery, diced

5 cloves garlic, minced

4 bay leaves

2 sprigs of fresh thyme (leaves only), or 1 teaspoon dry

1 tablespoon Worcestershire sauce

Salt, cayenne, and black pepper, to taste

¼ cup chopped parsley

1 bunch of green onions, green part diced

2 cups cooked rice, for serving

1. Peel and devein the shrimp, reserving the shells. Place the peeled, uncooked shrimp in the refrigerator for later use. Place the shells and 1 gallon of lightly salted water into a large pot. Bring to a boil and then turn the heat down to low and simmer for 15 minutes. Remove shells from pot and reserve the cooking liquid.

{CONTINUED}

2. Meanwhile, to make the roux, heat the oil on low heat in a large skillet. When warm, add the flour and stir continuously until it's a peanut butter brown color, about 25 to 30 minutes. (Please note that you cannot stop stirring once you start making the roux or it will burn.)

3. When the roux is peanut butter brown, add the onions to the pan. Cook on low heat for 5 minutes while stirring and then add the okra, bell pepper, and celery. Cook while stirring for another 5 minutes.

4. Slide the roux and vegetables into the shrimp broth. Add the garlic, bay leaves, thyme, and Worcestershire sauce to the pot. Bring the pot to a boil and then simmer uncovered for 2 hours. Taste and add salt, cayenne, and black pepper.

5. Ten minutes before serving, add the reserved uncooked shrimp, parsley, and green onions. Cook the gumbo until the shrimp have turned pink. Add salt, cayenne, and black pepper to taste. Serve gumbo poured over ¼ cup cooked rice.

NOTE: If you don't want to stand in front of the stove babysitting your roux for 25 minutes, you can whisk together the oil and the flour in a heavy, ovenproof skillet, place the skillet uncovered in an oven set at 350 degrees, and cook it for an hour and a half. Remove the skillet from the oven, stir the roux a couple of times, and then proceed with the recipe.

VARIATION

If you're the kind of person who doesn't like okra, you should probably have some filé powder (ground sassafras root) on hand to help thicken the gumbo and give it its distinct flavor. Add this to taste at the end of cooking. You can also throw in some andouille, cooked oysters, and/or crabmeat if you like. That's the fun with gumbo—just about anything goes!

SIDES, HOT AND COLD

10

A friend told me that she had been to Texas only once in her life. And since she had been a vegetarian at the time, she'd hardly eaten a thing.

Now, raise your hand if you agree with the sentiment that Texas is a place unfriendly to vegetarians. Well, I do believe that you've been led down the wrong path. Let me explain.

Sure, Texas is cattle country, and there are plenty of us who love our beef—whether it comes in the form of chicken-fried steak, smoky brisket, or a plate of chile con carne enchiladas. Yes, we eat lots of pork, chicken, and seafood as well. But Texas is also a fertile land with millions of acres set aside for growing fruits and vegetables, and this bounty is definitely reflected on a Texan's plate.

I come from farm folk, and at my family's table, every meal will be comprised of a protein along with a mess of side dishes. And you know what? As much as I love meat, I have to admit that the sides are usually my favorite part.

In late March, when the bluebonnets and other Texas wildflowers begin to liven up the landscape with their annual festival of color, you know that it's time to plant the crops that will be harvested throughout the late spring and summer. And sure enough, the last time I paid a July visit to my grandma at the farm, as I was eating breakfast, she walked into the dining room with a silver tray loaded with tomatoes, squash, garlic, peppers, and herbs. "Look at what I picked in the garden this morning," she said. As I surveyed the tray, I knew this bonanza would make for mighty fine eating that day.

My introduction to gathering food happened at an early age. My family always put me to work picking black-eyed peas and pulling potatoes, as I was closer to the ground than the adults. I reckon in some places this could be construed as a violation of child labor laws, but I never minded—I always thought it was great fun working outside to help provide food for that day's dinner.

Even as I grew older and became a bit lazy about helping out my family, I still appreciated their food ethic. My grandpa in his later years was confined to moving around with a walker. But one summer day my grandma helped him out to the garden, and side by side they planted potatoes so we'd have fresh ones to eat at Thanksgiving. Nothing could stop him from working on the land that had provided so well for him all his life.

Of course, during the harvest season, going out and picking your food isn't that unusual—it's just part of the day's work. Even if they don't live on a farm, many Texans keep backyard gardens or shop at farmers' markets and roadside vegetable stands, because we love the fresh produce that our state produces.

Now, I will admit that we do sometimes add a bit of meat to our vegetables to make them more robust, but this isn't a necessary measure for deep flavors. I've come up with some recipes that use chiles and aromatics to deliver that hearty mouthful that a ham bone or a side of bacon might otherwise lend a pot of, say, collard greens. Heck, even my great-grandma Blanche, who was no stranger to a ham bone, observed that greens could taste just as good without the addition of pork.

So to anyone who thinks that Texans eat only meat, I think they'd be surprised at all of the nonmeat options on our table. And if you're not satisfied after feasting on fresh Green Beans with Cilantro Pesto, Ancho Creamed Corn, Fried Okra dipped into a buttermilk dressing, Cactus Salad, creamy Tomatillo Cheese Grits, or a slice of Tomato Cobbler, I reckon there's always dessert.

BLACK-EYED PEAS

1 pound dried black-eyed peas

½ pound bacon

1 large onion, diced

3 jalapeño chiles, seeds and stems removed, chopped

4 garlic cloves, minced

½ cup chopped cilantro

1 teaspoon ground cumin

¼ teaspoon cayenne

Salt and black pepper, to taste

2 tablespoons lime juice

This southern staple has nourished me my whole life. Traditionally, black-eyed peas are served on New Year's Day for a promise of good fortune in the New Year. But as my grandma grows them on her farm, nary a dinner at her house is complete without a heaping bowl of this humble field legume.

In the summer, we'll eat them freshly picked with some of the pods broken and added to the pot, much like green beans. The rest of the year, we'll feast on our supply of dried black-eyed peas, sharing them with friends and families who stop by to visit.

Here is a basic pot of black-eyed peas, which takes a little bit of time to make but nowhere near as long as pinto beans or black beans. If you're fortunate enough to have a supply of fresh black-eyed peas, you can cut the cooking time in half.

1. Rinse and sort through the peas, removing any stones and shriveled peas. Place the peas in a large pot and cover with 2 inches of water. Turn the heat down to low and simmer, covered, for 30 minutes.

2. Meanwhile, in a skillet on medium heat, cook the bacon until crisp. Drain bacon on paper towels and reserve 2 tablespoons of bacon grease in the skillet. Add the onions and jalapeños to the skillet, turn the heat down to medium-low, and cook for 5 minutes while stirring occasionally. Add the garlic and cook for 30 more seconds. Add the onions, jalapeños, and garlic to the black-eyed pea pot. Break the bacon into ½-inch pieces and add it to the pot as well. Stir in the ground cilantro, cumin, cayenne, and salt and black pepper to taste and continue to simmer, covered, for 30 minutes longer. Before serving, stir in the lime juice.

GREEN BEANS
WITH CILANTRO PESTO

4 TO 6 SERVINGS

When I lived in Austin, I had a friend who would bring her green beans tossed with pesto to every potluck. Whether this dish was served hot or cold, it was always a welcome addition to the table. When we'd heap praise on her, she'd demur and say that she was merely using up the bounty of her garden. But no matter what her impetus, this simple yet elegant combination always reminds me of Austin.

I started making this dish soon after I moved to New York, but after a while I started tweaking it a bit. While my friend made her pesto with basil, I make mine with cilantro. I've also added pecans instead of pine nuts and thrown in a serrano chile because I can never resist a bit of heat. So while it may not be exactly the same dish I ate back in Austin, I find that with its addition of Texan ingredients, these green beans tossed with cilantro pesto taste even more like home.

1½ cups cilantro leaves
¼ cup olive oil
2 cloves garlic
1 serrano chile, seeds and stems removed, roughly chopped
¼ cup roasted pecans
1 tablespoon lemon juice
Salt, to taste
1 pound fresh or frozen green beans, preferably long and thin

1. In a blender or food processor, mix together the cilantro, olive oil, garlic, serrano chile, pecans, and lemon juice until a paste is formed. Add salt to taste.

2. Bring a large pot of salted water to a boil and then add the green beans. Cook until bright green, about 5 minutes. Drain and run cold water over the green beans to stop them from cooking any longer. Return the green beans to the pot and toss with the cilantro pesto. Add salt to taste.

NOTE: If you don't want to use all the cilantro pesto, it keeps in the refrigerator for a week and can be frozen.

CRANBERRY CONGEALED SALAD

12 SERVINGS

1 pound cranberries

1½ cups granulated sugar

2 tablespoons gelatin (2 packets)

1 cup orange juice

1 cup chopped celery

1 cup chopped unpeeled apple

1 cup chopped pecans

You can't have a Texan cookbook without at least one congealed salad, as it's a staple of potlucks, church suppers, funerals, holidays, and backyard gatherings. And true to form, as I was going through my family's files I discovered enough congealed salad recipes to do a whole chapter, if I wanted; but that's for another time, perhaps.

When deciding which one to choose, I went with this cranberry congealed salad—a recipe that's been in my family for almost a hundred years. We serve it every Thanksgiving, but I find it's just as welcome throughout the season and not just on that special day. And yes, it's been a favorite for so long because it's a crowd pleaser. Kids who ordinarily turn up their noses at cranberries will enjoy it because it wiggles; those who are watching their weight feel virtuous because there's celery in the dish; and I like it because there are pecans, which are a perfect complement to the tangy cranberries and crunchy apples.

Because it's an old recipe, it calls for plain gelatin instead of the flavored, artificially colored stuff. But if you've never worked with plain gelatin, please don't worry, as it's just as easy as instant.

1. Grind the cranberries in a food processor and add sugar. Let the cranberries stand a few minutes to macerate, stirring occasionally. Then pour into a bowl.

2. In a pot, dissolve the gelatin in orange juice and cook on low heat until hot.

3. Pour warm gelatin into the cranberry bowl and stir in celery, apple, and pecans. Pour into a mold and chill for at least 8 hours. Serve cold.

CABBAGE AND RADISH SLAW

4 TO 6 SERVINGS

Along the Texas-Mexico border, cabbage and radish slaw is a common side dish to hearty meals such as stacked enchiladas. Crisp cool cabbage is tossed with sharp radishes and bathed in a tangy vinegar dressing; it's a fine foil to a rich, cheesy dish. I've taken this classic border dish and tossed it with a bit of my Jalapeño Buttermilk Dressing, making it perfect for any backyard barbecue, basket of fish tacos, and, if you wish, that plate of West Texas Stacked Enchiladas (page 161).

4 cups shredded green cabbage
1 teaspoon kosher salt
1 bunch of radishes (about ¾ pound), greens discarded and radishes diced
1 tablespoon apple cider vinegar
1 teaspoon cumin seeds
½ cup Jalapeño Buttermilk Dressing (page 49)

1. Toss the shredded cabbage with 1 teaspoon of salt and let it sit unrefrigerated for 1 hour.

2. Drain off the excess liquid and then toss the cabbage with the radishes, apple cider vinegar, and cumin seeds. Stir the slaw with the Jalapeño Buttermilk Dressing and refrigerate for an hour before serving.

MEXICAN CORN (ELOTE EN VASO)

4 SERVINGS

Whenever I'm visiting my mom in Houston, I'll always volunteer to go to the grocery store. When I arrive at her neighborhood Fiesta, my first order of business is to make a stop at the food cart that has painted ELOTE EN VASO on the side, for a quick treat.

Elote en vaso, which translates as "corn in a cup," is a Mexican street dish where cooked corn is topped with butter, mayonnaise, Cotija cheese, salt, cayenne, and a squirt of lime. It's crunchy, creamy, salty, and spicy—the perfect snack.

Sometimes, however, you'll find this same combination of toppings placed on corn on the cob. And while the eating may be more of a challenge, it is still brilliant.

2 cups corn kernels (fresh or frozen) or 4 cobs of corn
2 tablespoons unsalted butter, room temperature
¼ cup mayonnaise
½ cup Cotija cheese, crumbled
Salt and cayenne, to taste
4 lime wedges
Hot sauce and chopped cilantro, for serving

1. To serve the corn in a bowl or glass, bring ½ cup of water to a boil in a saucepan. Add the corn and cook until tender, about 5 minutes. Drain and then pour into four individual bowls or glasses. Top each serving with a quarter of the butter, mayonnaise, Cotija cheese, and salt and cayenne to taste. Finish with a squirt of lime, hot sauce, and cilantro.

2. If you're serving the corn on the cob, preheat the oven to 350 degrees and lightly grease a sheet. Place the corn still in its husk on the sheet and cook for 15 minutes. After taking the corn out of the oven, let the corn cool for 5 minutes and then pull the husks down, leaving them attached to the base of the cob, which can act as a handle. While warm, spread ½ tablespoon unsalted butter and 1 tablespoon of mayonnaise all over the cob. Take ⅛ cup of cheese and sprinkle it on the cob, then sprinkle on some salt and cayenne. Finish with a squirt of lime, hot sauce, and cilantro.

CUCUMBER SALAD

4 TO 6 SERVINGS

2 unpeeled cucumbers, cut into
　¼-inch round slices
1 teaspoon kosher salt, plus more
　to taste
½ cup sour cream or thick,
　Greek-style yogurt
1 clove garlic, minced
1 tablespoon white wine vinegar
1 teaspoon yellow or Dijon mustard
¼ cup chopped cilantro
¼ medium red onion, diced
¼ teaspoon dill seed
¼ teaspoon ground cumin
¼ teaspoon cayenne
Black pepper, to taste

The delicate nature of a cucumber salad would probably slot it into the category of dishes my grandma calls ladies' food. But once you add the bite of red onion, the earthiness of cumin, and the fire of cayenne, this crisp and cool salad appeals to all palates.

Cucumber salad works well both for quick dinners and bringing to parties, especially as the flavors only deepen the longer it sits. And there's a reason cucumber salad is on offer at small-town cafés and barbecue joints, as this classic side dish helps cut through the richness of hearty fare such as Fried Chicken Livers (page 204) or Dr Pepper Ribs (page 199). Though if I'm looking for a light meal, I've been known to eat it simply by itself.

1. Cover the sliced cucumbers with salt and allow to sit refrigerated for at least 1 hour. Rinse well and drain.

2. Mix together the sour cream, garlic, vinegar, mustard, cilantro, red onions, dill seed, cumin, and cayenne. Taste and add salt and black pepper. Add the cucumbers, toss, and chill.

NOTE: Want to make it even spicier? Add a diced jalapeño or serrano chile to the salad.

TEXAS POTATO SALAD

4 TO 6 SERVINGS

2 pounds red new potatoes, cubed

¼ cup apple cider vinegar

1 teaspoon kosher salt, plus more
to taste

¼ cup yellow prepared mustard

¼ cup mayonnaise

2 celery stalks, diced

2 green onions, sliced, green part
only

¼ cup Bread and Butter Jalapeño
Pickles, diced (page 22)

1 teaspoon bread and butter
jalapeño pickle juice

½ teaspoon paprika

Black pepper, to taste

When I asked my family how they make their potato salad, they all provided recipes that called for similar ingredients: chunky unpeeled potatoes, green onions, celery, hard-boiled eggs, sweet pickles, mustard, and mayonnaise.

This is the potato salad that always graced the table at our family barbecues—a thick mouthful that was soft and crunchy, tangy and sweet. What makes this potato salad distinctly Texan, however, is the amount of mustard in the dish. I've also added Bread and Butter Jalapeño Pickles, which inject a sweet and spicy Texan touch.

1. In a large pot, cover potatoes with cold water, bring to a boil and cook until tender, about 15 minutes. Potatoes should be tender but not mushy. Drain potatoes and rinse in cold water. Toss with vinegar and salt, and let cool in the refrigerator for 30 minutes.

2. After the potatoes have cooled, gently stir the mustard and mayonnaise into the potatoes and then add the celery, green onions, jalapeño pickles, pickle juice, and paprika. Add salt and black pepper to taste.

VARIATION

Many barbecue places across the state serve their potato salad as a mashed version, using a scoop to dole out perfectly round portions. To make a potato salad in this style, after cooking the potatoes, mash them and then proceed with the rest of the recipe.

TEXAS CAVIAR

8 SERVINGS

There are countless ways to serve black-eyed peas, but one of my favorite preparations is something called Texas caviar. Helen Corbitt, the Neiman-Marcus chef who wrote many books on entertaining (and even catered my cousin's wedding back in the 1960s), is credited with inventing this dish, which is always a crowd-pleaser. It's a cinch to make: you toss cooked black-eyed peas with jalapeños, cilantro, garlic, and some diced tomatoes, and then douse it all with a hearty squirt of lime juice. Some people like to eat it as a side salad, but I find that it also makes for a wonderful dip for tortilla chips. And since it's gluten free and vegan, it can appeal to just about anyone.

4 cups cooked black-eyed peas, drained, or 2 15-ounce cans, drained

8 green onions, thinly sliced, green part only

½ cup chopped cilantro

3 fresh jalapeño chiles, stems and seeds removed, finely diced

2 plum tomatoes, diced, or ½ cup canned diced tomatoes, drained

1 yellow bell pepper, seeds and stem removed, diced

3 cloves garlic, minced

2 tablespoons olive oil

2 tablespoons lime juice

1 teaspoon ground cumin

Salt and black pepper, to taste

1. In a bowl, stir together the black-eyed peas, green onions, cilantro, jalapeños, tomatoes, bell pepper, and garlic.

2. Whisk together the olive oil, lime juice, and cumin and stir into the black-eyed peas. Taste and add salt and black pepper. Chill for 4 hours. Serve cold either as a side salad or with tortilla chips.

CACTUS SALAD

4 SERVINGS

1 pound cactus paddles (2 cups), or
  1 15-ounce jar cactus paddles
1 ripe plum tomato, diced, or ¼ cup
  canned diced tomatoes, drained
2 cloves garlic, minced
¼ medium red onion, diced
½ cup chopped cilantro
2 tablespoons olive oil
2 tablespoons lime juice
¼ teaspoon ground cumin
¼ cup Cotija cheese, crumbled
Salt and black pepper, to taste

If you've never had the pleasure of eating cactus, known as *nopal* in Spanish, you're in for a treat. This plant has a smooth yet crunchy texture with a flavor that's reminiscent of green beans. In San Antonio and along the border, cactus is prepared in a host of dishes, such as eggs, tacos, and soups. My favorite way to serve cactus, however, is in this cool and refreshing salad.

This salad goes well with hearty beef dishes such as Pasilla Tomatillo Braised Short Ribs (page 195) and Tacos al Carbon Small-Apartment Style (page 169). I also like to serve it with a bowl of charra beans. Don't be intimidated by the fact that it's cactus—the dish comes together in just a few minutes, and will please most palates, from the timid to the adventurous.

1. If using fresh cactus paddles, first you'll need to remove the thorns from the cactus. To do this, trim off the thick base and the edges of the paddle, about ⅛ of an inch all around. Wearing a glove, hold each paddle one at a time over the sink and while running water over it, scrub it with a vegetable or pot scrubber on both sides until all the thorns are gone. You can also scrape the paddle with a paring knife, but be careful not to scrape off too much of the green skin.

2. Dice the cleaned paddles and place in a pot of water. Bring to a boil and then turn the heat down to low and simmer for 15 minutes. Drain and rinse well under cold water. If using jarred paddles, skip the boiling step and simply drain them, then rinse with cold water.

3. Toss the cactus paddles, either fresh or jarred, with tomato, garlic, red onions, cilantro, olive oil, lime juice, cumin, and Cotija cheese. Taste and add salt and black pepper. Place the cactus salad in the refrigerator and allow it to marinate for 1 hour.

POBLANO MACARONI AND CHEESE

8 SERVINGS

Macaroni and cheese is one of those dishes I ate almost every day when I was young, though I have to confess that it usually came from that blue box. Even though my mom was against packaged food, she'd stock up on the boxed macaroni and cheese for food pantry donations. When she wasn't looking, I'd swipe a box and whip up a batch.

Mom, of course, soon got wise to my shenanigans, and in an attempt to wean me from the boxed stuff, she decided to start making it from scratch. And once you've had homemade macaroni and cheese, you'll never go back.

This recipe is very similar to hers in that it has a béchamel sauce base. But I've also added some roasted poblano chiles, along with a bit of dried mustard powder, cumin, lime zest, and cayenne. I won't lie—this is one decadent dish. But don't we all deserve a bit of indulgence sometimes?

2 poblano chiles
8 ounces elbow pasta (2 cups)
2 tablespoons unsalted butter
4 cloves garlic, minced
2 tablespoons all-purpose flour
1½ cups whole milk
1 teaspoon mustard powder
¼ teaspoon cayenne
½ teaspoon ground cumin
1 teaspoon lime zest
½ cup chopped cilantro
Salt and black pepper, to taste
4 cups grated white cheddar cheese (12 ounces)
½ cup Cotija cheese, for serving

1. Roast the poblano chiles under the broiler until blackened, about 5 minutes per side. Place chiles in a paper sack or plastic food-storage bag, close it tightly, and let the chiles steam for 20 minutes. Take the chiles out of the bag and rub off the skin. Remove stem and seeds and chop the chiles into 1-inch-long pieces.

2. Bring a large pot of salted water to a boil and add the pasta. Cook according to your package's directions and then drain the pasta. (You want the pasta to be cooked but not mushy; I cook my pasta for 5 minutes.)

{CONTINUED}

3. Preheat the oven to 375 degrees. Grease a large baking dish or a large cast-iron skillet, and pour the drained pasta into the dish.

4. In a pot (you can use the pot the pasta cooked in or you can do this while the pasta boils), on low heat melt the butter. Add the garlic and cook for 1 minute. Whisk in the flour and cook until a light brown, toasty paste is formed, about 1 minute. Whisk in the milk and stir until it's thickened a bit but still fluid, about 1 to 2 minutes. Remove the pot from the heat and stir in the mustard powder, cayenne, cumin, lime zest, cilantro, and chopped poblano chiles. Adjust seasonings and add salt and black pepper.

5. Slowly add half of the cheddar cheese and stir until it's melted and well combined into the sauce. (If the sauce has cooled too much and the cheese won't melt, return the pot to low heat on the stove. If, however, the sauce gets too thick, like a custard, you can thin it by stirring in milk, a teaspoon at a time.) Pour sauce over pasta and top with the remaining half of the cheddar cheese and bake uncovered for 20 minutes or until brown and bubbling. Sprinkle with Cotija cheese, and serve immediately.

VARIATION

Try adding cooked bacon, chorizo, chicken, squash, or corn to the macaroni and cheese before baking. You can also substitute pepper Jack for some of the cheddar if you like. And if you like a crunchy top, add crushed tortilla chips before baking.

TEX-MEX SQUASH CASSEROLE

8 SERVINGS

If you serve me squash that's been grilled, steamed, or lightly sautéed, I may not get very excited. But if you serve me a wedge of warm squash casserole, I will eat the whole pan.

I am not alone in this love. Squash casserole is a creamy, crunchy mass that's much closer to the fattening family than the vegetable family. You'll find it at potlucks, backyard barbecues, downtown cafés, and most likely at your family's Thanksgiving dinner, too.

I've tweaked the classic recipe, which is about as lively (and comforting) as a bowl of oatmeal, by adding some jalapeños for heat and tortilla chips for crunch. And yes, while the recipe your mom makes may call for a can of cream of mushroom soup, I've made mine with a simple béchamel sauce, which does not change the creamy end result at all.

1. Preheat the oven to 350 degrees and lightly grease a casserole dish.

2. Heat the butter in a large skillet on medium heat. When melted, add the yellow squash, zucchini, onions, and jalapeños, and sauté until onions are translucent and the squash is soft, about 10 minutes.

3. Add the garlic, cumin, chili powder, and cayenne, and cook for a minute. Add salt and black pepper to taste.

2 tablespoons unsalted butter

1 pound yellow squash and
   1 pound zucchini, sliced

1 medium yellow onion, diced

2 jalapeño chiles, seeds and stems
   removed, diced

2 cloves garlic, minced

1 teaspoon ground cumin

1 teaspoon chili powder

½ teaspoon cayenne

Salt and black pepper, to taste

2 tablespoons all-purpose flour

1 cup chicken or vegetable broth

2 cups crushed canned tomatoes,
   preferably fire roasted

½ cup half-and-half

½ cup sour cream

½ cup chopped cilantro

2 cups crushed tortilla chips

1 cup grated pepper Jack cheese
   (4 ounces)

1 cup grated cheddar cheese
   (4 ounces)

{CONTINUED}

4. Stir in the flour and cook until a light brown paste forms, about a minute. Add the broth and tomatoes and stir until the mixture thickens, which should happen in a couple of minutes. Stir in the half-and-half, sour cream, and cilantro, and turn off the heat.

5. In the casserole dish, layer the bottom with the crushed tortilla chips. Pour the creamy squash mixture on top of the chips, and then cover the whole dish with the grated cheese. Cook uncovered for 30 minutes or until top is brown and bubbling.

ANCHO CREAM CORN

4 TO 6 SERVINGS

The last time I visited my friend Robb Walsh, he prepared a feast. He was in the middle of recipe testing for a cookbook he was writing, and I'd say in the few hours I spent with him and his family, he probably concocted about twenty-five dishes. OK, I may be exaggerating, but there was a lot of food, and all of it was very good.

I got the idea for this ancho cream corn when I was at his house. He grilled ears of corn on the cob and smeared them with a spread of ancho-garlic butter. The combination of the chiles with the corn was superb, and I decided to apply that approach to my cream corn, which in my mind could use a little makeover.

Cream corn is a classic southern side dish, though I often find that it can be not only too rich, but also too bland for my liking. I've taken liberties and added not only an ancho chile and garlic for flavor, but a dash of cumin for depth, along with a healthy squirt of lime juice to both lighten and brighten up the dish. Finished with a sprinkle of salty Cotija cheese crumbles, this side dish will rise to the occasion and please everyone.

1 dried ancho chile, stem and seeds removed
4 tablespoons unsalted butter
2 cloves garlic, minced
5 cups corn, fresh or frozen (about 8 cobs shucked)
1 cup heavy cream
4 ounces cream cheese
¼ teaspoon ground cumin
⅛ teaspoon cayenne
1 tablespoon lime juice
Salt and black pepper, to taste
Cotija cheese, crumbled, for garnish

1. In a dry skillet heated on high, toast the ancho chile on each side for about 10 seconds or until it starts to puff. Fill the skillet with enough water to cover chile. Leave the heat on until water begins to boil and then turn off the heat and let the chile soak until soft, about 30 minutes. Once rehydrated, discard the soaking water, rinse the ancho chile, and dice.

2. In a large skillet on medium-low heat, melt the butter. Add the garlic and cook for 1 minute. Add the corn, cream, cream cheese, cumin, cayenne, and diced ancho chile. While stirring occasionally cook for 15 minutes. Add lime juice. Taste and adjust seasonings and add salt and black pepper. Serve with Cotija cheese sprinkled on top.

TOMATILLO CHEESE GRITS

6 SERVINGS

1 pound fresh tomatillos, husks removed, or 1 11-ounce can, drained

2 tablespoons unsalted butter

¼ medium yellow onion, chopped

4 cloves garlic, chopped

1 serrano chile, stems and seeds removed, diced

½ cup chopped cilantro

¼ teaspoon cayenne

2 tablespoons lime juice

1 cup grits

2 cups milk

2 cups water

1 cup grated white cheddar cheese (4 ounces)

Salt and black pepper, to taste

When I lived in Austin, my friends and I would go to Threadgill's on Sundays. And while Threadgill's offers many fine foods from the Texan food canon, I have to admit that the main attraction for me was their cheese grits.

Grits, if you've never had the pleasure, are a type of porridge that comes from stone-ground corn. There are white grits, which are considered more refined in certain circles, and yellow grits, which are the kind that I prefer. They're an ancient food, introduced to the European settlers by the Native Americans, and yet you seldom find them outside the South.

Grits on their own are pretty bland, which makes them a willing receptacle for a wide array of flavors. Many serve them with red-eye gravy, though I'm more inclined to eat them with melted cheese, which probably explains why I loved Threadgill's cheese grits so much. Here is my version of cheese grits, tarted up with tomatillos and serrano chiles. And while grits are traditionally served at breakfast, I find that these are delicious anytime of the day.

1. If using fresh tomatillos, on high heat, bring a pot of water to boiling and cook tomatillos until soft, about 5 minutes. Drain and place into a blender. (If using canned tomatillos, go ahead and put them into the blender now, too.)

2. In a skillet, heat the butter on medium-low heat and while stirring occasionally, cook the onions until translucent, about 5 minutes. Add the garlic and cook for 30 more seconds.

3. Add the onions and garlic to the blender along with the diced serrano chiles, cilantro, cayenne, and lime juice. Add ¼ cup of water and blend until ingredients make a smooth puree.

4. Cook the grits according to the package directions using 2 cups milk and 2 cups water. When the grits are done, stir in the tomatillo puree and cheese. Add salt and black pepper to taste and serve immediatcly.

NOTE: There are three types of grits. There are slow-cooking grits, which can take 45 minutes to cook; quick-cooking grits, which take about 15 minutes; and instant grits, which take about 5 minutes. The slow-cooking grits taste the best but obviously call for the most work. I cook with quick-cooking grits most of the time, especially as slow-cooking grits aren't readily available in my NYC grocery store.

TOMATO COBBLER

8 SERVINGS

The inspiration for this dish occurred after an evening of making fruit cobblers with summertime peaches. As I was placing the fruit in the skillet, it struck me that if we can have savory pies, why not savory cobblers as well? Faced with a bounty of tomatoes, I decided to pair them with a cornmeal crust, and threw in some cilantro and jalapeño to give it a Texan twist.

I like to serve this as a side with fare such as Tex-Mex Meat Loaf with a Chipotle-Tomato Glaze (page 196) or Redfish on the Half Shell (page 229), though it's filling enough to be a vegetarian main dish as well. If tomatoes aren't in season, I find the cobbler isn't adversely affected by using canned tomatoes.

1 pound tomatoes, peeled, cored, and diced, or 2 cups canned diced tomatoes, drained

1 jalapeño chile, seeds and stems removed, diced

2 cloves garlic, minced

¼ cup chopped cilantro

¼ teaspoon ground cumin

1 teaspoon lime juice

Salt and black pepper, to taste

8 tablespoons unsalted butter (1 stick)

½ cup all-purpose flour

½ cup cornmeal

2 teaspoons baking powder

¼ teaspoon kosher salt

1 cup whole milk

1. Preheat the oven to 350 degrees.

2. Toss together the diced tomatoes, diced jalapeño, garlic, cilantro, cumin, and lime juice. Add salt and black pepper to taste.

3. In a large ovenproof skillet, preferably cast-iron, melt the butter on low heat. Once melted, remove from heat.

4. In a bowl, mix together the flour, cornmeal, baking powder, and salt. Add the milk and stir until a thick, smooth batter forms. Pour the batter over the melted butter in the skillet. Do not stir. Spoon the tomato mixture on top of the batter. Bake for 30 minutes, uncovered.

NOTE: To peel tomatoes, cut an x at both ends of each tomato, drop carefully into a pot of boiling water for 30 seconds, remove with a slotted spoon, and then plunge the tomato into ice water. The skin will easily peel off after this.

FRIED OKRA

1 pound okra, fresh or frozen

1 cup all-purpose flour

½ teaspoon ground cumin

1 teaspoon kosher salt, plus more
to taste

1 teaspoon black pepper, plus more
to taste

½ teaspoon cayenne

1 large egg

½ cup buttermilk

2 cups finely crushed saltines

Vegetable oil, for frying

One day, my grandparents and I stopped at a barbecue joint to grab a take-out dinner. We asked for brisket by the pound, along with containers of pickles and potato salad. I thought we were done when my grandpa said, "Hold on! I'd also like an order of fried okra." My grandma gave him a look, then said he shouldn't be eating fried okra, as it's not the healthiest food. They argued for a while, and then my grandpa laughed and said, "I'm eighty-seven years old and if I want fried okra, I will have fried okra." My grandma sighed and as we drove back to the farm, my grandpa happily sat popping the pieces of fried okra into his mouth like popcorn or candy.

If you love fried okra as much as my grandpa, try this recipe, which has cumin and pepper added for flavor, and is breaded in crushed saltines for extra crunch.

1. Cut the okra into ¼-inch-wide slices, discarding the stems. (If you're using frozen okra, it will probably already be cut into slices.)

2. In a large plastic food-storage bag, mix together the flour, cumin, salt, black pepper, and cayenne.

3. Place the okra slices in the bag and shake until they are well coated. Mix together the egg with the buttermilk. Place the crushed saltines on a plate. In batches, dip the flour-coated okra into the egg mixture and then lightly dredge in the saltines. Place coated okra on a large plate or sheet. Repeat until all the okra are coated.

4. In a large heavy skillet, preferably a cast-iron skillet, heat ½ inch of oil on medium heat until it reaches 350 degrees. Cook the okra for 2 minutes, turning once.

RED CHILE RICE

4 TO 6 SERVINGS

¾ cup canned crushed tomatoes, drained

¼ medium yellow onion

2 cloves garlic

1 canned chipotle chile in adobo

½ teaspoon ground cumin

Pinch of ground cloves

1 tablespoon lime juice

1 tablespoon lard or vegetable oil

1 cup uncooked rice

2 cups chicken broth

Salt, to taste

Everyone in Texas knows that your enchilada plate isn't complete without a serving of refried beans and rice. This rice is my version of the Mexican rice you'll find paired with refried beans on the typical Tex-Mex combination platter. I cook the rice in a tomato sauce flavored with onion, garlic, chipotle chiles, cumin, and cloves, which gives the rice a bright, earthy flavor. But you don't have to be eating enchiladas to enjoy this rice, as it also makes a great side to Tex-Mex Meat Loaf with a Chipotle-Tomato Glaze (page 196), and Redfish on the Half Shell (page 229).

1. Add to a blender the tomatoes, onion, garlic, chipotle chile, cumin, cloves, and lime juice. Puree until a thick paste forms. Remove tomato puree from blender and measure. You should have about ½ cup.

2. Heat up the lard or vegetable oil in a heavy-bottomed pot on medium-low heat. Add the rice and sauté for 30 seconds. Add the tomato puree and while stirring, cook for 1 more minute.

3. Pour in the chicken broth, bring to a boil, and then cover the pot, turn the heat down to low, and simmer for 20 minutes. Turn off the heat and let it sit for 10 more minutes. Stir the rice to incorporate any tomato puree that's accumulated on top and then salt to taste.

NOTE: It's important that your pot has a heavy bottom, otherwise the rice may burn.

GREEN CHILE RICE

4 TO 6 SERVINGS

Green chile rice isn't the most common Tex-Mex side; you're more likely to see a version of red chile rice instead. But in Austin it makes its appearance on Tex-Mex menus, and my family serves it at Christmas to add a festive touch to our holiday feast. If you're looking for something new, this fragrant rice is terrific with a host of dishes. I adore it with Carnitas (page 201), though it also makes a fine accompaniment to Spinach and Mushroom Enchiladas with Tomatillo Salsa (page 155), Jalapeño Mustard Roast Chicken (page 205), and Austin-Style Black Beans (page 124).

2 poblano chiles
1 jalapeño chile, stem and seeds
   removed, roughly chopped
2 cloves garlic
½ teaspoon ground cumin
¼ cup cilantro
1 tablespoon lime juice
1 tablespoon lard or vegetable oil
1 cup uncooked rice
1¼ cups chicken broth
Salt, to taste

1. Roast the poblano chiles under the broiler until blackened, about 5 minutes per side. Place the poblano chiles in a paper sack or plastic food-storage bag, close it tightly, and let the chiles steam for 20 minutes. Take the chiles out of the bag and rub off the skin. Remove stem and seeds and chop the chiles. Place in a blender. Add to the blender the jalapeño, garlic, cumin, cilantro, lime juice, and 1 tablespoon of water. Puree until a thick paste forms.

2. Heat up the lard or vegetable oil in a heavy-bottom pot on medium-low heat. Add the rice and sauté for 30 seconds. Add the poblano puree from the blender and while stirring, cook for 1 more minute. Pour in the chicken broth, bring to a boil, and then cover the pot. Turn the heat down to low and simmer for 20 minutes. Turn off the heat and let it sit for 10 more minutes. Stir the rice to incorporate any puree that's accumulated on top and then salt to taste.

NOTE: It's important that your pot has a heavy bottom, otherwise the rice may burn. If they're in season, Hatch chiles can be substituted for the poblano chiles.

HOME

MADE

11

BREADS ★

My mom has always loved baking bread. In the mornings she'll make a batch of scones for breakfast; for lunch she'll serve sandwiches on one of her homemade loaves; and for supper, there's often a skillet of hot corn bread to go with our chili or beans.

Now, I will admit that I did go through a period when I was embarrassed to take a sandwich to school not made from store-bought white bread. But as I grew older, I appreciated my mom's baking prowess, a skill she learned from her mother and one that she has thankfully passed down to me.

Mom taught me the joy of kneading, how it not only works out your arms but also gives you the satisfaction of transforming something shaggy and rough into a pliant, smooth dough. It was from her that I also learned that sizzling your oil in a cast-iron skillet is part of making the best batch of corn bread. But perhaps most importantly, she showed me the joy of having a home filled with the comforting aroma of freshly baked bread from scratch.

I lived in Iowa for a spell after college, and it was there that her lessons in bread making came in handy. While I had no problem finding buns, muffins, and scones, in Iowa there was a complete absence of decent tortillas—both corn and flour. If you're a Texan, a tortilla is just as much a part of your daily bread intake as a slice from a yeasty loaf. No proper tortillas? I was devastated.

Naturally, I turned to my mom for a solution. In Texas we usually bought our tortillas at the store, as they were made in-house throughout the day, sometimes so fresh the bag was still warm. But she'd also dabbled in making tortillas at home and had a vintage tortilla press and a host of recipes to show for

this period in her culinary exploration. Graciously, she offered to send these items to me so I could begin my own tortilla-making experiments.

It was hard work, I have to admit. For the life of me, I couldn't make an acceptable flour tortilla—the dough was rubbery, and it snapped back into a small size every time I tried rolling it out into its proper round shape. At the time, I assumed that the bread-baking gene had just passed me by, and I gave up on making tortillas. But I started baking other breads—hearty loaves filled with cheese and sausage, cinnamon rolls, and muffins—and realized that I could bake bread after all. I just couldn't make flour tortillas.

When I moved to New York and suffered another dearth of tortillas, I decided to try my hand at making them again. As I now knew more about baking, I realized that the recipes I had used before had the wrong ratio of fat to flour. The recipes that I had been using were a foolish attempt at low-fat tortillas. I won't lie to you—if you want to make a decent flour tortilla, you need the fat in it to be pliant. You also need time for the glutens to relax so you can roll it out to a proper thickness and shape. But once I cracked the code, I began making flour tortillas often; I suggest you do the same.

Lest you think I've forgotten about that backbone of Tex-Mex—the corn tortilla—I haven't, and you'll find a recipe for them in this chapter as well. I've also included yeast-based breads such as a Chorizo Asadero Bread and Ruby Red Sweet Rolls. Of course, there are also my recipes for biscuits and corn bread, two things that are as common on the Texan table as a tortilla.

If you're not accustomed to making your own bread, I think you'll be surprised at how simple it is. And once you get into the rhythm of doing it, you may never return to store-bought loaves, biscuits, or tortillas again.

BISCUITS

10 TO 12 BISCUITS

2 cups all-purpose flour, plus more
for kneading

1 tablespoon baking powder

1 teaspoon granulated sugar, plus
more to taste

½ teaspoon kosher salt

8 tablespoons unsalted butter, cold
(1 stick)

¾ cup half-and-half or buttermilk

In the South, there are as many biscuit recipes as there are people—everyone has an opinion on how they should be made. Mine are not radical, though I do opt for butter over the more common lard or shortening, as I find it yields a more tender, flavorful crumb.

I also like to harken back to the old tradition of beaten biscuits, which was a method of beating the dough to get it to lift in the absence of baking powder or soda. Though I admit that I only slap my biscuit dough around for a few minutes.

Do I make the best biscuits? I have no idea. What I do know is that baking them always brings big smiles to people's faces. And if you're not careful, there will be one person who may be inclined to eat the whole batch, as I found out at a party I gave. But that's OK; to me it says that they are indeed pretty darn good.

1. Preheat the oven to 450 degrees and grease a baking sheet or a cast-iron skillet.

2. Mix together the flour, baking powder, sugar, and salt.

3. Cut the stick of butter into pieces and work it into the flour mixture with your hands or a pastry blender until it resembles pea-size crumbs. Add the half-and-half or buttermilk, mixing until the dough is a bit loose and sticky.

4. Pour the dough out onto a floured surface and knead for a minute. Dough should be smooth and no longer wet. You can sprinkle more flour on the surface if you find it's sticking. Make the dough into a ball and hit it with a rolling pin, turning it and folding it in half every few whacks. Do this for a couple of minutes.

5. Roll out the dough until it's ¼ of an inch thick, then fold it in half. Using a round biscuit cutter (you can use a glass or a cup if you don't have a biscuit cutter), cut out the biscuits from the folded dough. Place on a greased baking sheet or in a cast-iron skillet close together, about ⅛ of an inch apart (so they rise up not out), and bake for 15 minutes or until the tops are golden brown.

NOTE: If you don't want to roll and cut them out, after kneading and beating the dough you can drop the dough onto the baking sheet with a spoon. They're not as symmetrical (dropped biscuits are also known as cat-head biscuits), but they're no less delicious.

PAN DE CAMPO

1 LOAF

2 cups all-purpose flour

½ tablespoon baking powder

½ teaspoon granulated sugar

¼ teaspoon kosher salt

6 tablespoons lard or shortening, room temperature

¾ cup buttermilk

Did you know that Texas has a state bread? It's called pan de campo. Cowboys have traditionally made pan de campo, which translates in English to "country bread." As its ingredients are simple, and since it can be baked in a cast-iron skillet set over a fire, it's perfect for those working on the range. But don't worry, you can make it at home in your kitchen as well.

To eat the pan de campo, you can either cut it into slices or just tear off pieces. Its flavor is similar to a biscuit, which makes it great with honey or for dipping into beans. I've known people to get fancy with it and use it as a base for pizza, too.

1. Preheat the oven to 400 degrees and grease a large cast-iron skillet.

2. Mix together the flour, baking powder, sugar, and salt. Stir in the lard or shortening until the flour is lumpy and resembles crumbs. Stir in the buttermilk and blend until a smooth dough is formed. Heat up the skillet on medium.

3. Meanwhile, pat or roll out the pan de campo until it's a 9-inch-wide circle or large enough to almost fill out the skillet. Add the pan de campo to the heated skillet, cooking for 5 minutes on each side. Place the skillet in the oven and cook for 15 more minutes.

NOTE: You can jazz up the pan de campo by throwing in herbs such as oregano or rosemary. Toasted cumin seeds add a smoky note.

HUSH PUPPIES

ABOUT 20 HUSH PUPPIES

When you're serving fried fish, hush puppies are the perfect accompaniment. It's been said that these balls of fried corn bread are called hush puppies because cowboys used to feed them to their barking dogs in an attempt to get them to be quiet. "Hush, puppy!" they'd say as they tossed the fritters to the dogs. But whether or not that's true doesn't change my affection for this addictive fried bread, which I've made a bit spicier with jalapeños.

Oil, for frying
¾ cup yellow cornmeal
½ cup all-purpose flour
½ teaspoon baking powder
¼ teaspoon baking soda
½ teaspoon kosher salt
1 large egg
½ cup whole milk or buttermilk
1 jalapeño chile, stems and seeds removed, finely diced
¼ medium yellow onion, diced

1. In a large pot or Dutch oven, heat about 1 inch of oil until it's 300 degrees.

2. While the oil is getting hot, make the hush puppy batter. First, mix together the cornmeal, flour, baking powder, baking soda, and salt. Beat together the egg and milk and combine with the cornmeal mixture. Stir in the diced jalapeño and onions.

3. To fry the hush puppies, place tablespoon-size balls of dough in batches in the hot oil and fry until crisp and golden brown (about 2 minutes). Drain on paper towels.

CORN BREAD

8 SERVINGS

I don't want to start a debate about corn bread—but it is a fact that there are differences between northern and Texan corn breads: northerners like it sweet, while Texans like it savory. We are also known to liven it up with jalapeños, green chiles, or cheese. But the one thing a Texan will never, ever put into their corn bread is sugar. Corn bread is for dinner, not dessert.

Here's a classic Texan corn bread recipe that's baked in a cast-iron skillet, of course. Be sure to get the skillet good and hot, as that's what sears the butter and makes for a crisp, crunchy crust.

¼ cup bacon drippings or vegetable oil
2 cups cornmeal
½ cup all-purpose flour
2 teaspoons baking powder
½ teaspoon baking soda
1 teaspoon kosher salt
1 large egg, beaten
2 cups buttermilk

1. Preheat the oven to 450 degrees.

2. While the oven is heating, put the drippings or oil into a cast-iron skillet and place it in the oven for a few minutes until the oil is sizzling.

3. Meanwhile, mix together the cornmeal, flour, baking powder, baking soda, and salt. Whisk together the egg and buttermilk and pour into the dry ingredients. Stir until well combined.

4. Take the cast-iron skillet out of the oven, pour the hot oil in the skillet into the batter and stir until well combined. Pour batter into the hot cast-iron skillet and bake for 15 to 20 minutes or until an inserted knife comes out clean.

CHORIZO ASADERO BREAD

1 LOAF

1 tablespoon or 1 packet of yeast

¼ cup warm water

4 tablespoons unsalted butter

1 cup whole milk

1 large egg, room temperature

3 cups all-purpose flour, plus more for kneading

1 teaspoon kosher salt

½ pound Mexican Red Chorizo, crumbled and cooked (page 213)

1 or 2 canned chipotle chiles in adobo, diced

2 cups asadero or Muenster cheese, grated (8 ounces)

Mom and I were in Houston shopping at the Fiesta Market on Alabama when I had the idea for this bread. Fiesta, which caters to Houston's Hispanic community, had on display a whole case of Mexican chorizo. That's something you just don't see in New York City. And next to the chorizo was a bounty of Mexican cheeses, such as the creamy melting cheese asadero. Add these two ingredients to a loaf of soft white bread, along with some chipotles for a bit of heat, and you've got yourself the perfect vehicle for sopping up soups and beans.

This bread is best served warm out of the oven, though it's also great the next day toasted. If you can't find Mexican chorizo, make your own—that's what I do. And Muenster is an excellent substitution for the asadero. It can last a few days, but if you have a house full of guests, I doubt it will remain that long.

1. Dissolve the yeast in the warm water in a large bowl. Melt the butter on medium-low heat and then whisk in the milk and egg. Add the milk mixture to the yeast. Add the flour and salt to the liquids and stir until incorporated. Turn out the dough onto a lightly floured surface and knead until smooth.

2. Place dough in a bowl, cover, and let rise until it's doubled in size, about 1½ hours. Knead into the dough the chorizo, chipotle chiles, and half of the grated cheese, a little bit at a time. When well incorporated, place dough in a greased 9-by-5-inch bread pan and sprinkle the remaining cheese on top. Cover and let rise again until it's a little over the top of the pan, about 1½ hours.

3. Heat the oven to 400 degrees and bake bread for 35 to 40 minutes, or until the top is lightly browned and it sounds hollow when you thump it.

RUBY RED SWEET ROLLS

15 ROLLS

For my birthday, my mom always used to make me orange sweet rolls. I loved how the tangy citrus complemented the sweet and spicy cinnamon. But the best thing about these rolls was that they came from a can

I know, I know! But growing up in a household where bread was usually made from scratch, there was something magical about instant dough. Of course, if I had these rolls now, I'd probably not like them as much. And there's really no need to pop open a can when with a little planning and a bit more work, you can make far superior sweet rolls from scratch.

I brighten these sweet rolls up with Texas's native Ruby Red grapefruit, a fruit so juicy it can ruin you for other grapefruits. If, however, you can't find Texas grapefruit where you live, I'd substitute a sweet orange or a combination of orange and pink grapefruit.

1. Mix the yeast with the warm water and let it sit for 5 minutes.

2. Stir in the zest, juice, sugar, salt, egg, butter, and 1 cup of the flour. Mix together until a lumpy batter is formed. Slowly add the remaining flour until a soft, pliable dough comes together. Don't worry if it's sticky.

3. Cover and let it rest for 15 minutes. After it's rested, turn dough out onto a floured surface and knead for 5 minutes until it's smooth. Place dough in a bowl, cover, and let rise until it's doubled in size, about 1½ hours.

{CONTINUED}

FOR THE ROLLS

1 tablespoon or 1 packet of yeast

½ cup warm water

1½ teaspoons Ruby Red grapefruit zest

½ cup Ruby Red grapefruit juice

¼ cup granulated sugar

½ teaspoon kosher salt

1 large egg, beaten

2 tablespoons unsalted butter, melted

3 cups all-purpose flour, plus more for kneading

FOR THE FILLING

2 tablespoons granulated sugar

1 teaspoon ground cinnamon

1 teaspoon Ruby Red grapefruit zest

4 tablespoons unsalted butter, room temperature

FOR THE ICING

2 cups powdered sugar

6 tablespoons unsalted butter, room temperature

¼ cup Ruby Red grapefruit juice

2 teaspoons Ruby Red grapefruit zest

1 teaspoon vanilla extract

¼ teaspoon kosher salt

4. Grease a 9-by-13-inch baking dish. On a floured surface, roll out the risen dough into a large rectangle, about 9 by 13 inches, with the longer side facing you. For the filling, mix together the sugar, cinnamon, and zest. Spread the butter on the dough and then sprinkle the cinnamon mixture over the butter.

5. Starting on one of the long sides, roll the dough and pinch ends to seal. Cut off 1-inch slices from the rolled dough and place sliced rolls in the baking dish. Cover and let rise for an hour.

6. Preheat the oven to 375 degrees. Bake rolls until golden brown, about 15 minutes. While rolls are baking, for the icing whisk together the powdered sugar, butter, juice, zest, vanilla, and salt. Spread onto rolls when they come out of the oven.

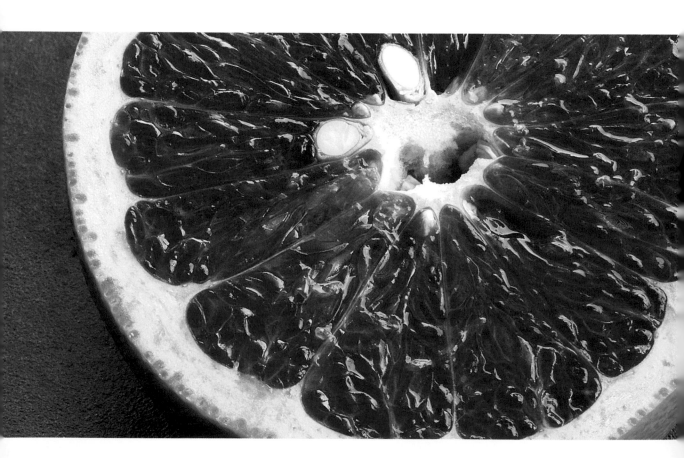

KOLACHES

12 KOLACHES

Almost halfway between Austin and Dallas is a hamlet called West, which was settled by Czech immigrants. Their descendants continue to make one of the tastiest pastries ever—the kolache. This sweet, soft, filled pastry is always an excellent excuse to stop the car, stretch your legs, and chow down.

Everyone loves kolaches, and while you can find them all over the state, for some reason they just taste better in West. Perhaps it's the water, perhaps it's the history, perhaps it's the competition among all those Czech bakeries serving their interpretation of the same treat—but most will agree that if you want the best kolaches, you must travel to West.

The kolache comes from a large family. I'd say it's a distant relative to many pastries, such as a Danish, a *klobasnek*, or even a hamantaschen (the two seem to favor the same fillings), but there's just something about that roll, a certain flavor that makes it unique.

So while making kolaches in Manhattan is akin to making bagels in West, I do think these kolaches are about as close to that little town in Texas as you can get. For me, it's a taste of road trips, wildflowers in bloom, and a hint of warmer days on the horizon. And if you're looking for a sweet escape, perhaps you will enjoy them, too.

FOR THE PASTRY
1 tablespoon or 1 packet of yeast
1 cup whole milk, warmed
¼ cup granulated sugar
3 cups all-purpose flour, divided, plus more for kneading
12 tablespoons unsalted butter, divided (1½ sticks)
2 large eggs
1 teaspoon kosher salt

FOR THE CRUMBLE TOPPING (KNOWN AS *POSYPKA*)
2 tablespoons all-purpose flour
2 tablespoons granulated sugar
1 tablespoon unsalted butter
⅛ teaspoon ground cinnamon

1. In a large bowl, combine yeast, warm milk, sugar, and 1 cup of the flour. Cover and let rise until doubled in size, about 20 minutes.

2. Melt 8 tablespoons unsalted butter. Beat the butter together with the eggs and salt. Add eggs to flour mixture and blend. Slowly add the remaining 2 cups of the flour. The dough should be soft and moist. Knead dough for about 10 minutes on a floured surface. Put dough in a greased bowl and let rise covered until it's doubled in size—about an hour.

{CONTINUED}

3. After the dough has risen, punch it down and divide into 12 even-size pieces. In your hands, roll the pieces into balls and then flatten to about 3 inches in diameter. Place flattened pieces on a greased baking sheet, cover, and let rise again for another half hour.

4. Meanwhile, make the fillings (see following) and mix together the flour, sugar, butter, and cinnamon for the *posypka* topping.

5. After second rising, preheat the oven to 375 degrees. With your finger gently make an indention in the center of each dough ball (be careful not to flatten it too much) and fill with 1 tablespoon of filling and sprinkle with *posypka*. Bake for 12 to 15 minutes. While baking, melt the remaining 4 tablespoons unsalted butter. Brush with melted butter when you take the kolaches out of the oven and serve warm.

KOLACHE FILLINGS

DRIED FRUIT FILLING

⅛ pound dried fruit such as apricots
or prunes
2 tablespoons granulated sugar
¼ teaspoon ground cinnamon
½ teaspoon lemon zest

1. Cover the dried fruit with water for 1 hour to rehydrate.

2. When the fruit is rehydrated, cook on low for 15 minutes, adding sugar, cinnamon, and lemon zest. Place in the blender and puree.

CREAM CHEESE FILLING

8 ounces cream cheese, softened
¼ cup granulated sugar
3 tablespoons all-purpose flour
1 large egg yolk
½ teaspoon lemon zest

Beat the cream cheese and sugar together until fluffy. Add the flour, egg yolk, and lemon zest.

SOPAPILLAS

ABOUT 24 SOPAPILLAS

Sopapillas are total decadence for me. You'd think after concluding a stomach-swelling multicourse Tex-Mex meal of chips and salsa, queso, guacamole, tamales, rice, beans, and enchiladas that it would be impossible to find room for one more dish. But I can never refuse a warm, steamy basket of this sweet fried bread that's been dusted with cinnamon sugar and is drowning in honey. It's a Tex-Mex classic.

If you've never had them, sopapillas are a puff of light and flaky fried dough that is perfect for catching pools of honey. And if you've never made them, it's like magic watching them puff as they fry, transforming from a flat dough into an airy, golden delight.

1. Mix the yeast with the warm water and let it sit for 5 minutes. Meanwhile, combine the flour, sugar, and salt. Add the melted butter to the yeast and then slowly stir the liquid into the flour mixture. Mix until well combined. Knead the dough for 2 minutes until it is smooth and elastic. Cover and let rise in a greased bowl for 1 hour, or until dough is doubled in size.

2. After dough has risen, punch it down on a floured surface; then roll it out into a ¼-inch-thick rectangle. Using a knife or pizza cutter, cut out 3-inch squares and then cut squares on the diagonal into triangles.

3. Heat 3 inches of oil in a large pot or Dutch oven to 350 degrees. Fry two triangles of dough at a time in the oil for 1 minute on each side. The dough should puff when it hits the oil. Drain the sopapillas on a paper towel, then sprinkle with cinnamon and sugar. Serve hot with honey.

FOR THE SOPAPILLAS

1 tablespoon or 1 packet of yeast
1½ cups warm water
4 cups all-purpose flour, plus more
 for kneading
1 tablespoon granulated sugar
1 teaspoon kosher salt
1 tablespoon unsalted butter, melted
Vegetable oil, for frying

FOR TOPPING

2 tablespoons granulated sugar
2 tablespoons ground cinnamon
Honey, to taste

CORN TORTILLAS

Corn tortillas are the workhorses of Tex-Mex cooking. Without them you wouldn't have enchiladas, chalupas, tacos, or tortilla chips. Of course, finding fresh corn tortillas in Texas is not a problem, but I've found that in many places outside Texas the corn tortillas on offer have the texture and flavor of paper.

I make my corn tortillas at home with masa harina and a tortilla press that's been in my family since I was a little girl. Once you get the hang of it, making corn tortillas takes little time. And heck, anyone who has had a fresh corn tortilla hot off the skillet will agree—there's no comparison to the machine-pressed ones you buy at the store. They're so different in texture and taste, you almost wonder how the two are related.

2 cups masa harina
1¼ cups warm water
Pinch of salt

1. Mix the masa harina, warm water, and salt until a dough is formed. Knead the dough for a minute until smooth. Divide into 12 equal-size balls and cover with a damp cloth.

2. On medium-high, heat a dry skillet, preferably cast-iron, until very hot, which you can test by flicking a bit of water into the pan. If it dances and sizzles, it's ready.

3. Cut two pieces of parchment paper that cover the width of a tortilla press. Place a piece of the cut parchment paper on the press, put a ball of dough on it, and then lay the other piece of parchment paper on top. Press out the tortilla. Take the tortilla, which is now wrapped in parchment paper, off the press, gently peel off the two pieces of paper, and place the tortilla into the hot skillet.

{CONTINUED}

4. Cook for 30 seconds on one side, flip it, and then cook for 1 minute on the other side. It should start to puff a bit. Flip it again and cook for 30 more seconds. Place cooked tortillas in a basket lined with cloth or in a tortilla warmer. Repeat process for remaining balls of dough. Can be stored in the refrigerator for a week. They can also be frozen for 6 months.

NOTE: If you don't have a tortilla press, you can pat the balls into flat discs or roll them out with a pin. You can also place the balls (with the parchment paper) between two very heavy books and press them out that way.

VARIATION

HOMINY TORTILLAS

1 cup canned hominy, drained
1 cup masa harina
1½ cups water
Pinch of salt

If you're looking for a more robust corn flavor, try adding hominy to your corn tortilla dough.

1. In a blender or food processor, grind the hominy until it's a paste. Mix it with the masa harina, warm water, and salt until a dough is formed.

2. Divide into 12 balls and proceed with the regular corn tortilla recipe.

HOUSTON-STYLE FLOUR TORTILLAS

8 TORTILLAS

You can always tell where you are in Texas by the type of flour tortilla. While it may be a bit simplistic to divide the state into two flour-tortilla camps, in my experience that's what I've seen. This recipe is for the Houston-style tortilla, which is soft and pliant. These tortillas are a bit sweet and flaky, which makes them excellent for eating warm off the comal (a Mexican cast-iron griddle), no adornment necessary.

A simple combination of lard, water, and flour is what gives these tortillas their signature texture and taste. You can definitely substitute shortening if you like, but they won't taste *as* good.

The key to flour tortillas is patience. The glutens in the dough will need time to relax, so do not skip the dough-resting step.

These tortillas pair well with Carnitas (page 201), Tacos al Carbon, Small-Apartment Style (page 169), and other roasted or grilled meats. They're wonderful rolled and dipped into a bowl of Houston-Style Green Salsa (page 59), as well.

¼ cup lard or shortening

1 cup water

2 cups all-purpose flour, plus more for kneading

1 teaspoon kosher salt

1. Place the lard or shortening and water into a pot on medium heat and cook until it has melted.

2. In a bowl, stir together the flour and salt. Pour in the melted lard or shortening and water and stir until a loose ball is formed. Place dough on a floured surface and knead for 2 minutes until dough is supple and smooth. Cover the dough and let it rest for 1 hour.

(CONTINUED)

3. After an hour, divide the dough into 8 pieces. Cover again and let it rest for 30 minutes. After dough has rested, place each dough ball one at a time on a floured surface, pat it out into a 4-inch circle, and then roll with a palote or a rolling pin from the center until it's thin, about 8 inches in diameter. Don't overwork the dough, or it will be stiff. Keep rolled-out tortillas covered until ready to cook.

4. In a dry cast-iron skillet heated on high, cook each tortilla for 30 seconds on one side, flip it, and then cook for 1 minute on the other side. It should start to puff a bit. Flip it again and cook for 30 more seconds. Place cooked tortillas in a basket lined with cloth or a tortilla warmer. Repeat process for remaining balls of dough.

SAN ANTONIO–STYLE FLOUR TORTILLAS

8 TORTILLAS

2 tablespoons unsalted butter

¾ cup milk

1 tablespoon vegetable oil

2 cups all-purpose flour, plus more
   for kneading

1 teaspoon baking powder

½ teaspoon kosher salt

In Corpus Christi, San Antonio, and Dallas, the flour tortillas tend to be puffier and thicker than their Houston and border brethren. This is your true Tex-Mex tortilla, as you won't find it in Mexico. Likewise, when companies aim to reproduce a flour tortilla, this is the model they use.

Of course, if you've had only a flour tortilla from a plastic bag, you've never had a good flour tortilla. This style of tortilla is good if you're adverse to lard, and while it's different from the Houston-style tortilla, it's just as delicious.

I had spent many years trying to find a recipe for a puffy flour tortilla, but it wasn't until I made a recipe found in *The Border Cookbook* by Cheryl Alters Jamison and Bill Jamison that I achieved puffy-tortilla bliss. I've adapted their recipe here, adding a little butter for flavor and toning down the baking powder. If you're looking for a flour tortilla that's lower in fat, this is your recipe. Not to mention that it's so soft and flavorful, you won't even miss the extra calories.

1. Place the butter and milk into a pot and on medium-low heat cook until butter has melted. Turn off the heat and stir in the vegetable oil.

2. In a bowl, stir together the flour, baking powder, and salt. Pour in the melted butter, milk, and oil and stir until a loose, sticky ball is formed. Place dough on a floured surface and knead for 2 minutes until dough is firm and smooth. Stir until well combined. Cover the dough and let it rest for 1 hour.

3. After an hour, divide the dough into 8 pieces. Cover again and let it rest for 30 minutes. After dough has rested, place each dough ball one at a time on a floured surface, pat it out into a 4-inch circle, and then roll with a palote or a rolling pin from the center until it's thin, about 8 inches in diameter. Don't overwork the dough, or it will be stiff. Keep rolled-out tortillas covered until ready to cook.

4. In a dry cast-iron skillet heated on high, cook each tortilla for 30 seconds on one side, flip it, and then cook for 1 minute on the other side. It should start to puff a bit. Flip it again and cook for 30 more seconds. Place cooked tortillas in a basket lined with cloth or in a tortilla warmer. Repeat process for remaining balls of dough.

APPLE CHEESE SCONES WITH JALAPEÑOS

ABOUT 8 SCONES

When I was young, my mom went through an Anglophile phase, and one of the results was her replacing our usual biscuits with the English scone. People say that a scone is simply a biscuit with an egg added to the dough, though I find that scones do lend themselves more to embellishment.

That's what I've done with these, filling them with diced green apples, grated cheese, and bits of Jalapeño. I love the late-summer, early-autumn combination of chiles with apples—the two were made for each other. And while scones originally may be from across the pond, adding jalapeños and cheddar cheese to these makes them decidedly Texan.

2 cups all-purpose flour
¼ cup granulated sugar
2 teaspoons baking powder
½ teaspoon kosher salt
¼ teaspoon ground cinnamon
½ cup unsalted butter, chilled, cut into slices
¼ cup buttermilk
1 large egg, beaten
1 jalapeño chile, seeds and stems removed, diced
½ cup Granny Smith apple, peeled, cored, and finely diced
½ cup grated sharp cheddar cheese

1. Preheat the oven to 425 degrees and grease a baking sheet or a cast-iron skillet.

2. Mix together the flour, sugar, baking powder, salt, and ground cinnamon.

3. Cut the butter into pieces, and work into the flour mixture with your hands or a pastry blender until it resembles pea-size crumbs. Stir the buttermilk and egg into the dough. Stir in the diced jalapeño, apple, and cheese and mix until well combined. If the dough is too sticky and wet, simply add a bit more flour. Spoon hand-size balls of dough onto the greased sheet and bake until lightly brown, about 15 minutes.

LEMON LAVENDER BREAD

2 LOAVES

FOR THE BREAD

1 cup buttermilk

½ teaspoon baking soda

1 cup unsalted butter, room
temperature

2 cups granulated sugar

4 large eggs

3 cups all-purpose flour

1 teaspoon dried lavender

2 teaspoons lemon zest

1 cup pecans, chopped coarsely

FOR THE GLAZE

¾ cup lemon juice

1½ cups granulated sugar

My great-aunt Mary's signature dish was her lemon bread. Mary was the family iconoclast who would drink and smoke to get a rise out of her Baptist relatives. Yet her sharp wit and ability to turn any event into a story made her a blast to be around.

In a way, this lemon bread is much like her: a bit tart and a bit sweet. I like to eat this bread for breakfast, though it's also very good as a dessert. It tastes best cold from the refrigerator, though you can certainly eat it warm. And while Mary never added lavender to her lemon bread, I don't think the family rebel would have minded my tweaking her recipe one bit.

1. Preheat the oven to 350 degrees and grease and flour two 9-by-5-inch loaf pans.

2. Stir together the buttermilk and baking soda and set it aside. Cream together the butter and sugar. Beat the eggs and slowly add to the creamed butter. Stir in the buttermilk, then slowly add the flour. Mix until a smooth batter is formed. Stir in the lavender, lemon zest, and pecans. Pour the batter into the pans and bake until a tester comes out clean, about 50 minutes. Remove the bread from the oven and cool for 10 minutes.

3. For the glaze, mix together the lemon juice and sugar. Once the bread has cooled, take it out of the pans, place each loaf on a sheet of foil, top with the glaze, and wrap. Place in the refrigerator for at least 12 hours. Serve cold.

NOTE: You can usually find dried lavender in the spice section of the grocery store or at specialty markets.

SWEET POTATO MUFFINS

12 MUFFINS

These muffins are a family favorite; you can always find a plate of them in my grandma's kitchen. They are best served warm from the oven on an especially cold morning. The combination of sweet potato, brown sugar, dates, and pecans reminds me of late fall and early winter holidays.

1¾ cups all-purpose flour

1 teaspoon baking soda

¼ teaspoon kosher salt

½ teaspoon ground cinnamon

2 large eggs

1 cup granulated sugar

½ cup brown sugar

1 teaspoon vanilla extract

½ cup vegetable oil

1 15-ounce can of sweet potato,
   well drained and mashed

½ cup pecans, chopped

1 cup dates, chopped

1. Preheat the oven to 350 degrees and grease and flour a muffin pan.

2. Combine the flour, baking soda, salt, and cinnamon in a large bowl. Beat together the eggs, granulated and brown sugars, vanilla, and oil. Stir in the mashed sweet potato until well blended. Add the liquid ingredients to the dry ingredients and stir until moist. Stir in the pecans and dates.

3. Spoon batter into the muffin pan until three quarters full. Bake for 25 to 30 minutes. Remove from pan immediately.

12

SWEETS

There's a photo of me cooking with my mom when I was a toddler. I'm standing on a chair, helping her scoop out balls of cookie dough. The next photo taken that day shows my face plastered with chocolate and a wide grin. I like to say that I do not have a sweet tooth. But as my mom is fond of reminding me, I've been enjoying both baking and eating sweets my whole life, which these photos prove.

My baking experiences also extended to visiting my grandma, who is so well versed in pie making that she could roll out a crust in her sleep. And while I was less help to her in the kitchen, you would always find me at her side taking mental notes while patiently waiting for that moment when she'd let me lick the bowl.

So yes, I do love to eat sweets, and I'm also quite fond of making them as well. I reckon my supposition that I don't have a sweet tooth stems from the fact that I'm not one to frequent bakeries or order desserts when I go out to eat. But upon reflection, I've realized that I don't order desserts when I'm out because I was taught at a young age that the best baked goods are prepared by loving hands at home.

The sweets on offer in Texas are as far ranging as the state itself. From our southern heritage, we have a vast collection of pies, such as chess pie, chocolate pie, or that county-fair favorite, the fried pie, which I enjoy making from apples grown at my family's farm.

We also take inspiration from our Mexican heritage with tres leches cake, a sponge cake that's been soaked in three different types of milk. And then there's chocoflan, a delicious miracle of science in which you bake a cake with the custard swirled into the batter, only to have the two separate once the cake is done.

No summer day in Texas would be complete without a serving of homemade ice cream, which my family's been making for generations. In the old days, we'd have to crank it by hand and fool with rock salt, which many still consider a superior method for making ice cream. Fortunately, new ice cream makers eliminate much of this effort while still yielding excellent results. Two of my favorite flavors are a robust Mexican coffee, made deep and warm with brown sugar and cinnamon, which I'll top with an ancho-chile hot fudge. Though when the dewberries are in season, a dewberry-cobbler ice cream combines two of my favorite desserts into one.

When it's cold, I like to keep warm by baking cookies. At the holidays, I'll serve a platter of chocolate chewy cookies, made fiery with a bit of chipotle. And no gathering at the farm would be complete without shortbread, which I enhance with a bit of lime juice to give it zing.

The Texas tradition of making desserts is long and varied. I have stacks and files filled with recipes from my ancestors; it would take me quite a while to bake them all. Even though many of my recipes are old, however, it doesn't mean they're necessarily old-fashioned, as a good sweet seldom goes out of style.

ARROZ CON LECHE

4 TO 6 SERVINGS

Rice pudding is the ultimate comfort food. Its soft and sweet nature poses no challenge to both the palate and the mind—you can just eat it, relax, and enjoy. Many rice puddings are baked, but the Mexican interpretation of this dessert is created on the stove, which makes for a looser, creamier texture.

At its most basic, arroz con leche is simply rice with milk, as the name means in Spanish. Some, however, add a hint of spice by adding a cinnamon stick or citrus peel. I've followed that lead and also added a bit of vanilla to round out the flavors. Though I'm a big fan of the arroz con leche's soothing texture, I've sprinkled some candied almonds on top for a bit of contrast and crunch.

You'll often find arroz con leche at Tex-Mex restaurants, though I think of it more as a home-cooked treat. Sure, it goes well after an evening meal, but it would not be unusual to serve it for breakfast, too. Just be cautious if you do serve it early in the day—after you tuck into a comforting bowl of arroz con leche, you may be ready to curl up on the couch and simply relax.

FOR THE PUDDING

1 cup rice, uncooked
1 cinnamon stick
1 strip of orange peel, ½ inch wide
4 whole cloves
4 cups whole milk
¼ cup granulated sugar (plus more to taste)
½ teaspoon kosher salt
2 tablespoons unsalted butter
1 teaspoon vanilla extract
Ground cinnamon, for serving

FOR THE CANDIED ALMONDS

½ cup almond slivers
1 tablespoon granulated sugar
¼ teaspoon kosher salt
¼ teaspoon ground cinnamon
¼ teaspoon grated orange zest

1. In a large pot, add the rice, cinnamon stick, orange peel, and cloves, and cover with 3 cups of water. On high heat, bring to a boil and then turn down the heat to low. Cover and cook for 5 minutes. After 5 minutes, remove the cover from the rice and continue to simmer until all the water is gone, about 10 to 15 more minutes.

2. Meanwhile, to make the candied almonds, place the almond slivers in a skillet heated on medium low. While stirring, cook the almonds just until they start to brown, about 2 minutes. Sprinkle the sugar over the almonds and continue to cook while stirring for 1 minute or until sugar melts.

{CONTINUED}

3. Remove from heat, toss with the salt, cinnamon, and orange zest and lift the almonds out of the skillet to cool in one layer on a flat surface.

4. Once the water is gone from the rice pot, keeping the heat on low, pour in the milk and sugar. Cover the pot and cook for 10 minutes, then remove the cover and while occasionally stirring, cook until the rice is fluffy and the liquid has been reduced to a thick sauce, about 25 minutes. Taste and add more sugar if you like and then stir in the salt, butter, and vanilla. Serve warm, sprinkling the top with ground cinnamon and the candied almonds.

BLUEBERRIES WITH CORNMEAL SHORTCAKES

8 SERVINGS

Texas may not be known for its blueberries, but make no mistake—blueberries do grow in Texas, and they are big, full, and juicy. Texan blueberries are primarily found in East and Northeast Texas with the peak of the season happening in June, a time marked by the annual Blueberry Festival in the East Texas town of Nacogdoches.

I'm a big fan of shortcake desserts, when fresh fruit is paired with a biscuitlike cake and topped with fresh whipped cream. The most common iteration of this form is of course strawberry shortcake. But I love the combination of blueberries with corn, so I present to you blueberry shortcake with cornmeal biscuits.

There's a bit of lime juice squirted in to brighten this dish, and I've also added some cinnamon and vanilla to the whipped cream for warmth. But the real star of this dessert is the blueberries. When they're in season, I can think of no better way to showcase this charming fruit—other than just eating them when freshly picked.

1. Toss the blueberries with the sugar, lime juice, and cinnamon. Let the blueberries sit at room temperature for half an hour so they can become soft and juicy.

2. Preheat the oven to 400 degrees. Grease and flour a large cast-iron skillet or baking sheet and place a metal mixing bowl in the freezer.

3. To make the cornmeal shortcakes, mix together the flour, cornmeal, baking powder, sugar, and salt. Cut the stick of butter into pieces and work into the flour mixture with your

FOR THE BLUEBERRIES
2 cups blueberries
2 tablespoons granulated sugar
1 teaspoon lime juice
¼ teaspoon ground cinnamon

FOR THE CORNMEAL SHORTCAKES
1 cup all-purpose flour, plus more for kneading
1 cup cornmeal
1 tablespoon baking powder
3 tablespoons granulated sugar
½ teaspoon kosher salt
8 tablespoons unsalted butter, chilled (1 stick)
¾ cup half-and-half

FOR THE WHIPPED CREAM
2 cups heavy whipping cream
2 tablespoons granulated sugar
¼ teaspoon ground cinnamon
¼ teaspoon vanilla extract
½ teaspoon lime juice

{CONTINUED}

hands or a pastry blender until it resembles pea-size crumbs. Add the half-and-half, mixing until the dough is a bit loose and sticky.

4. Pour dough out on a floured surface and knead for a minute. Dough should be smooth and no longer wet. You can sprinkle more flour on the surface if you find it's sticking. Roll or pat out dough until it's ¼ of an inch thick and then fold it in half. Using a round cutter that's about 2 inches wide (you can use a glass or a cup if don't have a biscuit cutter), cut out the biscuits from the folded dough. This should yield 8 cornmeal biscuits.

5. Place the biscuits close together, about ⅛ of an inch apart, in the cast-iron skillet or baking sheet (so they rise up, not out) and bake for 15 minutes or until the tops are golden brown. Let biscuits cool for 10 minutes.

6. Meanwhile, take the metal mixing bowl out of the freezer. Pour in the whipping cream and whisk in the sugar, cinnamon, vanilla, and lime juice. With an electric mixer, whisk, or eggbeater, beat the cream until it triples in size—thick with soft peaks.

7. To assemble the shortcakes, slice a cornmeal biscuit in half. Place ¼ cup of blueberries on one half of the biscuit and top with whipped cream and the other half of the cornmeal biscuit.

GRANDMA'S PIE CRUST

2 cups all-purpose flour
1 teaspoon kosher salt
½ cup vegetable oil
¼ cup whole milk

I come from a long line of pie people. Oh, sure, we enjoy eating cakes, cookies, and ice creams, but it's pies that make us swoon. My grandma has been rolling out pies with a pin that was hand carved for her as a wedding gift over sixty years ago. Now, that's a pin that's seen a lot of action!

This is my grandma's basic pie-crust recipe, which is unusual in that it calls for oil and milk instead of the usual butter, shortening, or lard. But everyone who eats it admits that it's definitely the best pie crust they've ever tried.

1. In a bowl, mix together the flour and salt. Add to the dry ingredients the oil and milk, and stir until well combined. (If the dough is too dry, you can add a bit more milk, about a teaspoon at a time.)

2. Halve the dough into two balls. If you need only one crust, you can freeze the other crust for up to 6 months.

3. To line the pie pan, take one ball, place it between two sheets of wax paper, and roll it out into about an 11-inch circle. Lift the top sheet of wax paper off the rolled-out dough and then flip the dough into the pie pan, lifting off the other piece of wax paper. Press until smooth and trim the edges, using a fork or your fingers to crimp for decoration.

CHESS PIE

8 SERVINGS

8 tablespoons unsalted butter
  (1 stick)
3 large eggs
1 cup granulated sugar
1 teaspoon vanilla extract
1 tablespoon yellow cornmeal
½ cup lemon juice
1 teaspoon lemon zest
1 unbaked Grandma's Pie Crust
  (page 318)

One pie that always reminds me of Texas is chess pie. It was my grandpa's favorite pie, and when we weren't eating it at home you could guarantee that he'd get a slice for dessert at a Sunday-night supper at the cafeteria.

Now, before we discuss this pie, let's talk a little bit about eating at the cafeteria. I'm not sure how it is in other places, but most Texans—no matter if they hail from small towns or the big cities—love going to the cafeteria. Whether you're trying to feed a family on a budget, or just want a home-style meal without having to cook, pushing your tray down the long line and choosing from the vast display of dining selections is always a blast.

If you're not familiar with chess pie, it's a custard-based dessert that is made with the simplest ingredients—eggs, butter, a bit of lemon, and cornmeal. Yet its humble origins belie the rich results.

The origin of its name is a mystery, but most concede that it has nothing to do with the game of kings. Some say that it may be named after the town of Chester, England, while others claim that it's a rendition of how a southerner would sound if saying, "It's jes' pie." But honestly, I'm not too bothered about why it's called chess pie, just as long as you'll save an extra slice for me.

1. Preheat the oven to 350 degrees.

2. On low heat, gently cook the butter until it's melted. In another bowl, beat the eggs with the sugar, vanilla, cornmeal, lemon juice, and zest. Pour in the melted butter and mix until creamy and well combined.

3. Pour filling into unbaked pie shell and bake uncovered for 50 minutes or until the custard is set. Let cool for 20 minutes before serving. It can be eaten either warm or cold.

GRANDMA'S CHOCOLATE PIE

8 SERVINGS

There are pies, and then there is my grandma's chocolate pie.

It's a luscious chocolate custard resting on a flaky, almost salty, crust topped with a springy meringue. For me, it's the pièce de résistance, and whether times are good or times are bad, it's always welcome and appropriate. It has always been my favorite dessert.

I sometimes think that only my grandma can make this pie taste so good, though she has been gracious in sharing her recipe. Please note, however, that the secret ingredient is love. Here is my grandma's advice for serving: "It's real good hot, wonderful cold, and you can even eat it frozen—then it's like a Popsicle!"

1. Preheat the oven to 350 degrees.

2. Poke holes into the unbaked pie crust with a fork and bake it for 15 to 20 minutes or until it's lightly browned. Some people prefer to weigh it down with pie weights or dried beans as it may bubble a bit.

3. Meanwhile, mix together the sugar, flour, salt, cocoa or baking chocolate, egg yolks, and milk with a whisk. Cook in a pot on medium heat while occasionally stirring until it bubbles and thickens, about 7 to 10 minutes. If it starts to become lumpy, just beat out the lumps. (It will not get any thicker in the oven, so cook it in the pot until it's your desired thickness.)

4. Remove from the heat and stir in the vanilla and butter.

{CONTINUED}

1 unbaked Grandma's Pie Crust (page 318)
¾ cup granulated sugar
5 tablespoons all-purpose flour
¼ teaspoon kosher salt
4 tablespoons unsweetened cocoa or 1½ squares of unsweetened baking chocolate
2 egg yolks, beaten slightly
1½ cups whole milk
½ teaspoon vanilla extract
1 tablespoon unsalted butter

MERINGUE INGREDIENTS
2 egg whites
⅛ teaspoon kosher salt
4 tablespoons granulated sugar

5. To make the meringue, beat the egg whites with the salt until they are smooth, light, and fluffy; they should have soft peaks like whipped cream. This can take anywhere from 5 to 10 minutes. (If you don't have a stand mixer, a strong arm with a whisk or an eggbeater can accomplish this task, too. Please note that by hand it will take much longer than 10 minutes.) Stir the sugar into the meringue.

6. Pour the chocolate custard into the baked pie shell and top with the beaten egg whites. Bake it until the peaks on the meringue are lightly browned, about 10 to 15 minutes.

APPLE FRIED PIES

10 PIES

Texans' reputation for deep-frying everything probably originated at our annual state fair, where indeed, everything from butter to beer is battered and dipped in hot oil. I will not comment on those egregious edibles, but I will say that there is one fried dessert that does hold sway over my heart, and that would be fried pies.

Fried pies are known as hand pies in certain circles up north, and I think the latter name might do this dessert more justice, as that describes a fried pie's nature perfectly—it's a pie you can eat with your hands.

"Wait! Isn't that an empanada?" you may be saying to yourself. And yes, the two do have much in common. But what differentiates a fried pie from its Hispanic cousin is the fried pie's pastry, and as the name implies, a fried pie is fried, whereas an empanada is usually baked.

Fried pies are found in Texas wherever people are on the move, such as at gas stations, county fairs, football games, and rodeos. Ideally there is someone making them fresh to order, but fried pies do have a bit of a shelf life, so you can eat these cold as well. As for fillings, you're limited only by your imagination. I'm fond of apple, so that's the filling I've included for this recipe, but you can substitute any filling you prefer.

FOR THE CRUST

2 cups all-purpose flour
½ teaspoon kosher salt
½ cup lard, chilled
¼ cup cold water

FOR THE FILLING

4 tablespoons unsalted butter
2 cups cooking apples such as
    Granny Smith, peeled, cored, and
    diced (about ½ pound of apples)
1 tablespoon all-purpose flour
¼ cup granulated sugar
¼ teaspoon ground cinnamon
¼ teaspoon ancho chile powder
½ teaspoon kosher salt

FOR THE PIES

Vegetable oil, for frying
Powdered sugar and ground
    cinnamon for sprinkling

1. To make the crust, mix together the flour and salt. Add the lard, either with a fork, your hands, or a pastry cutter. When the flour is clumped together, slowly add the cold water, a tablespoon at a time, until the dough is moist enough to come together. Form the dough into a ball, then wrap and place the dough in the refrigerator to chill for at least an hour.

(CONTINUED)

2. Meanwhile, in a large ovenproof skillet, preferably a cast-iron skillet, melt the butter on low heat. Add the apples, flour, sugar, cinnamon, ancho chile powder, and salt, and while occasionally stirring, cook until the apples are soft, about 5 minutes. Taste and adjust seasonings.

3. To make the fried pies, roll out the chilled piecrust until it's no more than ⅛ of an inch thick. Cut out 3-inch-diameter circles. Roll out any leftover scraps and continue to cut 3-inch circles until all the dough has been used. You should have about 10.

4. Place 2 teaspoons of filling in the center of each crust. Moisten the edges and fold the crust over, sealing the edges with your fingers, and then press down on the edges with a fork.

5. In a cast-iron skillet, heat 1 inch of oil to 350 degrees. With a spatula, gently place each pie into the hot oil, and turn over after a minute. Cook on the other side for another minute, and then drain on a rack or paper-towel-lined plate. You can sprinkle powdered sugar and/or cinnamon over pies if you like.

PEACH COBBLER

8 SERVINGS

No matter where you are in Texas—from the panhandle to the Rio Grande Valley—you will always find one dessert that everyone agrees is wonderful: peach cobbler. I've seen it at West Texas taquerias, East Texas small-town cafés, in Dallas cafeterias, and on offer after a Houston crawfish boil. Texans love their peach cobbler.

There are many ways to make peach cobbler. I recall when I first moved to New York and asked my grandma how she made hers, which was always a Saturday-evening favorite at her house, she said, "Just take peaches and add a crust. It's simple."

Indeed, peach cobbler is a cinch to make. I offer here a version found in my great-grandma Blanche's collection of recipes, in which you make a batter and then lay the peaches on top. As the cobbler bakes, the batter rises and wraps itself around the peaches, so when you pull the cobbler out of the oven you have peaches nestled in a buttery pastry. This is my favorite version of peach cobbler, as the ratio of pastry to peaches is balanced. I've been known to work my way through a whole pan in one sitting, and if you're not careful, you may find yourself doing the same.

8 tablespoons unsalted butter, melted (1 stick)
1 cup all-purpose flour
1 cup granulated sugar
1 cup milk
2 teaspoons baking powder
2 cups sliced fresh peaches, peeled and pitted
1 teaspoon ground cinnamon
1 teaspoon ground ginger

1. Preheat the oven to 350 degrees.

2. Pour melted butter into a large cast-iron skillet or a 9-inch-square baking pan. Mix together the flour, sugar, milk, and baking powder, and pour the batter over the butter.

3. Toss the sliced peaches with the cinnamon and ginger. Place the peaches on top of the batter and bake uncovered for 45 minutes.

PUMPKIN EMPANADAS

ABOUT 15 EMPANADAS

FOR THE CRUST

8 ounces cream cheese,
   room temperature
8 tablespoons unsalted butter,
   room temperature (1 stick)
1½ cups all-purpose flour
½ teaspoon kosher salt

FOR THE FILLING

1 15-ounce can of pumpkin
1½ tablespoons heavy cream
¼ cup chopped pecans
½ cup brown sugar
½ teaspoon ground cinnamon
¼ teaspoon ground ginger
¼ teaspoon ground allspice
¼ teaspoon orange zest
½ teaspoon vanilla extract
½ teaspoon kosher salt

FOR THE EMPANADA TOPPING

1 large egg
2 tablespoons whole milk
1 teaspoon ground cinnamon
1 tablespoon granulated sugar

Whenever two homesick Texans get together, it's inevitable that they will discuss what they miss most from home. Take my friend Amy, a homesick Texan who now resides in Mississippi. She adores the pumpkin empanadas found at Fiesta grocery stores in Houston and has let me know on many occasions how much she pines for these Mexican sweet treats. And I have to agree with her—it's always a joy to eat these pastries.

If you're not familiar with empanadas, they're a Mexican turnover that is stuffed with fillings both sweet and savory. They're similar to a fried pie, although they're not fried and the pastry is fluffy rather than flaky. I like to serve them at the end of the year when pumpkin-flavored dishes are most common. Fiesta sells them year-round, so there's certainly no reason why you can't eat them year-round, as well.

1. To make the crust, mix together the cream cheese and butter until smooth. Stir in the flour and salt until a smooth dough is formed. Wrap in plastic wrap and refrigerate for 30 minutes.

2. Meanwhile, for the filling, mix together the pumpkin with the cream, pecans, brown sugar, cinnamon, ginger, allspice, orange zest, vanilla, and salt. Taste and adjust seasonings.

3. To make the empanadas, preheat the oven to 375 degrees and lightly grease a baking sheet.

4. Take the dough out of the refrigerator, and roll it out on a floured surface until it's ⅛ inch thick. Cut into 5-inch rounds and then gather the scraps, roll out again, and cut more 5-inch rounds until all the dough has been used.

5. Place 2 teaspoons of the filling in the center of each dough circle and fold the dough to the other side so it forms a half-moon shape. Crimp the edges with a fork to seal.

6. For the topping, whisk together the egg and milk and brush this on top of the empanadas. Mix together the cinnamon and sugar and sprinkle on top. Bake for 25 minutes or until top is browned.

VARIATION

If you prefer, you can substitute $1^{3}/_{4}$ cups cooked sweet potato for the pumpkin.

CHOCOFLAN

12 TO 20 SERVINGS

The first time I encountered chocoflan was at a Mexican taqueria in Houston. Sitting on the counter was a round chocolate cake topped with a layer of creamy flan, which is a Mexican custard. I ordered a slice and was blown away by the combination of the fluffy custard and light yet moist chocolate cake.

Beyond tasting wonderful, what makes chocoflan all the more incredible is how it's made. You bake both the flan and the cake batter at the same time. Through a miracle of science, the flan separates from the cake and creates a separate layer. It's pretty amazing to witness. But science aside, chocoflan is an impressive dessert that doesn't take that much effort yet makes a huge impression.

I've tweaked the basic recipe by adding orange and lime juices to my flan custard. As cola cakes are popular in Texas because of their rich flavor and light texture, I made my cake base with Mexican Coca-Cola, a beverage that is made from cane sugar instead of corn syrup.

In Mexican communities, chocoflan is known as a celebration cake and is served at birthdays, holidays, and other special events, but there's certainly no reason why you couldn't make this whenever you have the time.

1. Preheat the oven to 350 degrees and grease and lightly flour the cake pan. Coat the bottom of the pan with the *cajeta* or caramel.

2. To make the cake batter, in a large mixing bowl cream together the butter and the sugar. Add the eggs, mixing well. Sift together the flour, cocoa powder, baking soda, salt, and cinnamon and stir into the bowl. Add the Mexican Coca-Cola (or regular cola) and buttermilk and stir until a thick batter is formed. Pour the batter into the pan.

(CONTINUED)

FOR THE CAKE

½ cup *cajeta* or caramel topping
1 cup unsalted butter, room temperature (2 sticks)
1 cup granulated sugar
2 large eggs, beaten
2 cups all-purpose flour
¼ cup unsweetened cocoa powder
1 teaspoon baking soda
1 teaspoon kosher salt
½ teaspoon ground cinnamon
1 cup Mexican Coca-Cola (or regular cola, not diet)
½ cup buttermilk

FOR THE FLAN

4 ounces cream cheese, room temperature
4 large eggs
1 12-ounce can of evaporated milk
1 14-ounce can of sweetened condensed milk
½ tablespoon vanilla extract
2 tablespoons orange zest
1 tablespoon lime zest
¼ teaspoon kosher salt

SPECIAL EQUIPMENT

1 Bundt cake pan, 1 10-inch-round pan, or 1 tube pan that can hold 12 cups, along with a larger pan to create a water bath

3. For the flan, in a blender mix the cream cheese and eggs until smooth. Blend in the evaporated milk, sweetened condensed milk, vanilla, orange zest, lime zest, and salt. Slowly pour the flan mixture over the cake batter (it's fine if some of it sinks and some of it stays on top) and cover the cake pan tightly with foil.

4. Place the cake pan in the larger pan and fill the larger pan with 1 inch of warm water to create a water bath, which will help the flan bake evenly. Bake for 1 hour or until an inserted knife pulls out clean. Allow the cake to cool for 1 hour.

5. To serve, run a knife along the edges of the cake pan then invert the cake pan over a serving tray and lightly shake until the cake slides out. The cake can either be served warm or you can refrigerate it for a few hours and serve it cool.

NOTE: This cake is very rich and makes a ton, which is perfect for a large gathering. The recipe, however, can easily be cut in half. If you choose to do this, bake it in a 9-inch-square or round pan. Premade cajeta, which is a Mexican goat's milk caramel sauce, or regular caramel can be found at most Mexican groceries or large grocery stores.

COCONUT
TRES LECHES CAKE

12 SERVINGS

Tres leches cake is quite the luxury. One bite of this sponge cake after it has absorbed the eponymous three milks and you'll easily see why it has become one of the most popular desserts in Texas.

Its provenance is unknown—some say it hails from South America, while others insist that food company executives developed the recipe so they could sell more canned milk in Mexico. No matter, it's a cinch to make and is always a crowd pleaser.

Tres leches cake is known for its moist, smooth texture. But as I like a little crunch in my desserts, I throw in some toasted coconut flakes to both my cake batter and my whipped-cream topping. I also add some tangy lime zest to brighten the heaviness of this rich and creamy cake.

1½ cups flaked coconut

1 cup all-purpose flour

1 teaspoon baking powder

2 teaspoons lime zest

¼ teaspoon ground nutmeg

¼ teaspoon kosher salt

8 large eggs

½ cup brown sugar

4 tablespoons unsalted butter, melted

1 teaspoon vanilla extract

FOR THE THREE-MILK SYRUP

½ cup coconut milk

1 12-ounce can of evaporated milk

1 14-ounce can of sweetened condensed milk

FOR THE WHIPPED CREAM TOPPING

2 cups heavy cream

2 tablespoons granulated sugar

1 teaspoon vanilla extract

1 tablespoon lime zest

1. Preheat the oven to 350 degrees, grease a 9-by-13-inch cake pan, and place a metal bowl in the freezer.

2. In a large ungreased skillet heated on medium low, place the coconut in an even layer and sauté until lightly toasted, about 3 to 5 minutes. Remove from heat. Sift together the flour and baking powder. Stir into the flour ½ cup of the toasted coconut, lime zest, nutmeg, and salt.

3. Beat together the eggs and brown sugar in a mixing bowl with a stand mixer, using the wire whisk attachment, for about 10 minutes until they are smooth, light, and fluffy; they should have soft peaks like whipped cream. (If you don't have a stand mixer, a strong arm with a whisk or an eggbeater can accomplish this task, too. Please note that by hand it will take much longer than 10 minutes.) When the eggs are fluffy,

(CONTINUED)

slowly pour in the melted butter and stir in the vanilla extract. Then slowly stir in the flour mixture until the batter is an even shade of brown.

4. Pour the batter into the 9-by-13-inch baking pan and bake for 20 to 25 minutes or until an inserted knife comes out clean. Let the cake cool for 15 minutes.

5. While the cake cools, stir together the coconut milk, the evaporated milk, and the sweetened condensed milk to make the three-milk syrup.

6. Once the cake has cooled, with a fork, poke holes all over the top of the cake. Slowly pour the three-milk syrup over the cake. Let the cake absorb the milk syrup for 10 minutes. Cover and refrigerate for 8 hours. (You might not need all of the milk; if there's any left it makes a fine drink.)

7. To make the whipped cream topping, in the chilled bowl, beat the cream with the sugar and vanilla. Once whipped, gently stir in the lime zest. Spread over cooled cake and top with the remaining 1 cup of toasted coconut. Store the cake in the refrigerator. Will last for several days.

TEXAS SHEET CAKE

12 TO 20 SERVINGS

I don't know if Texas sheet cake originated in Texas, but you'd be hard-pressed to find a Texan who doesn't serve this rectangular chocolate dessert. It's a mainstay at potlucks, birthday parties, bake sales, picnics, or at any event where you'll need a portable sweet that can feed tons of people.

One of the hallmarks of this moist, fine-crumbed cake is that the icing is always poured on right when you take the cake out of the oven. So depending on how fast you work, you can usually whip this up in under forty minutes, which makes it perfect for those steamy summer days when you don't want to spend too much time laboring in the kitchen.

1. Preheat the oven to 400 degrees and grease a 9-by-13-inch pan.

2. Sift the sugar and flour together in a bowl. Melt the butter on low in a saucepan, and when melted add cocoa and water and heat until boiling. Pour cocoa mix over sugar and flour, and mix well with a spoon. Add eggs, buttermilk, baking soda, vanilla, cinnamon, and ancho chile powder, if using. Mix well with a spoon.

3. Pour batter into greased pan and bake for about 30 minutes, checking it at 20 minutes. The cake will be done when an inserted knife comes out clean.

4. Five minutes before the cake is done, make the icing. Bring to a boil the butter, cocoa, and milk. Remove from heat, and mix in powdered sugar, vanilla, cinnamon, and pecans. Beat well and then spread over cake while both are still warm.

FOR THE CAKE

2 cups granulated sugar

2 cups all-purpose flour

1 cup unsalted butter (2 sticks)

4 tablespoons unsweetened cocoa

1 cup water

2 large eggs, lightly beaten

½ cup buttermilk

1 teaspoon baking soda

1 teaspoon vanilla extract

1 teaspoon ground cinnamon

1 teaspoon ancho chile powder (optional)

FOR THE ICING

8 tablespoons unsalted butter (1 stick)

4 tablespoons unsweetened cocoa

6 tablespoons whole milk

1 pound powdered sugar

1 teaspoon vanilla extract

1 teaspoon ground cinnamon

1 cup chopped pecans

DATE BARS

16 BARS

1 cup granulated sugar

½ teaspoon kosher salt

2 large eggs

1 tablespoon unsalted butter, melted

1 tablespoon hot water

1 cup all-purpose flour

1½ teaspoons baking powder

1 teaspoon vanilla extract

½ pound dried dates, finely chopped (1½ cups)

1 cup pecans, chopped

Powdered sugar

Whenever I look through my family's recipe files, I'm struck that there are some desserts my ancestors made that have never gone out of fashion, desserts like peach cobbler or chess pie. But then there are the desserts that seem to have slipped through the cracks, unloved and forgotten.

Now, I reckon some of these treats are no longer cooked simply because they didn't make a good impression even when they were popular. Raisin pie comes to mind. But then I'll come across a dessert such as these date bars and I'm instantly intrigued.

I had no idea what to expect when I made this recipe found on a card scribbled in my great-grandma Gibson's handwriting. But I'm a fan of bar cookies and I adore dates, so I decided to give the recipe a try. What turned out was a buttery, cakelike cookie punctured by caramel-sweet bites of dates. It's not fussy or complex but graceful and agreeable enough to be equally at home in a lunch box or at a holiday party.

I'm glad I found this recipe, and if you like dates and soft cookies, I bet you'll be glad to have found it as well.

1. Preheat the oven to 350 degrees. Line a 9-inch-square baking pan with foil and lightly grease.

2. Mix together the granulated sugar, salt, and eggs until creamy. Add the butter, water, flour, baking powder, vanilla, dates, and pecans and mix until a thick, very sticky batter is formed. (You can do this by hand, but it's much easier using a stand mixer with the paddle attachment.)

3. Pat the batter into the greased pan until even. Bake at 25 to 30 minutes or until browned. Once cool, lift the foil out of the pan, cut into bars, and sprinkle with powdered sugar.

MEXICAN CHOCOLATE CHEWIES

ABOUT 36 COOKIES

Chocolate chewies are light, crisp, and, yes, chewy chocolate cookies that are studded with chocolate chips and pecans. You see them at bakeries all over Texas, and yet not too many people make them at home. There's really no reason for this, especially as they're a snap to make. I've added a bit of cinnamon and chipotle chile powder to give them a bit of spice and heat.

2 cups pecans, roughly chopped
2½ cups powdered sugar
½ cup unsweetened cocoa powder
½ teaspoon ground cinnamon
¼ teaspoon chipotle chile powder
¼ teaspoon kosher salt
3 large egg whites
1 teaspoon vanilla extract
2 cups semisweet chocolate chips

1. Preheat the oven to 350 degrees and line a baking sheet with parchment paper.

2. While oven is heating, arrange the chopped pecans in a skillet and place in the oven for 5 minutes or until they've turned a bit darker brown (but not black) and smell fragrant. Mix roasted pecans with the powdered sugar, cocoa powder, cinnamon, chipotle chile powder, and salt.

3. Stir the egg whites into the dry mixture by hand (or beat with a stand mixer on low) just until the batter is well mixed. Stir in the vanilla extract and chocolate chips. Drop tablespoon-size portions of batter on the sheet an inch apart, about six per sheet, as these cookies will spread while baking. Bake for 15 minutes or until crackling on the surface.

4. Remove sheet from oven, lift the parchment paper with the cookies still on it off the sheet, and cool on a rack. Allow cookies to cool for 20 minutes before removing from paper, as they're very delicate. They will keep for a few days in an airtight container.

SHORTBREAD WITH LIME ZEST

1 cup unsalted butter, room
temperature (2 sticks)
½ cup granulated sugar
2 cups all-purpose flour
1 tablespoon cornmeal
¼ teaspoon flaked sea salt
1 tablespoon lime zest

My cousin Susan makes a fabulous shortbread cookie that she brings to all the family gatherings. They're crisp and buttery, and I always have a difficult time restraining myself from eating more than one.

It's not a complicated recipe, but what makes it different from others I've seen is that it calls for cornmeal, which adds a bit of crunch to the texture. And as I've long been a fan of buttery cookies with a hint of citrus, I've added lime zest to Susan's basic recipe. I bet they'll be a big hit at your next family gathering, though they also go well with a morning cup of coffee or tea.

1. Preheat the oven to 300 degrees and grease a large baking dish.

2. Cream together the butter and the sugar and stir in the flour, cornmeal, sea salt, and lime zest.

3. In the baking dish spread the mixture so it's ½ inch thick. Prick holes all over the dough with a fork. Bake for 1 hour or until it's lightly browned. While warm, cut into squares and remove from pan.

DEWBERRY COBBLER
ICE CREAM

1 QUART

If you grew up in Houston, you know about dewberries. These wild berries that arrive in the spring can be found by the bayou, along the road, in vacant lots, behind buildings, or if you're lucky, even in your own backyard.

My friends and I used to pick them in the wilder parts of my suburban neighborhood, braving thorns, poison ivy, and chiggers to get to this luscious fruit, which is similar to a blackberry. Many times we'd eat most of our harvest before returning home, but if we were smart, we'd save enough for dewberry cobbler.

Every summer, Blue Bell, the beloved Texan creamery based in Brenham, issues a flavor called Southern Blackberry Cobbler, to which this recipe pays its respects. And not to boast or anything, but I dare say this might even be better.

1. Cook the cream and half-and-half on medium heat until warm; do not let it come to a boil.

2. Beat the egg yolks with the sugar and vanilla. Add to this ½ cup of the warm cream mixture, and then stir the egg mixture back into the remaining cream mixture still in the pot.

3. Heat this on medium low for 5 minutes or until it gets slightly thick. Do not let it come to a boil. You'll know it's ready when it coats the back of your spoon. Cool in the refrigerator for 4 hours.

4. While the custard base is cooling, place rinsed berries in a blender and puree with the half-and-half until smooth. Pour the berry puree into a pot through a mesh strainer to

FOR THE ICE CREAM BASE

1 cup heavy cream

2 cups half-and-half

2 egg yolks (save the whites for another use)

¾ cups granulated sugar

1 teaspoon vanilla extract

FOR THE DEWBERRY FILLING

1 cup dewberries or blackberries, rinsed

¾ cup half-and-half

3 tablespoons granulated sugar

1 teaspoon cornstarch

Pinch of cinnamon

¼ teaspoon lemon juice

FOR THE COBBLER CRUST

½ cup all-purpose flour

Pinch of kosher salt

2 tablespoons vegetable oil

1 tablespoon whole milk

½ teaspoon granulated sugar

¼ teaspoon ground cinnamon

(CONTINUED)

remove the seeds. Whisk into the puree the sugar, cornstarch, cinnamon, and lemon juice. Heat sauce on medium, stirring occasionally until thickened, a couple of minutes. Place in the refrigerator to cool for 4 hours.

5. To make the cobbler crust, heat the oven to 350 degrees and grease a baking sheet. Mix together the flour, salt, oil, and milk until well combined. Let it rest for 10 minutes and then roll out the crust until it's ¼ inch thick (you don't have to worry about it being round, as you'll be breaking up the pieces). Poke holes in it with a fork, sprinkle the top with sugar and cinnamon, and bake for 20 minutes or until brown. Place in the refrigerator to cool for 4 hours.

6. After the custard has chilled, prepare as per your ice cream maker's instructions. When it's done, swirl in the dewberry mixture and then crumble in the crust (you don't have to use all of it; I find any leftovers make a delicious sweet snack).

MEXICAN COFFEE ICE CREAM WITH ANCHO CHILE HOT FUDGE

1 QUART ICE CREAM / 2 CUPS HOT FUDGE

FOR THE MEXICAN COFFEE ICE CREAM

2 well-chilled cups heavy cream

1 well-chilled cup whole milk

¾ cup brown sugar

1 teaspoon vanilla extract

¾ cup well-chilled strong coffee (you can use decaffeinated)

1 teaspoon ground cinnamon

FOR THE ANCHO CHILE HOT FUDGE

8 tablespoons unsalted butter (1 stick)

4 ounces unsweetened baking chocolate

2½ cups granulated sugar

1 12-ounce can of evaporated milk

1 teaspoon vanilla extract

1 teaspoon ancho chile powder

Flaked sea salt, such as Maldon, to taste

My favorite ice cream flavor always has been coffee. While my family never made coffee ice cream at home, as soon as I started making my own, I realized what a cinch it was. But I didn't want to make just any coffee ice cream—I wanted the ice cream to taste like Mexican coffee.

If you've never had Mexican coffee, it's a strong brew comprised of dark-roasted coffee beans, *piloncillo* (a Mexican dark-brown sugar), and cinnamon. The sweetly caramelized flavor of the coffee and brown sugar gets a nice kick from the cinnamon. These flavors pair very well with a hot fudge that's been fired up with a bit of ancho chile powder.

1. To make the ice cream, mix the cream, milk, brown sugar, vanilla, coffee, and cinnamon in a mixing bowl. Freeze and churn according to your ice cream maker's instructions.

2. To make the hot fudge, melt the butter and chocolate in the top of a double boiler. Stir in the sugar and the evaporated milk. Cook until sugar is melted and the sauce is smooth. Stir in the vanilla, ancho chile powder, and salt to taste. Serve warm over the ice cream.

NOTE: The hot fudge will harden a bit once it's cold. If you like, dip your spoon into this for a fudgy treat.

PINEAPPLE SHERBET

1 QUART

When I was young and we ate out at a Mexican restaurant, the only desserts on offer were pralines, sopapillas, and sherbet in flavors such as orange, lemon, or pineapple. Sherbet is sort of an old-fashioned frozen dessert that you seldom see anymore, but this doesn't mean that it's any less refreshing than it used to be.

Some recipes for sherbet are simply pureed fruit mixed with eggs. I, however, have made a pineapple sherbet with buttermilk, as I find the texture is the same and I don't have to worry about serving raw egg whites. I've also added a bit of mint to my sherbet, as I love how its bright bite adds a bit of spark to the sweet pineapples. Though it's mighty fine on its own, it's also fabulous when scooped on top of a halved Ruby Red grapefruit.

1 20-ounce can of crushed
  pineapple, drained
1 cup heavy cream
1 cup buttermilk
¼ cup granulated sugar
1 teaspoon lemon juice
1 teaspoon fresh mint, finely diced
Pinch of salt

1. In a blender, mix together the pineapple, heavy cream, buttermilk, sugar, and lemon juice until smooth.

2. Stir in the mint and salt. Freeze according to your ice cream maker's instructions.

PRALINES

ABOUT 15 PRALINES

4 cups pecans
2 cups granulated sugar
2 cups brown sugar
2 teaspoons vanilla extract
6 tablespoons light corn syrup
1 tablespoon unsalted butter
⅔ cup whole milk

SPECIAL EQUIPMENT
Candy thermometer

If your family is anything like mine, the annual Thanksgiving game between the University of Texas and Texas A&M can cause some bickering.

I remember one year, my grandma Ashner—a lifelong Aggie—sat at the head of the table shaking her head at her children and grandchildren, who had gone against her wishes and became Longhorns instead. There was a bit of boasting between the two sides about who was going to win the game that year. But just before things became too ugly, my aunt Julie passed around her homemade pralines.

We all took a break from our quarreling and took a bite. And as this creamy, nutty confection melted in our mouths, you could feel the pregame tension melting away, too. We might not have agreed about football, but we were all in accordance that Julie's pralines were indeed the best. You don't find this candy often in New York City, but thankfully, Julie gave me her recipe. Her pralines are a cinch to make, and in under an hour you'll have trays laden with these candies that are perfect for sharing.

1. Line a baking sheet with parchment paper. In a dry cast-iron skillet heated on medium, toast the pecans while stirring for 5 minutes. Don't let them burn.

2. In a pot, place a candy thermometer and add the toasted pecans, granulated sugar, brown sugar, vanilla, corn syrup, butter, and milk. Turn the heat to medium and while stirring cook until the thermometer reads 234 degrees. Remove from heat and continue stirring until the mixture loses its glossy shine and has cooled down to 140 degrees. Drop ½-cup-size spoonfuls of the candy onto the lined sheet. Let cool for 20 minutes and then remove.

PEANUT PATTIES

ABOUT 15 PATTIES

If you stop at any gas station across Texas, you'll see a display of round red peanut patties stacked by the register. If you're not familiar with peanut patties, they are simply a handful of peanuts combined with nougat to make a crisp yet creamy candy.

I love the flavor and texture of peanut patties, but one thing that's always bothered me about them is that they're dyed red. I'm not sure why candy makers do this, but because they're red, I've always expected a little heat to be present. Unfortunately, there's no heat, as this is an old-fashioned confection and our great-grandparents weren't especially known for preparing fiery foods.

Well, I've remedied that oversight by adding a bit of cayenne to my recipe. So while these may not be exactly the peanut patties you'll pick up when you fill your tank, I daresay they're a welcome variation.

2 cups granulated sugar
¾ cup half-and-half
½ cup corn syrup
¼ teaspoon kosher salt
½ teaspoon ground cinnamon
2 cups roasted, salted peanuts
2 tablespoons unsalted butter
1 teaspoon vanilla extract
½ teaspoon ground cayenne
4 drops red food coloring (optional)

SPECIAL EQUIPMENT
Candy thermometer

1. Cover a large baking sheet with parchment paper.

2. In a pot, place a candy thermometer and combine the sugar, half-and-half, corn syrup, salt, cinnamon, and peanuts. Cook on medium heat while stirring until the thermometer reads 240 degrees. This should take about 10 to 15 minutes.

3. At this point, immediately remove the pot from the heat and stir in the butter, vanilla, cayenne, and if you're using it, the red food coloring. Keep stirring until the candy loses its glossy shine and has cooled down to 140 degrees, about 5 to 10 minutes. (You may want to have a partner on hand to help if your arm gets tired.)

4. Once the candy turns opaque, quickly drop ½-cup-size spoonfuls onto the sheet and let cool an hour before eating. Will last for 1 week stored in an airtight container.

RESOURCE GUIDE

Many of the ingredients in this book can be found at a regular grocery store or a Mexican grocer. If, however, you have a hard time sourcing certain items, such as dried chiles or crawfish, here are places where you can mail order these ingredients.

AMAZON
http://www.amazon.com/ (US)
Cast-iron cookware; chili powder; dried chiles; tortilla presses; and masa harina

http://www.amazon.co.uk (Europe)
Canned jalapeños; dried chiles; masa harina; and pecans

CAJUNGROCER
http://www.cajungrocer.com/
Crawfish and frog legs

DUBLIN DR PEPPER
http://www.dublindrpepper.com/
Dr Pepper

LICON DAIRY
http://licondairy.com/
Asadero cheese

LODGE
http://www.lodgemfg.com/
Cast-iron cookware

MEXGROCER
http://www.mexgrocer.com/ (US)
http://www.mexgrocer.co.uk/ (Europe)
Beans; cactus; *cajeta*; canned chipotle, jalapeño, poblano, and serrano chiles; corn husks; dried chiles; masa harina; Mexican chocolate; posole (hominy); spices; tortilla presses; and tortillas

MILLICAN PECAN COMPANY
http://pecancompany.com/pecans.htm
Pecans

PENDEREY'S
http://www.penderys.com/
800-533-1870
Chili powder; corn husks; dried chiles; spices; and vanilla extract

TEXMEX.NET
http://www.texmex.net/Rotel/main.htm
Chili powder; corn husks; corn tortillas; and Ro-Tel tomatoes

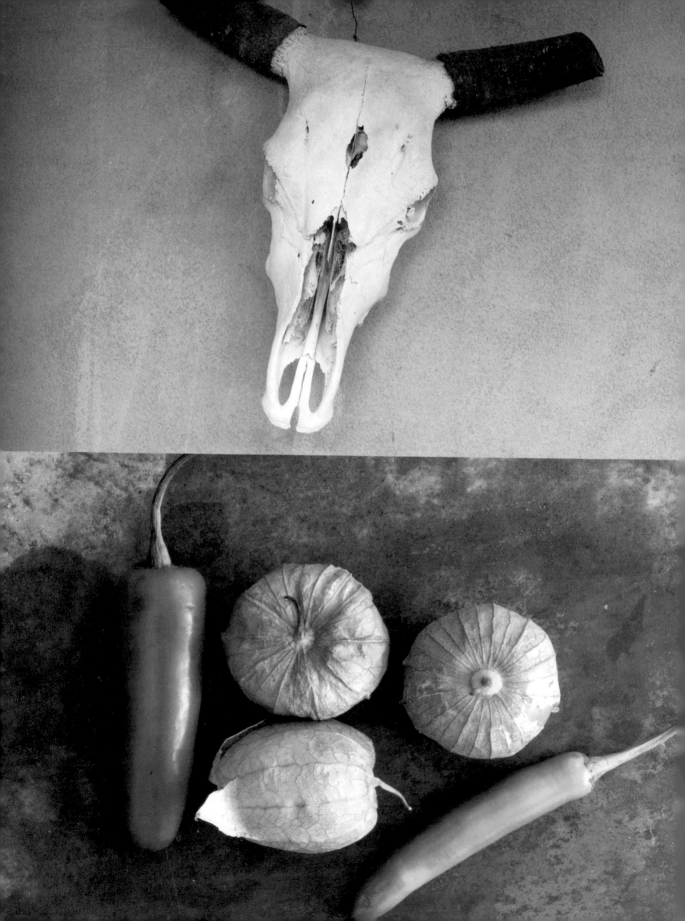

INDEX